BEYOND TERROR

BEYOND TERROR

A Battered Wife on Trial for the
Alleged Murder of Her Husband

RAOUL D. REVORD, ESQ.

Copyright © 2023 by Raoul D. Revord, ESQ.

All rights reserved. No part of this book may be reproduced in any form or by any electronic or mechanical means, including information storage and retrieval systems, without permission in writing from the author and publisher, except by reviewers, who may quote brief passages in a review.

ISBN: 978-1-961395-07-7   (Paperback Edition)
ISBN: 978-1-961395-06-0   (Hardcover Edition)
ISBN: 978-1-961395-05-3   (E-book Edition)

Some characters and events in this book are fictitious and products of the author's imagination. Any similarity to real persons, living or dead, is coincidental and not intended by the author.

Book Ordering Information

The Media Reviews
99 Wall Street #2870
New York, NY, 10005 USA

www.themediareviews.com
press@themediareviews.com
+1 (315) 215-6677

Printed in the United States of America

Contents

Dedication vii
Acknowledgments ix
Prologue xi

Chapter 1: An Interruption at Upper Twin Lake 1
Chapter 2: Investigation at the Scene 14
Chapter 3: An Early Arraignment 20
Chapter 4: Private Investigator's Investigation 25
Chapter 5: The Theories of the Case 29
Chapter 6: The Preliminary Examination 34
Chapter 7: A Search for Experts 52
Chapter 8: Discovery 57
Chapter 9: Pretrial Motion Regarding Voir Dire 64
Chapter 10: Jury Selection 72
Chapter 11: Opening Statements 86
Chapter 12: The Prosecution's Case 98
Chapter 13: The Case is with the Defense 102
Chapter 14: Rebuttal Witnesses 165
Chapter 15: Closing Argument for the Prosecution 167
Chapter 16: Closing Argument for the Defense 175
Chapter 17: Prosecution Rebuttal 190
Chapter 18: Judge Roode's Instructions to the Jury 194
Chapter 19: The Verdict 206
Chapter 20: Sentencing 210
Chapter 21: The Appeal and Court of Appeals Decision 213
Chapter 22: Jean's Release from Prison and Homecoming 215

End Notes 217
About the Author 219

Dedication

To the social workers, doctors, psychologists who work with battered women, helping them to escape from the abusive environment in which they live, and to the prosecutors, lawyers, law students, and law enforcement men and women who truly support the U.S. Constitution with its Bill of Rights and dedicate their professional lives to the pursuit of justice.

Acknowledgments

After fifty years as a trial lawyer, I want to acknowledge and thank the many friends and acquaintances who had encouraged me to write this novel. Special thanks for the encouragement of my children and ex-wife. I also want to thank Ms. Helen Peters, former creative writing teacher, for her encouragement, expert review, and editing of my manuscript.

PROLOGUE

It was 6:30 p.m., a Saturday evening—*September 22, 1984*—he was drunk, dressed in his jeans and T-shirt, with stocking feet. He had fallen asleep at the kitchen table in a drunken stupor at about 4:00 a.m. that morning, and he had started drinking again at 6:30 a.m. and throughout that day. His drink of choice was Petri Brandy. It was a favored drink of many of the people who regularly drank alcohol in the Upper Peninsula of Michigan. The brandy was usually mixed with a little water or taken straight with a "snit"—*a short glass of beer as a chaser*. After beating her up in the morning and threatening her with a knife, he was again threatening to kill her along with her brother Bill and son Robert and then commit suicide in the late afternoon. She had been repeatedly asking him to leave the home and sober up, but he would not leave. She had endured his beatings quite regularly over the past three years, many times hospitalized with injuries and sometimes near death. "I can kill you and then commit suicide; the police won't be of any help to you. They won't do nothing to stop me," John said, while glaring at her with a hateful look in his eyes and a very weird look on his face. Jean—*standing at the threshold of the bedroom door, nearly five feet away*—had a rifle held at her right hip, screaming, trembling, demanding that John leave the house until he could get sober, telling him that she refused to be beaten again. *What will he do*, thought Jean. She previously believed she would be beaten if she stayed, and killed if she left. Now, he was convincing in his thoughts of suicide and she feared she would be killed even if she stayed. *If she didn't get him out of the house now, he would surely kill her in her sleep.* "I'm going to kill you, your brother, and Robert too, now give me that f—gun," he said, as he got up off the bed and lunged at her, grasping for the rifle she held at her hip.

Oh! Pain in my chest . . . my back . . . What's this . . . blood, thought John, as he looked at the front of his white T-shirt, rapidly becoming soaked with blood dripping from his mouth and nose. The weird look on his face, suddenly becoming an astonished and terrified look, as he looked at Jean while he staggered backwards, falling upon the bed, thinking, *oh, God! (coughing) She . . . she shot me. I can't breathe—choking—gurgling. I should have killed that bitch before she fired, can't breathe, can't see . . . (hearing screaming) . . . can't hear what they're saying . . . light's fading . . . can't . . . I can't . . .* "I'm sorry, Jean. Oh God . . . Oh God . . . I'm sorry." *(coughing, choking) . . . can't breathe . . . anymore . . . I . . . I . . . Oh God!* As he lay on the bed, violently threshing and dying, his eyes then were becoming a fixed stare. No more sounds, coughing is over, no more blood splattering on the walls, blood now just oozing from his nose and mouth. Jean stayed at the threshold of the bedroom door, while screaming, and seemed paralyzed, nearly five feet away, a rifle still held at her right hip. She continued screaming, trembling, frightened, and unsure whether she was still alive. *Was he going to get up, or was he really dying?* Afraid that he would grab her if she bent down to him to try to stop his bleeding, not sure if he was still alive, Jean was unable to move. While still holding the rifle, she yelled at their seventeen-year-old son—*who was crying and checking on his dad for any signs of life*—"Robert, call the ambulance." She then thought, with a slight sense of guilt . . . *the beatings are over . . . she would not be beaten tonight . . . or ever again.* Her thoughts of not having to endure a beating again produced a very slight momentary smile in a corner of her mouth. However, she collapsed and crawled away from the bedroom door into the living room, dragging the rifle with her. Rising to her feet, she stumbled into the kitchen and collapsed at the kitchen table, dropping the rifle to the floor, her head in her hands, hysterical, frightened, still trembling, and struggling for a full breath of air.

Chapter 1

An Interruption at Upper Twin Lake

Two hours later that evening, Ann called from the kitchen, "David, there is a client on the phone wanting to speak with you."

"Thank you," he replied, as he reached for the phone on the end table next to him in the living room of the cabin.

Ann was just about to clean up the table on the porch, overlooking the Upper Twin Lake, and start washing dishes, while David had begun playing his guitar, sitting in his favorite chair, near a blazing fire in the stone fireplace, his father-in-law singing "Old Shep." The family was just beginning to relax with music and song after a dinner of grilled steaks, baked potatoes, salad, and corn-on-the-cob. In addition to David and his wife, both their parents, and their three children, were at the cabin. David expected that the telephone caller might be a client who wanted to talk to him about drafting a will, or perhaps a drunken-driving arrest or some mundane real estate matter.

"This is Attorney David Chartier, who is calling?"

In a barely audible, but highly distressed voice, a woman replied, "This is Jean Davis . . . I'm . . . (sobbing) at the State Police Post, I had to shoot that son of a bitch (sobbing loudly), he was going to kill us."

"What . . . John? Is he alive?" David inquired.

"No!" she stated.

"I've been arrested for murder."

David paused for a moment, not knowing what to say. What a shock! He finally got command of his thoughts and his voice and he barked over the phone. "Jean, I'll be right down; don't speak to the officers, except to tell them that you do not want to be questioned further, and that you want counsel. Do you understand?" David asked.

"Yes," she said.

David grabbed a pen and a yellow pad that was on the end table near the phone, leaving his guitar, the cabin, and his family, amid questions about who and what the telephone call was about, telling them only, "I have to see a client who has been arrested for murder."

"Do you have to go now?" inquired Ann.

"Yes, Ann . . . my client is being held by the Michigan State Police for murder; she has asked for me, as her attorney," David replied, really feeling badly about leaving the whole family, when he had been looking forward to spending the entire evening with them.

David had defended several clients facing the charge of domestic violence. With this call, however, the tables have turned. He thought about that phrase—*domestic violence*—and did not recall ever hearing those two words used together, prior to ten years ago. It is not that there was not such a thing as domestic violence, but the label—*domestic violence*—just did not seem to David to have been a familiar phrase to describe *Dick kicking the shit out of Jane, during the 1970s*. It must have been when the abused wives and domestic partners began standing up for themselves, refusing to live in a hostile home environment.

"Domestic violence" was in recent times on the front pages of newspapers every other day, it seemed; the public sees it on the television and they read books about it. People who did not live with violence in the home did not hear much about it. People, who did live with violence in the home, did not talk about it. It is like an elephant in the living room—everyone knows it is there, but no one wants to talk about it.

The Upper Peninsula of Michigan (U.P.) has vast regions of total forest and lakes with only a sprinkling of small towns, bordering the north shore of Lake Michigan and the south shore of Lake Superior. Most of the U.P. towns are separated by about twenty-five to forty miles distance from its nearest neighboring town. Many old-timers say that was about the distance a horse could travel in a day. Persons born and raised in the U.P. are sometimes referred to as Yoopers, while people from downstate coming to the U.P. are referred to as Trolls—*living in Michigan's Lower Peninsula, below the Mackinac bridge, at the Straits of Mackinac, the connecting waters between Lake Michigan and Lake Huron.* David and Ann's cabin, built in the early 1930s from hand-hewn pine logs—*having a small kitchen, with a wood-burning cook stove, living room with a stone fireplace, two bedrooms, and a glassed-in porch, overlooked the Upper Twin Lake in the Upper Peninsula of Michigan's Hiawatha National Forest.* The cabin had neither running water, nor an indoor toilet—*it had a picture pump in the kitchen and there was an old outhouse, just fifty feet east of the cabin*—it was David's favorite place to be, offering a real repose from the stress of a busy law practice. It had been a perfect autumn day, sunny; all of the trees—*except the evergreen*—were in full color.

David left the cabin knowing that Ann would be upset at his leaving, his heart palpating, driving down the sandy drive, through the mixed red and white pines, to the Buckhorn Road, and on to Federal Forest Highway 13, heading north toward the Michigan State Police Post, in the city of Pictured Rocks, Michigan. That evening, David did not look much like a trial lawyer; he was wearing shorts, a sweatshirt, and sandals.

Pictured Rocks is a small town—*approximately 3500 people*—situated on the southern shore of Lake Superior, in the North Central part of Michigan's Upper Peninsula. The town is surrounded on the east, south, and west by tall hills completely covered with mature hardwood—*beach, maple, oak, and a sprinkling of evergreen trees throughout*—displaying a beautiful scene of small town and forest. To the north is Lake Superior, vast, blue, and beautiful, with Grand Island, just three miles north of the town—*forty-five square miles of forest and natural beauty*—in Lake Superior, and the Pictured Rocks National Lakeshore—*with its 200-foot cliffs of breathtaking colored sandstone*—to the northeast, a favorite tourist attraction.

David was driving through the beautiful pristine forest that lined both sides of Highway 13, the late afternoon sun was blazing through the trees, illuminating the fall colors of the leaves of the maple, oak, and beach trees, the tamarack displaying their golden yellow needles, soon to be dropped, in preparation for the long winter ahead. His mind wondering, he thought it odd, that when looking at the fall colors of the forest, the mixture of the colors did not seem to clash, but imagined that placing the same mixture of colors in an unnatural setting, might seem unsettling.

It was David's twelfth year as a practicing attorney in the Upper Peninsula of Michigan, handling a considerable caseload representing a wide variety of legal matters for many clients. Over the years, this variety of law cases included corporate, criminal, probate, real estate, personal injury, wrongful death, products liability, medical malpractice, workers disability, social security disability, bankruptcy, and contract matters, but never a murder case, a fact that now left David feeling somewhat insecure as a criminal defense attorney. What would a good criminal defense attorney do next?

First, thought David, the client must retain him, as trial counsel. Next, meet the client, get the basic story, and insure that she does not make any further admissions to the police and learn what admissions, if any, she had already made to the police and the circumstances under which they were made. David knew that he needed to get to the scene where the shooting occurred and hopefully talk to someone who might have witnessed it, record as much of the event as possible, have the witness tell of his or her observations in minute detail, minimizing the possibility that the story might change with time.

Many of the lawyers in the remote communities of the U.P. are general practitioners, handling a great variety of legal matters, whereas lawyers from the more metropolitan downstate communities often are specialists, handling a very narrow aspect of the law.

Ann and David had married in 1960, while he was a freshman in undergraduate school. They had worked hard and saved to finance his way through college. David's father had given him twenty dollars once and a pair of new tires for his car upon graduation from Michigan State University with his bachelor degree, cum laude, in industrial security administration. He worked in management for a number of corporations, prior to beginning law school; his first position was supervisor of security for a defense contractor at White Sands Missile Range, New Mexico. He was not able to attend law school right after getting his BS degree, as he and Ann then had a child—*their son Jerome was born in David's senior year at MSU*—and he had to get a full-time position to support the family and repay his educational debts.

Five years after getting his bachelor's degree, he was working for another defense contractor in Ann Arbor, Michigan, and he was able to attend the Detroit College of Law in Detroit—*now Michigan State University College of Law*—in the evenings, while working in full-time security management positions for companies in Ann Arbor and later in Detroit.

David's work in defense industrial security management for research laboratories at White Sands Missile Range, New Mexico, and later at the Aerospace Corporation in Ann Arbor, Michigan, were both extremely important positions, requiring the highest level of security clearance and good management skills. David developed his management skills early in his career between the ages of twenty-three to twenty-eight, supervising many people in the classified document accountability sections, keeping track of hundreds of thousands of highly classified documents, writing security manuals, conducting security education programs and investigations. David has never talked much about his work during those years, although he enjoyed his work very much and developed very patriotic feelings for the United States of America, while protecting research and development (R & D) secrets, believed to be extremely important to the national defense of the U.S. and its allies. David did not have to go to Viet Nam; he was married with children—*and was working where it was necessary that he have access to highly classified information, documents, equipment, and missiles*—and he was taken off the list for the draft, for the duration of the war.

After four and a half years in law school, David graduated and received his Juris Doctor degree in law and began studying for the bar exam. He was able to pass the exam on the first attempt and was admitted to the practice of law in all the Michigan courts, as well as the federal courts within the state, soon after.

His practice began in the city of Detroit, handling mostly federal criminal court appointments, representing defendants charged with a variety of drug offenses. It was not much of a practice; he did not have a real law office. All of his law clients lived in dangerous neighborhoods in Detroit, and David was not about to visit them on their turf—*while dressed in his three-piece suit and tie*—but would arrange to meet them in the lobby of the federal building, downtown Detroit—*although not very private*—a much safer place to meet and discuss their particular cases.

In the spring of the year following his admission to the Michigan bar, he and his family—*Ann and he then had three children, their son Jerome, their two daughters Mae and Jeanine*—moved back to their hometown of Pictured Rocks, in the U.P. He joined a friend of his who had a very active law practice, and for the next ten years, he immersed himself in the law. Ann was never very happy about moving back to the U.P. David and Ann had a new three-bedroom tri-level home in Ypsilanti, Michigan, in a new subdivision. Ann liked the school system where son Jerome and daughter

Mae were attending. Ann believed that moving back to the U.P. would result in the loss of their independence, their privacy, and the security of corporate employers, who paid David well. After living away from parents and other close family members, one experiences a new adult identity consistent with the level of responsibilities of becoming parents, having a home, demanding employment, and education pursuits. Moving back to one's hometown where parents and other senior family members still reside frequently causes a sense of instant age regression and a loss of the once separate adult identities that gave David and Ann that great feeling of independence, responsibility, and privacy. Although David experienced those feelings too, he did not experience them to the extent that Ann did, David being active in the practice of law. Ann being at home with the children was subjected to recurring unannounced visits from parents and other family members, with their carefully pointed criticisms and their seeming obsession at attempting to take control of just about every adult decision that arose in her or the children's lives.

As David continued to drive, he was thinking about the elements of the crime of murder—*the burden of proof that a prosecutor would need to overcome to prove a defendant guilty, beyond a reasonable doubt*—and, thinking also, about possible theories of defense, of a wife killing her husband—*was she insane . . . was it self-defense . . . an accident, or was it murder?*

David was acquainted with both Jean and John Davis. He had represented both of them in different civil cases involving automobile-related personal injuries in the past. John was a forty-nine-year-old former ironworker, injured in a head-on car collision—*the oncoming vehicle had crossed the centerline and collided with John's car*—causing extensive serious injuries that prevented him from ever returning to work. David represented John in litigation against his own Auto No-Fault Insurance Company, as well as against the wrongful driver and owner of the offending vehicle. The cases settled, but David left the door open for future medical claims, for the balance of John's life.

John was a high school dropout who had worked hard to become an ironworker, and he provided for his wife and three children with his hard-earned wages, less of course what he and Jean spent on their weekend drunks in the local bars.

John's whole sense of worth and masculinity seemed associated with his pride of being an ironworker. In David's dealings with him, John always seemed to be a big but gentle man, with a silly little grin on his face, as if he were hiding some small secret that he really wanted to tell David. David had heard that in recent times, however, that John had become very violent with Jean and his kids when drunk—*which was most of the time.* John must have felt quite desperate after finding that his injuries were likely to permanently disable him from returning to work as an ironworker. Confined to the house most every day and night would have been unbearable for any man accustomed to iron working at considerable heights in the larger cities of Marquette, Escanaba, Sault Ste. Marie, Iron Mountain, Menominee, and Green Bay. Physically healthy persons seem to suffer from mental and emotional depression in the U.P. at a greater rate per capita than in other parts of the state. It could be the sense of isolation felt by many living through the long winters with snow depths of two hundred fifty to three hundred inches of accumulated snowfall on average in the Pictured Rocks County area. At any rate, add to that problem soft tissue brain damage resulting from a head-on collision of two automobiles. The prognosis for a normal life is extremely challenging for the strongest and most conscientious of individuals. At the time of John's accident, there was very little medical support for the concept of "closed head injury." For some odd reason, doctors would not give much thought to changes in personality resulting from a head injury that did not fracture the skull. It took years of research and much litigation in personal injury cases to get the medical doctors to recognize and treat brain injuries in patients having soft tissue head injuries without skull fractures.

    David had been Jean and John's lawyer on behalf of their eight-year-old deceased son—*Clifford Davis—killed while crossing the highway to board his school bus.* Jean was standing on the front porch of their home—*as any attentive mother might do while watching their youngster crossing the highway to board a waiting school bus, with red lights flashing*—watching as an eighteen-wheeler—*disregarded the flashing lights of the school bus*—struck and killed her eight-year-old son.

    A horrified Jean Davis ran to her son as he lay on the highway. Knelt, picked him up, and held him, as he died in her arms. She screamed and screamed, it seemed endlessly.

    As she held her son, Jean felt a sharp, disabling pain in her chest and left arm. She fell over on the highway with her dead child lying across her chest. Jean lost consciousness, a victim of a massive heart attack. Ambulances had been called by a neighbor—*one for the deceased boy and the other for Jean*—which took them both to the Pictured Rocks Memorial Hospital, where, after a brief emergency examination of Jean and the routine treatment for heart attack victims, she was transported to Iron Town General Hospital and underwent heart surgery for a double coronary heart bypass. Dr. Bruce Hunt, performed the surgery, and she was in the continuing care of a renowned cardiologist, Robert LaGale, MD. Five days later, Jean returned home following her heart surgery; she attended the funeral for her son.

David represented the couple, applied for Michigan no-fault benefits for Jean, and commenced litigation on behalf of her deceased son's estate. Thereafter, David also commenced an action for third-party noneconomic damages—*against the trucking company and the driver*—flowing from the negligent use of a motor vehicle.

David prepared their cases well, and, although preparing for trial, was able to negotiate a large settlement that was paid to both Jean and John for the loss of society and companionship of their deceased son, and their mutual loss of consortium, because of Jean's heart surgery and mental depression, following her heart attack and double-bypass surgery. David obtained a separate settlement, compensating Jean for her loss of earnings, beyond the three-year period of receiving no-fault lost wage benefits, replacement services, her fright and shock, feelings of impending death, posttraumatic stress, and loss of enjoyment of life. It was hardly the kind of settlement that the case would warrant in Chicago or Detroit, but for the Upper Peninsula of Michigan, it was a large settlement.

It is, indeed, sometimes depressing to realize that in certain rural areas of the state, jury verdicts and settlements are perhaps one-tenth of the verdict or settlement, which could be expected in a metropolitan area of the state, as if rural life and good health were not as valuable as life in the city. In the U.P., it seemed very difficult to find a jury that would award a seven-figure award in personal injury cases. David had always found Upper Peninsula juries to be reluctant to take money out of one party's pocket and place it into the other party's pocket, unless they are outraged at the gross negligent and outrageous conduct of the defendant.

Although John and Jean were already living on the old Davis farm, they subsequently purchased the seventy-seven-acre farm from John's family members with monies received from the settlement of their civil case against the offending truck driver.

The farm is located in a farming area southwest of the city of Pictured Rocks, in the Township AuTrain. John never did farm that land, but he had purchased a new tractor and plow for winter snowplowing, and perhaps he had thoughts of using it to cultivate some of the land in the future. After purchasing the old farm, Jean became quite protective toward her home and her children. She found herself more and more concerned about John's erratic and destructive behavior, following his accident.

The disabling in juries that John sustained in his auto accident—*confining him to their home and no longer able to work*—caused him to go into a deep depression. Although he and Jean were both drinkers—*both of them are probably alcoholics*—his drinking kept him in a near constant state of drunkenness. He became physically assaultive and emotionally abusive to Jean and their boys, frequently threatening to kill them and threatening suicide.

Jean was forty-two years old, grew up on a run-down farm nearby, and was a school dropout, working on occasion as a server or barmaid. She and John had been married eighteen years, and in the years following John's accident, the marriage became a rocky one, frequent drunkenness was commonplace, with recurring violence between the two of them a predictable occurrence. David thought that for many years Jean expected to get more than her share of beatings and had long ago come to accept it all . . . *until today.*

Considering not only his legal education, but also David's twelve years of trial experience and his years of handling numerous management matters and investigations in the military defense industry, before becoming a trial attorney, made him a capable criminal trial attorney for Jean Davis, in this high profile case, involving a wife killing her husband.

As David arrived at the Michigan State Police Post, the sun was no longer shining—*having dropped behind the hills to the west*—and it was getting dark. He parked the car and went into the post and said to Sergeant Wallace at the desk, "I am here to see my client, Mrs. Davis."

David did not have to identify himself, as most all of the troopers were acquainted with him. Some of them had been a prosecution witness in a criminal case, in which David was defense counsel, and had, at one time or another, been subjected to David's vigorous cross-examination. They did not like him and David did not respect some of them for what he saw, in some cases, as unprofessional conduct, a tendency to *bend reality* or exaggerate facts to get convictions.

Police officers take an oath to support and defend the U.S. Constitution and the Constitution of their respective state, which includes citizens' rights to due process and the right to be free of unlawful searches and seizures of their persons or property, without due process of the law. Further, defendants are to be advised of their right to remain silent, once the investigation has focused on them, and/or they are in a custodial situation or environment. However, when a criminal defendant's rights have been infringed or denied, there are some officers—*hopefully a small percentage, who conveniently forget their obligation to seek and disclose the truth*—who choose instead to ignore exculpatory evidence and exaggerate other evidence in hopes of getting a conviction. They may deny it, but David was convinced that some want a conviction—*at the price of justice*.

Did the police, despite her request for counsel, take a statement from Jean, or did they take the statement after she was placed in the backseat of the cruiser—*from which she cannot exit*—before being advised of her right to counsel? Right now, David needed to see and talk to her, and to see the home where the shooting occurred.

David was escorted to a room in the rear of the Michigan State Police Post and there saw Jean through a window, sitting at a small table, where the officers had been questioning her, regarding the shooting.

"Make it quick, Mr. Chartier, we're going to be taking her to the jail for booking soon," the interrogating officer stated, as he left the room and closed the door.

Jean was a farm girl, with reddish hair—*who dressed in pants and a sweatshirt most of her life*—who, David was quite sure, had never received any parental advice on feminine grooming. Good dental care did not seem to be an important priority in her life, as she had some cavities in her front teeth that detracted from an otherwise somewhat pleasant smile. One might question, why she would not have used some of the legal settlement monies to have her teeth fixed, instead of spending large sums at the casinos and on booze. David believed the answer to that question was rather simple—*she is probably also an alcoholic, and that is what alcoholics do, when living in their disease*—personal hygiene and health concerns were not their highest priority, when taverns, cars, tractors, television sets, furniture, and appliances lay in the balance.

David learned, however, that part of their money had been used to purchase the property and to remodel the house, purchasing new furnishings and appliances, as well as a new tractor and a new motor vehicle.

"Jean, where did this happen?" David asked.

"At home," she said.

"Was anyone else there?"

"Yes, my brother Bill and my son Robert were home."

"How old is Robert?"

"Seventeen," she stated, sobbing.

"Did he see the shooting?"

"I don't know. Bill and I were just trying to get John to leave the house."

"Christ, he was drunk-out-of-his-mind, threatening to kill me, my brother Bill, and Robert. Bill had found the gun upstairs and came downstairs, threatened John with it, but got scared and put the gun under my arm and left me all alone in the doorway to the bedroom."

"I was just trying to scare him with the gun and get him to leave the house at first, but he charged at me and the gun fired. Blood came to his mouth right away and he staggered backwards and fell onto the bed."

"That son-of-a-bitch said he was going to take the gun away from me and kill us all."

"I didn't know what to do . . . I wasn't going to let him kill us."

"Jean, you will not get a court-appointed attorney because you own property and have assets in the bank. You will have to hire private counsel," David said.

"Jean, if you would like me to defend you, I will have to ask you to pay me a retainer and sign an agreement concerning my legal fees," David explained.

"Jean, this case is going to be very costly to defend. It's not uncommon that the costs of defending a murder case might involve six figures or greater," David said.

"We lost a great amount of our settlement monies at the casino, but I have about $20,000 left over and I will pay you $10,000, if that is agreeable, and deed you the seventy-seven-acre farm," Jean stated.

David said that he would be agreeable to her payment of $10,000 and to receiving a *future interest* in the land, but he insisted that she reserve a *life estate*, in the land, for the rest of her lifetime.

"Would you agree to execute such a deed?" David inquired.

"Yes I would," she acknowledged.

David extended his right hand and they shook hands to seal the agreement—*In the remote Upper Peninsula of Michigan, many agreements are still verbal and sealed with a handshake*—a custom not found in most other parts of the country except, perhaps, in rural parts of Texas and Louisiana.

"Jean, I want you to do what the officers ask you to do tonight, but do not speak to them or anyone else about this matter. Do you understand?"

Jean swallowed hard and responded, "Yes."

"They will fingerprint you at the jail and lock you up, but I will come to see you in the morning."

"In the meantime, I am going to the house to look around."

David could not help feeling badly for Jean, confined to a small cell, segregated from other cells housing male inmates, as he saw her eyes fill with tears and she started to cry. David could not resist trying to comfort her and leave her with some kind of hope that she would soon be released, pending trial.

David then left Jean and drove to his office to make some phone calls. He wanted to get out to the Davis's house and enter, as soon as he knew that the police had finished their investigation at the scene.

David called a friend, Col. Don White, a retired Michigan State police detective—*then an auctioneer and private investigator, without much private investigation work*—and after telling him that he needed his help in a murder case, asked him to gather his evidence kit and to meet David at the Davis farmhouse, as soon as he could get there. David had been friends with Don since Don was a detective at the Redford Post, near Detroit, in the early '70s, when David, as the supervisor of Telephone Fraud Investigations and Internal Audits for Bell Telephone Company, had met him in the course of an investigation. Don is a friendly man, with a smile always on his face. He was an investigator and an auctioneer, always joking around, but serious in his work. David knew that it would be interesting working with him. With his generosity, heavy infectious laugh, and personality, people might have believed that they had just met Santa Claus.

Next, David called Robert—*the seventeen-year-old son of Jean Davis, through one of his uncles, living in the area*; *Robert was there*—and asked him if he would meet with David at the family home, so that Robert could tell David what he had observed at the home that afternoon and evening. Robert agreed to meet David there in forty-five minutes. It was then 9:30 in the evening and David suspected that the police would still be at the scene.

Later, David was driving on the highway, near the home, when he saw a couple of Michigan State police cars leave the Davis driveway and enter the highway, driving in the direction of Pictured Rocks, with their red lights flashing, as they passed him going in the opposite direction. He slowed his car until he could no longer see them in his rearview mirror and then spotted the Davis drive ahead, turned his car into the drive, and parked near the rear of the house. Neither Don White nor Robert Davis had shown up yet. He turned his car lights out and shut off the car. There did not appear to be any police barriers around the house nor any of the police tape warning about crossing onto a crime scene. He believed that the police investigation at the scene was complete and that it would be okay for him to enter the premises. It was 10:15 p.m. and his on-scene investigation was about to begin.

Chapter 2

Investigation at the Scene

It was 10:20 p.m. and Don White arrived. It was a mild evening and Don and David were standing in the dark talking about how David expected the investigation to proceed. David wondered if Robert was going to show. Robert had been through quite an emotional day, witnessing what had happened in that house that day, and realizing that his mother had killed his dad. David would not be too surprised if Robert chose not to come to the house to talk to him or his investigator.

At precisely 10:30 p.m., a car pulled into the driveway. It was Robert, accompanied by his great-uncle, Clarence Johnson, who had come to stay with Robert and be of emotional support for him.

Robert was a good-looking boy. He was much bigger than David had expected for a seventeen-year-old kid. Although he seems mild-mannered and gentle, he clearly had the strength of a grown man. Soon after meeting Robert, David sensed that the violence and drama that Robert had experienced that day had left him in a state of shock; his reaction and demeanor was flat and David wondered about the emotional scars that would haunt Robert from this day forward.

Finding that the police had locked the rear door when they left the house, Robert located a key in the attached shed hanging on a nail and opened the rear door to the house; turning on the lights, he led them into the kitchen. The house was a two-story frame farmhouse. It was built in the 1940s. Many improvements were evident in the interior of the house—*new kitchen cabinets, countertops, and new appliances in the kitchen*—it looked in good shape, except for the mess in the kitchen, where it was apparent that it had been the scene of violence that day; dishes and kitchen utensils had been thrown around, broken dishes and cups were strewn on the kitchen floor.

"Robert, I know that you have had a frightful day and that you feel bewildered regarding the death of your father and the arrest of your mother on the charge of murder. I would like my investigator, Col. Don White, to ask you questions as to what you had observed happening in the house between your mom and dad throughout the day, describing the fighting between them and their location in the home where the arguments and fighting occurred," David said.

Despite Robert's size and his obvious physical maturity, David was looking at a sensitive young man who was on the brink of an emotional collapse, nearly crying but trying desperately to appear in control of his emotions.

"Don White is a notary public, and I would ask you to swear that what you are going to tell him is going to be the truth, the whole truth, so help you God."

Robert held up his right hand and said, "Yes."

David explained to him that he most likely would not be asking the questions—*David had discussed with Don the questions that he wanted him to ask*—but would rely on his investigator to do that. Don began his questioning of Robert, while standing in the kitchen of his home.

"What time did you wake up this morning Robert?" asked Don.

"Nine o'clock," answered Robert.

"What did you first do after awaking?"

"I heard my parents arguing in the kitchen, but I was too tired to get right up. I dosed off until about 9:45, and I was awakened again by my parents yelling and throwing things in the kitchen. I heard my dad threaten to cut my ma with a knife. I got up, put my clothes on, and hurried downstairs to the kitchen. Dad was drunk, his eyes were bloodshot, his speech was slurred, and he and my ma were arguing about who had supported who the longest over the years.

"Dad was getting loud and hollered that he supported her more than she supported him, and after they had yelled some more, she threw the tea kettle at him and he caught it and threw it back, hitting her in the face; then she told him to get out of the house, until he cooled off.

"My dad had a hunting knife with about a seven-inch blade that he took out and said to my ma that he could slit her throat if he wanted and the police wouldn't do anything to stop him.

"That's when I stepped in, and took out my knife from my belt case and said that he would have to cut me first.

"Then I backed away from him and went and stood near my ma."

"Tell me about prior threats and assaults by your dad against your mother, that you observed or are aware of," asked Don.

"Before my dad got hurt—*both legs and both arms were broken as well as a skull fracture and injuries to his brain*—he wasn't mean, but after, he got real mean and drank a lot and was always saying that he was going to commit suicide. Sometimes he would get very crazy and try to burn the house down. He was in the house and fired a gun toward the firefighters when they came to put out the fire. He tried throwing gas on me once and said he was going to light me on fire. Once he shot at my ma and my uncle when they were driving out of the yard, because he did not want them taking the car to go to the bar. He hit my ma with his crutch once and fractured her skull, and once he threw her out of the car as he was driving down M-94 and it knocked her out. The next morning she woke up next to the guardrail and walked back to town to get to the hospital," he said, *while beginning to cry*.

Don stopped questioning Robert, to allow him to stop crying, and then continued his questions.

"What happened next?" asked Don.

"My ma said that she was going to get out of the house for a while and left in her car. I took my bike and went visiting a friend who lived a few miles away and stayed most of the rest of the afternoon."

"When did you return home?"

"It was about 6:30 when my ma, my uncle Bill, and I came back home.

"I had seen her car at the Village Tavern and went in to see her. When leaving, we put my bike into the trunk of the car and I rode home with them. When we got to the house, my dad had the door locked and I could hear him yelling that we could not come in.

"But, I knew where a key was hidden in the porch and I was able to open the door to the kitchen, just like I did tonight.

"We went inside the kitchen, and my dad came out of the living room and slugged my ma and started fighting with my uncle Bill, who was trying to protect my ma. She tried reasoning with my dad and my dad hit her in the face a couple more times and her face was swelled.

"He then stopped hitting her and went into his bedroom and I heard him say that he was going to kill her. My ma and Uncle Bill were telling my dad to leave the house until he sobered up, but my dad wasn't moving. My dad had a weird look on his face, and kept saying that he was going to kill us all and commit suicide. He slugged my ma and knocked her to the floor near the end of the bed and she needed help to get up. Her mouth was swelled. Uncle Bill hit my dad a couple times in the face, yelling at my dad to stop hitting my ma. My ma went back to the door of the bedroom and told my dad to leave the house again. I was standing next to my ma, near the bedroom door. My uncle Bill ran upstairs and he got a rifle from under the bed and came down the stairs with it, and when my dad saw the gun, he said that my uncle Bill didn't have the guts to shoot him. Uncle Bill turned and moved behind my ma and shoved the rifle under my ma's right arm, and she held it at her hip, not pointing it anywhere. I was sick and tired of the yelling and screaming and I left and walked into the kitchen.

"I heard my dad screaming at my ma that he was going to take that gun away from her and was going to shoot her, my uncle Bill, and me too. My ma told me that when he got off the bed, he lunged at her. I heard her scream and then heard the shot. I think that she must have shot right from the hip.

"Dad must have fallen backwards on the bed cuz I ran to the bedroom right after the shot was fired, and my dad was lying partly on the bed, on his back, and was coughing blood all over the room. I noticed a bullet hole near the top of his chest."

As Robert was telling us what he had observed, David stood at the threshold of the bedroom and could see the blood-soaked bed, approximately five feet away from the threshold of the bedroom doorway. Blood was splattered on the rear wall next to the bed, blood splattered on the wall and ceiling, near the head of the bed, apparently where John had been coughing up blood, before he died.

"What happened next?" asked Don.

"My ma was shaking, looked scared, but told me to go call an ambulance and I did. They told me to find a pressure bandage and place it on the wound pressing hard to stop the bleeding, but I didn't know what a pressure bandage was and I felt helpless."

"My ma's face was bruised and I could tell that she was really scared. She said that son-of-a-bitch would never beat her again."

Robert was crying...

Before leaving the area of the bedroom, Don—*always looking for details*—sighted a spot of what appeared to be blood, right at the threshold of the bedroom door. He photographed it and then collected the sample, placing it into a clean plastic baggie and marking the location where it was found and the date and time, on the outside of the baggie.

They then prepared to leave the Davis home, having completed their investigation at the home. David thanked Robert for talking to him and to his investigator. David told Robert how sorry he was that this tragedy occurred. Robert said that he would be staying with his great-uncle for a while. We all left the home and Robert locked it up before leaving. It was close to 1:00 a.m. and David wanted to see Jean in the morning and expected to have a very busy day at his office. Arraignment had been set for Monday morning, September 24, 1984, at 9:30 a.m. David was exhausted and needed sleep. When arriving home, David spent about a half an hour sitting in his reclining chair in the family room, trying to unwind some, so that when going upstairs to bed, he might actually fall asleep. Ann was awake, however, and wanted to discuss everything that transpired at the cabin after David left. She asked if there was anything David could discuss with her concerning the murder case. David told Ann of his meeting with Jean at the State Police Post and of going to the Davis home in AuTrain Township. David told Ann that he believed that the case was defendable, and with that, they both fell asleep.

On Sunday, David went to the office and began preparation of his appearance, demand for preliminary examination, and a speedy trial. He planned to take the pleadings to the district court clerk for filing on Monday morning, serving a copy of the same on the prosecuting attorney, whose office was on the second floor of the courthouse annex.

The preliminary exam is something that David could wave—*in which case there would be an automatic bind over to the circuit court*—and the matter would be set for pretrial wherein all motions would be heard by the judge, and if none of the motions were dispositive of the case, a trial date would be set.

David was not about to waive the preliminary exam in this case, as he wanted to hear and cross-examine the prosecution witnesses. He needed to do this to learn as much as he could about the prosecutor's case. However,

David would not be calling any witnesses to testify during the preliminary exam. David knew that he needed to play his cards "close-to-the-vest," not disclosing his trial strategy or his theories of defense prior to trial.

Many of David's cases would have to be set aside for a while. David made several calls to those clients whose matters could be delayed without any significant problems and did so where the individual clients consented. In those cases where a sustained legal effort was required in ongoing litigation, David continued to handle them, but in those matters where David was unable to reschedule matters or where the clients objected to delaying their cases, David's partner, Attorney Charles Regal, agreed to substitute as counsel. Charles was a very accomplished attorney whose father was a long-time practicing attorney in Pictured Rocks and had been a circuit judge covering four counties, comprising Michigan's Fourteenth Judicial Circuit Court. Charles and David were well-regarded trial attorneys throughout the Upper Peninsula of Michigan.

Chapter 3

An Early Arraignment

It was about 7:00 a.m., Monday, September 24, 1984, and David was just getting to the jail to meet with Jean. Jean appeared pleased to see him. He tried to show a degree of confidence to put her somewhat at ease.

"I was not able to sleep at all last night, and I have been so worried about going to court today; what am I supposed to do? Will the judge ask me anything? Do I have to wear these jail clothes into the courtroom?" Jean asked.

"Jean, we will soon be going into the district court for an arraignment before Judge Kaufman for the purpose of informing you of the charge being brought against you. The sheriff will bring you into the courtroom in the jail uniform that you are now wearing. Do not worry about your clothing. Speak to the judge only when he addresses you directly. I do not want you speaking to or reacting to any reporters that might be hanging around the courthouse or courtroom; I have prepared and filed my appearance and formal request for a preliminary examination. We will only be in the courtroom a short time," David stated.

After leaving Jean, David stopped at the prosecutor Wilfred "Will" Brenner's office to obtain a copy of the police report to review in advance of the arraignment. Will and his secretary arrived precisely at 8:00 a.m.

"Well, good morning, David, what can I do for you?"

"I would like a copy of the police report, prior to the arraignment. Do you think that you can get me a copy now?"

"Sure, David, I have an extra copy for you; I knew you would be asking for one."

"Would you also give me a list of the items taken from the Davis home?"

"I don't have that information yet. I will have to get it from the state police. In the meantime, file your motions," he declared, in quite a different tone than that which he had earlier expressed.

He handed David the copy of the police report, and said, "I will see you in court in a few minutes."

David went into the courtroom—*no one is in the courtroom yet*—and he spent the next few minutes reviewing his copy of the police report that he had just received from Will Brenner. The report indicated that the Pictured Rocks County Sheriff Deputy Bower had received a call from the Davis residence at 7:00 p.m., requesting an ambulance. The report stated that John Davis was shot and that Mrs. Davis had shot him. Deputy Bower called the Michigan State Police Post and advised the sergeant of the desk of the call from the Davis residence, explaining that the EMTs had been dispatched to the Davis home.

The report further indicated that an ambulance had gone to the Davis residence with EMT Beverly Whiley and Deputy Brian Cassidy in the ambulance, and that Michigan State Trooper Dale Rose was sent to the Davis residence as well.

The report said that Jean had said to Trooper Rose, as he entered the Davis home,

"I shot him, I shot him, he hit me, and I shot him. We couldn't leave him stay; he would have killed us in our sleep."

The side door to the courtroom opened. Sheriff Cromby was bringing Jean into the courtroom, wearing her bright orange jail uniform with her wrists in handcuffs and her ankles in shackles with ankle cuffs and chains. On her face was an expression of bewilderment and fear, as she looked at David.

Prosecutor Will Brenner sat at the prosecutor's table with a slight grin on his face as he watched Jean being escorted into the courtroom.

Will Brenner, a rather plump, good-looking man in his early sixties, had been the prosecutor in Pictured Rocks County for about fifteen years, and this was to be his last criminal prosecution, prior to assuming the position of the Pictured Rocks County probate judge, to which he had recently been appointed. David could tell by his looks that he wanted a conviction in this murder case, to cap off his prosecuting career. David was not going to get any further cooperation from him at any stage of these proceedings, and he suspected that Will was not going to be forthcoming in providing additional information that the investigating officers had obtained, at least not without a court order requiring a disclosure of his file.

David felt that he had a good sense as to how limited Will's cooperation was likely to be throughout this trial. After all, it was to be Will's last prosecution. David suspected that Will wanted people to remember him as a tough, winning prosecutor, and the last murder case of his career was going to be the case most people remembered.

The judge's chamber door opened and Judge Kaufman entered the courtroom.

"All rise!" commanded the bailiff.

"Hear yea! Hear yea! The district court for the county of Pictured Rocks is now in session, the Honorable Judge Kaufman presiding; please be seated," announced the bailiff.

The bailiff was an old sheriff deputy and had been appointed the district court bailiff about fifteen years ago to serve the district court when it was in session. It was a "great plum of a job" as a reward for long-time loyal service.

Judge Kaufman looked down at David and said, "Counsel, would you bring your client before the bench?"

David took Jean's arm and began leading her from behind the defendant table—*guiding her as she shuffled her shackled feet*—to a place beside him in front of the judge's bench.

"Are you Jean Davis?" the judge asked.

"Yes, I am, Judge," Jean replied.

"Now you have been charged with an open count of murder in the death of John Davis. Do you understand the nature of the charge?"

"Yes, I do, Your Honor."

"This charge carries with it a possible penalty of life in prison if you are found guilty by a jury in a circuit court trial, or if you later plead guilty, prior to or during the trial. You are entitled to a preliminary examination within fourteen days of this arraignment, and if the prosecution proves that the crime charged has been committed and that there is probable cause to believe that you committed it, you will be bound over to the circuit court for trial. Do you understand?" asked Judge Kaufman.

"Yes I do."

"I see that you have hired Attorney David Chartier to represent you in these proceedings; a smart move on your part, Mrs. Davis," stated the judge.

"I'm going to set this matter for preliminary examination ten days from today's date—*October 4, 1984*—unless there is a waiver of the fourteen-day period and a request from the defense to extend the time for it."

There are rare circumstances when a defense attorney may not wish to have a preliminary examination take place—*e.g. when a chief prosecution witness is sickly and/or of advanced age*—preserving the witness's testimony, that can be used later in the circuit court trial, in the absence of the witness.

In ordinary circumstances, however, the defense will want the preliminary examination to take place for two important reasons: to discover what the prosecution is going to be basing his case on, and to pin down the witnesses' testimony, to insure that there is a record of the particular testimony that can be expected at the later trial—*to be used by the defense for cross-examination*—in the event the witness tries to change his or her testimony, at the time of the later trial.

"Your Honor, I would like to direct the court's attention to the subject of defendant's bond, currently set at $250,000, and I request that it be reduced and that she be able to post ten percent of the bond for her release, pending trial in this cause," David said.

"My client is not a flight risk, nor is she a danger to anyone, she owns property in the county, has children and relatives in the county, and the prosecution, I suspect, will not offer any substantial argument that she would be of danger to any other person."

Will stood up and stated, "Your Honor, this is a murder case and the defendant is facing possible conviction and sentencing for murder, and should always be considered a flight risk."

The judge turning his attention back in David's direction, declared in response, "I will take the issue of bond under advisement, and may reduce the bond to $25,000.00, if the defendant can pledge assets to the court, valued at least as much as the bond."

"The defendant is remanded to the custody of the Pictured Rocks county sheriff, to be held in the Pictured Rocks County Jail, until further order of this court. Case continued, pending further order of this court," stated Judge Kaufman.

David could feel Jean trembling as he took her by the arm and escorted her away from the front of the judge's bench into the hands of Sheriff David Cromby. She looked over her shoulder at David as she was escorted out through the side door of the courtroom and her eyes conveyed to him her raising fear, and she asked, "Will you be coming to see me?"

"Yes, I will, Jean, but I have a lot of work to do."

The side door of the courtroom closed behind her, and David began collecting his notes from the defense table and prepared to leave the courtroom, bidding Will Brenner good-bye, as he left.

David noted the newspaper reporters as he was leaving the courthouse. A reporter for the Iron Town Mining Journal stopped David as he exited the courthouse and addressed him, asking, "Mr. Chartier, would you like to comment on today's arraignment of Jean Davis?" he asked.

"My client is not guilty of murder," David responded, as he made his way to his car.

David drove back to his office and asked his legal assistant, Sandy, to reschedule all of his appointments. Sandy had been David's paralegal and secretary for all of the twelve years that he had practiced law in the U.P. She was exceptionally competent, thorough, and resourceful in the ways in which she aided David in the preparation of his cases. David could not have handled the volume of complex cases that he did without her professional assistance. There were rumors too that David and Sandy had an even closer and intimate relationship outside the office—*a rumor never acknowledged nor substantiated.*

Sandy told David that Jean's brother, Bill Bakcum, had been arrested as an accessory to murder in this case, and was appointed counsel to represent him. David would not be able to represent him, as he and Jean would likely have conflicting testimony that could prejudice their respective defenses. However, David had concerns that proceedings in Bill Bakum's case could seriously prejudice Jean's case. David was subsequently informed by his investigator that Bill was trying to negotiate a plea deal with the prosecutor. David talked with Bill's lawyer and received his assurance that, if they did reach a plea arrangement, he would demand it in writing, but delay putting anything on the record, until the conclusion of a trial in Jean's case, avoiding prejudice to Jean's case.

Jean's brother Bill could not be summoned to testify in Jean's case, as he would assert his right not to testify under the Fifth Amendment.

Where a prosecutor knows that the witness will assert his right to remain silent, it would be improper to call him to testify—*For this reason, this story will not follow the course of Bill Bakcum's case, but will focus on the case involving Jean Davis.*

Chapter 4

Private Investigator's Investigation

While David was concerning himself with physical evidence and methods of discovery, as well as probable expert witnesses in the fields of psychiatry, spousal abuse, and firearm ballistics, Col. Don White was busy interviewing witnesses who might shed some light on the question of Jean and John's relationship, as known by others in the county.

David was in his office on Tuesday morning when Don entered his office, wanting to tell him of an interview he had had with a witness he had interviewed at the Lakeside Inn, on M-28, west of Sand River, Michigan.

"I contacted Janice Brown, a waitress at the Lakeside Inn. She did not want to have me interview her at that bar, so I saw her at the Tioga Bar instead," he stated.

—The Tioga Bar was located just a few miles east of the Lakeside Inn, on Highway M-28, in Iron Town County—

"She told me that about two months ago, Jean had come into the Lakeside Inn and told her that she had just gotten out of the hospital in Iron Town, after John had kicked the shit out of her and fractured her skull. She said that Jean had told her that she was afraid that John would kill her sometime, during one of his rages," Don Stated.

"Janice also said that more recently, Bill Bakum was in the bar, just before he was arrested as an accessory to murder, and he was saying that Jean didn't have to pull the trigger, but that she wanted John out of the house one way or another," said Don.

Don also said that he had been down at the state police post trying to get information and had requested a list of the effects taken from the Davis home, but he was denied access.

"Trooper Rose told me that I could not obtain any of that information and that you would have to seek a court order to obtain it."

"David, I do have something to show you."

Pulling out some papers from his briefcase, he said, "I was able to get my hands on these," he said, handing what appeared to be the Autopsy Report of John Davis prepared by J.P. Wiseman, MD, and a ballistics report, prepared by the Michigan State Police ballistics expert.

"Where did you get these?"

"A private investigator has certain trade secrets that are not to be disclosed regarding his investigation," he replied—*with that silly little grin on his face*—as if to tell *David not to look a gift horse in the mouth.*

"I appreciate this, Don, but you have to get out of here now and let me read these; I will call you later," David said.

Don left his office, looking back, giving him a stupid grin. David finished drafting the last will and testament he had been working on, picked up the reports, and began to read them with great interest. The autopsy report read in part:

AUTOPSY REPORT

Autopsy No. A-86-07
Name of Subject John William Davis
Age : 49
Sex: Male Race: White
Medical Examiner: Donald Krueger, MD
Date and time of Death: September 22, 1984 at 8:07 p.m.
(DOA) Date and time of Autopsy: September 23, 1984 at 1:15 p.m.
Autopsy Performed by: J.P. Wiseman, MD

DIAGNOSIS

1. Gunshot wound to the chest.
   A. Perforation of left 2nd rib, pericardium, posterior left atrim, left main stem branchus, and 7th vertebral body.
   B. Exsanguinations into left pleural cavity, posterior mediastinum.

1. Moderate centriacinar emphysema.
2. Moderate coronary atherosclerosis.

CAUSE OF DEATH

COMPLICATIONS OF GUNSHOT WOUND TO CHEST (BRONCHUS, HEART).

CLINICAL SUMMARY

A family feud led to the wife shooting the deceased patient in the chest with a .22-caliber bullet. Resuscitation efforts at Pictured Rocks Memorial Hospital were unsuccessful. Toxicology studies were performed at Pictured Rocks Memorial Hospital and were not repeated at Iron Town General Hospital, Inc . . . .

MICROSCOPIC EXAMINATION

Skin: A few small powder flecks are seen in the entrance wound.

FINAL ANATOMICAL DIAGNOSIS

1. Gunshot wound to the chest.
    A. Perforation of left 2nd rib, pericardium, posterior left atrim, left main stem bronchus, and 7th vertebral body.
    B. Exsanguination into left pleural cavity, posterior mediastinum.

1. Moderate centriacinar emphysema.
2. Moderate coronary atherosclerosis.

CAUSE OF DEATH

Complications of gunshot wound to chest (Bronchus, Heart)
J.P. Wiseman, MD Pathologist

In felony cases, motions for discovery and production of records and items under the prosecutor's control are not usually brought before the district court judge—*who will be presiding over the preliminary examination*—but are rather raised by motion before the circuit judge, if there is a bind over of the defendant.

Sandy was helping David separate some of his notes and prepare various files for his use, trying to maintain some sense of order in the case. David surmised that before this was over, his file was going to be one of the biggest of his career. Sandy opened a file and had an in-house case number assigned to the file. David then prepared the attorney fee retainer agreement, as well as the deed by which he was to obtain a future interest in the Davis property, subject to Jean's life estate in the home and land.

David had numerous other cases to work on while waiting for the time of the preliminary exam. Other legal matters took up most of his time, e.g. meeting with clients, drafting pleadings, and running to court in either Pictured Rocks County or three or four other counties in the Central Upper Peninsula.

CHAPTER 5

The Theories of the Case

Theory of the Prosecution

Will's theory of the case was likely that after arriving at the AuTrain Township residence at approximately 6:30 p.m. on September 22, 1984, Jean Davis had a confrontation with John Davis, the deceased. She had physically pushed him out of the entranceway to the dining room, whereupon he retreated into the bedroom and closed the door. Jean then pushed open the door, and she and her brother, William (Bill) Bakum, began fighting with John. They wanted him to leave the residence. Their son, Robert Davis, broke up the fighting, and Robert heard his uncle say that he was going to get a gun. He watched his uncle run up the stairs and then come down the stairs moments later carrying a rifle. Robert heard his father say that his uncle did not have the guts to pull the trigger. It was Will's theory that the defendant then grabbed the rifle from her brother and shot John Davis as he sat on his bed, five feet distance from her. Upon hearing the rifle shot, Robert, who had walked into the kitchen, turned and rushed to the doorway of the bedroom, where Jean was standing, holding the rifle. He saw his father, lying on his back across the bed, coughing blood in the air. He could not seem to breathe and laid there until he died.

The theory of the people would likely be that Jean unlawfully killed John Davis without any justification or excuse. John Davis had done everything in his power to retreat from the confrontation initiated by Jean and her brother Bill. He remained seated on the bed, while Jean shot and killed him. After shooting her husband, Jean made several statements to several persons, and to the police, admitting that she had shot her husband.

Theory of the Defense

David believed that the findings of the pathologist and the Michigan State ballistics expert would be important to a theory of self-defense, as the pathologist report indicates—there were flecks of gunpowder at the entrance wound. The pathologist wrote, "A bullet tract goes through the second rib 2.0 cm lateral to the midline. The bullet tract proceeds through the left main stem bronchus and the most posterior portion of the left atrim to pass out of the posterior portion of the pericardial sac, through the aorta, and embedded in the seventh vertebral body."

This pathologist's finding demonstrates a downward trajectory of the bullet *on the inside* of John Davis's body.

The Michigan State ballistic expert, however, conducted ballistic testing and wrote in his report that the decedent was a distance between eighteen inches and up to five feet away from the muzzle of the gun, and the trajectory of the bullet was downward.

His finding of a downward trajectory would seem to be supported by the pathologist's findings of a downward trajectory—*the bullet entering the upper left chest striking the second rib and ultimately lodging in the seventh vertebral body*—inside the thorax of John Davis.

Jean's story that John was on his feet and rushing her when the shot was fired is beginning to become clear, in spite of the report of the pathologist, concerning the trajectory of the bullet *inside* John's body. Jean said that the rifle was at her right hip when the shot was fired and that John was close to her, attempting to take the gun from her. Both Jean and John are approximately of the same height. The ballistics report identifies the presence of power burns on the shirt worn by John, and the pathologist's report identified flecks of powder in the entrance wound, indicating that John had to be close to the muzzle of the gun when the shot was fired, *with a slight upward trajectory of the bullet on its way to John's body.*

David was no expert in ballistics, but it seemed clear to him that to hit the second rib, a shot *from the hip* would have to have an *upward trajectory.*

Jean did say that blood came to his mouth as soon as she fired the gun—*a spot of blood was found near the doorway where Jean was standing at the time of the shooting*—and, that he staggered backwards and fell onto the bed, approximately five feet distance from the muzzle of the rifle.

Eureka! Suddenly, David remembered the case where on March 30, 1981, John Hinckley shot President Reagan with a small-caliber gun, and the bullet struck a rib and was deflected downward inside the body of the president, causing extensive damage to his internal organs. If that scenario occurred in this case, it would be consistent with Jean's statement.

David knew then that he was going to need a ballistics expert in this case to conduct his own testing of the ballistics evidence. Specifically, David wanted to know if the trajectory of a small-caliber bullet *inside* the body of a victim tells us anything about the trajectory of the bullet on its way to the body. He also needed to know whether the distance from the muzzle of the rifle and the shirt worn by John was a relatively short distance and not up to five feet, as the Michigan State Police ballistics report indicated.

California State University in Sacramento has a school for criminalists—*where they teach all aspects of forensic investigation of crime scenes*—and David thought that he was going to try to get a professor of ballistics there to re-conduct the ballistics study in this case. He would have to get Judge William F. Roode to order the Michigan State Police to release the gun, bullet, test patterns, and the shirt worn by John, to take to the California School of Criminalists for the study. He was not able to predict his chances of success, however, as he was not aware of a judge ordering the police to turn over their ballistics evidence to the defense in the past.

Col. Don White providing these reports to him gave him hopes of defending this case on the theory of self-defense. He believed that as an early move in this case, after arraignment in the circuit court, he would assert the claim of insanity as a defense. If the state's forensic psychiatrist finds Jean competent to stand trial, but does not find that Jean was temporarily insane—*the moment the shot was fired*—then he would dismiss that claim and proceed on the theory of self-defense alone. Doing so would also buy him some time to locate and talk with various experts, to get a "feel" for the direction of the case, supporting his theory of self-defense, prior to trial.

Further, he was thinking about hiring the same psychiatrist that testified in a case many years ago, wherein Mrs. Frances Hume—*a victim of years of spousal abuse*—was tried for the murder of her husband after she poured kerosene on the floor near the bed and lit it afire as he was sleeping off a drunken stupor. The psychiatrist found her to have been temporarily insane, and the jury acquitted her. The psychiatrist was from Lansing, Michigan, and David had no idea whether he was still in practice there or elsewhere.

When an insanity defense notice is filed with the court, in addition to the defendant undergoing a psychiatric examination by a state forensic examiner, each such defendant is entitled to have his or her own psychiatric examination by a psychiatrist of his or her own choosing to counter the testimony of the state forensic examiner, if needed.

David was going to look for a spousal abuse syndrome expert, with plenty of credentials—*preferably one with a PhD who has worked in the field for some time and ideally had published about the syndrome and had experience of testifying about the syndrome in the courtroom*—he felt that such a person might be helpful in this case.

David suspected that the prosecution would raise objections to such an expert testifying. *Spousal abuse syndrome is a fairly new field of study*—Will would likely argue that the syndrome does not exist in reality and is just a theory—*not shared among most in the practice of psychology*—and should not be allowed to contaminate the thinking of the jury with a syndrome, not universally adopted by most in the psychological field.

More than once, David needed to remind himself that the defense attorney does not have to prove that the defendant is innocent, but he does have an obligation to raise a reasonable doubt as to the defendant's guilt. A reasonable doubt is a fair honest doubt growing out of the evidence or lack of evidence. It is not merely an imaginary or possible doubt, but a doubt based on reason and common sense. Thus, a reasonable doubt is just that—a doubt that is reasonable, after a careful and considered examination of the facts and circumstances of the case.

When asserting the affirmative defense of insanity or self-defense, the burden is on the prosecution to prove—*beyond a reasonable doubt*—that the defendant *was not* insane or that the defendant *was not* acting in self-defense.

Even if the insanity defense might not prove applicable in this case, David was beginning to see a theory of self-defense, from which it might just be possible to raise sufficient doubt to convince a jury to acquit Jean. The case was going to take his full attention, ingenuity, and dedication to secure the experts that will support Jean's testimony and to advocate the expert testimony and the scientific proofs, convincing a jury that there is reasonable doubt as to her guilt. The guilt or innocence of a defendant is not the real question in a criminal trial, but more appropriately, it is whether guilt of the defendant *has or has not been proven*, beyond a reasonable doubt.

CHAPTER 6

The Preliminary Examination

David woke up early, having had a difficult time trying to sleep, worried about the upcoming preliminary examination. Although David did not expect to offer any testimony from witnesses at the preliminary exam, it was going to be his first real opportunity to tie the prosecution witnesses down to specific answers to direct questions—a process, the value of which cannot be appreciated, until the time of the trial.

"Hear yea! Hear yea! The District Court for the County of Pictured Rocks, State of Michigan, is now in session, the Honorable District Judge Ronald P. Kaufman presiding, please be seated," announced the bailiff.

"This is the matter of the People of the State of Michigan v. Jean Davis. File 84-15-504," decreed the judge.

"The defendant was arraigned before the court on September 24, 1984. Mr. Chartier was present at arraignment representing Mrs. Jean Davis. The matter is here for preliminary examination."

"Are the people ready to proceed with examination?"

"Yes, Your Honor, we are," replied Mr. Brenner.

"Is the defense ready to proceed, Mr. Chartier?"

"Yes, Your Honor, we are," David replied.

"Call your first witness, Mr. Brenner."

"The people call Master Robert Davis."

Young Robert Davis walked up to the witness chair with a concerned look on his face and seemed to avoid having eye contact with his mother sitting at the defendant's table.

"Please raise your right hand . . . Do you swear to tell the truth, nothing but the truth, so help you God?" inquired the court clerk.

"Yes, I do," replied Master Davis.

"For the record, please state your name and how old you are," requested Mr. Brenner.

"My name is Robert Davis and I am seventeen years old."

"Where do you live?"

"I lived with my ma and dad in AuTrain Township, southwest of Pictured Rocks, but am now staying with my uncle."

"Who is your father?"

"John Davis."

"Who is your mother?"

"Jean Davis."

"Do you see your mother in this courtroom?"

"Yes, she is right over there (gesturing to the defendant) seated next to Mr. Chartier."

"Were you at home on or about September 22, 1984, which was a Saturday?"

"Yes."

"Were you present during an incident that involved a shooting on that day?"

"Yes, I was home, but I wasn't in the bedroom when my ma shot my dad."

"And did this occur inside the house where you live?"

"Yes."

"Who all lives in this house?"

"My ma, my dad, my uncle Bill and myself."

"Were you, at any time, gone from the house during the afternoon of that day?"

"Yes."

"Did your mother leave the house too, that afternoon?"

"Yes."

"Were you and your mother visiting friends that afternoon?"

"Yes, I left on my bike and she left in her car; later in the day, I saw my ma's car at the Village Tavern and I went in to talk with her and to my uncle Bill. She wanted to go home, so I put my bike in the trunk of her car and rode home with my ma and my uncle Bill.

"My uncle Bill has been staying with us for a while, because my dad has been so mean when he drinks and has been beating up my ma; he sleeps in an upstairs bedroom."

"Tell me what happened when you got home."

"The door was locked and my dad was too drunk to open it and my ma was yelling at him asking him to open the door and my dad kept saying that we couldn't come in.

"I found a key hanging on a nail in the porch and I unlocked the door and we went in."

"What was your dad doing at that time?"

"He slugged my ma and my uncle Bill as soon as we entered the kitchen, from the back porch.

"He was looking for a fight as soon as we came into the house, standing like a boxer, with his fists clenched.

"He went into the bedroom and it looked like he was going to barricade himself in the bedroom, and my ma forced the door open and I guess he hit her, cuz she was yelling, and when I looked into the room, she was on the floor. I helped my ma get up, and she kept trying to get him to leave the house. My uncle Bill had tried to defend my ma, but he was no match for my dad. I saw my uncle run up the stairs and come down with a rifle yelling at my dad to leave the house and stop beating on my ma. He told my dad that if he did not leave the house, that he would shoot him. My dad said that he—*uncle Bill*—didn't have the guts to pull the trigger; my uncle Bill then turned and moved behind my ma, pushed the gun under my ma's right arm, and ran back upstairs, leaving my ma in the doorway of the bedroom alone.

"I went in the kitchen, but then I heard my dad say that he was going to kill her and me too. I watched them argue and fight so many times before and I was just sick of it and—*bang*—I heard the shot. I turned and went back into the bedroom and saw my dad sitting on the floor, and his upper part of his body and head were lying on the bed, coughing and bleeding all over, blood was running through his nose. My ma was in the doorway of the bedroom, holding the rifle on her right hip.

"I asked my ma where she shot him and she goes, 'Robert, I don't know; God, I don't know.'"

"My ma said to call an ambulance and I went into the living room and called 911."

"I told them that my ma shot my dad and that he was bleeding bad. They told me to put a pressure bandage on the wound and apply pressure to stop the bleeding, but I didn't know what a pressure bandage was."

"I went back to the bedroom and my dad looked like he was dead, cuz he wasn't breathing anymore. Blood was all over the bed and the walls and running down my dad's face cuz he was coughing up blood and his shirt was soaked with it."

"I could see a puncture wound on his upper left chest."

"I asked my ma why she didn't put a pressure bandage on him, and she said that she was afraid that he wasn't dead and that he would grab her if she bent down to help him. My ma was really shaking and she said that that son of a bitch would never beat her again."

"All right, did the ambulance finally come?"

"If it did, I wasn't home."

"You left after that?"

"Yes."

"Why did you leave?"

"I didn't want to stay there. I may have done something bad to my ma."

"That's all the questions I have, thank you," said Mr. Brenner.

"We will take a short recess, Mr. Chartier," announced the judge.

"You may step down, Master Davis, and we will be out for about ten minutes and then we will resume with cross-examination. Court will be in recess," declared the judge, as he slammed down his gavel with a *bang*.

(At about 11:04 a.m., court recessed and reconvened at about 11:17 a.m.)

"All rise," announced the bailiff.

"Master Davis, will you come forward, please, and have a seat again in the witness chair. You're still under oath," said Judge Kaufman.

"Mr. Chartier, you may proceed."

"Thank you, Your Honor."

David was not looking forward to cross-examining young Robert Davis. He had been through hell time after time, living in that crazy household, with two alcoholic dysfunctional parents.

What a life for a young boy. David would have bet that he did not often bring friends to his home, never knowing if his parents would be drunk or sober, whether there would be screaming, fighting, or threatening to kill one another. However, Robert had said things in Mr. Brenner's direct examination that placed his mother in a bad light. He seemed to be saying that his mother should not have shot his dad.

On the one hand, he testified how she appeared scared and was shaking with fear, but was blaming her for acting in obvious self-defense. David suspected that Will Brenner had spent considerable time coaching Robert about his testimony and had him so confused that he did not know what he had observed or how he felt about that terrible evening in his home.

David needed to get some straight answers from Robert if he was to have any hope of a favorable jury verdict in the circuit court, and he had to have those answers on the record now during the cross-examination of Robert.

"Master Davis, will it be all right if I call you Robert?"

"Yes."

"Robert, on the date of Saturday, September 22, 1984, what time did you awaken on that morning?"

"10:15."

"I beg your pardon?"

"9:45 maybe."

"Are you sure about that?"

"Yes."

"Do you recall your mother calling you to come downstairs?"

"Yes."

"What time did that occur?"

"Ten o'clock."

"Do you recall telling my investigator, in a prior interview . . . ?"

"I object, Your Honor, I think that question is improper. I think, while a certain amount of leading is proper, certainly, this shouldn't be, as to what transpired before, prior investigations," stated Mr. Brenner, with a concerned look on his face and the sound of some uneasiness in his voice.

"Overruled, he may cross-examine as to prior statements," Judge Kaufman declared.

"Robert, do you recall telling my investigator, in a prior interview, that you had awakened at 9:00, and that you were watching TV, and that you had heard your parents arguing, on the morning of September 22nd?"

"Yes."

"Well, now what is it, 9:45 or 9:00?"

"At 9:00, I woke up."

"Robert, I would like you to try to be precise."

"If you do not know the answer, don't be afraid to say that you don't know. If you cannot remember, don't be afraid to say that you can't remember."

"Now you heard arguing downstairs, between your mother and your dad, isn't that true?"

"Yes."

"And you went downstairs where the fighting was talking place?"

"Yes."

"Your father was quite drunk, was he not?"

"Yes."

"His eyes were bloodshot, were they not?"

"Yes."

"His speech was slurred, was it not?"

"To a point."

"Didn't you tell my investigator that his speech was slurred?"

"Yes."

"Your mother was asking him to leave the house, isn't that true?"

"Yes."

"I object, Your Honor. Again, I object to this line of questioning. While leading questions are permissible, this has absolutely no context with the direct examination, and I think that it is gross leading," Mr. Brenner cried out to the court.

"Overruled, it's cross-examination and, of course, leading is entirely appropriate in cross-examination," declared the judge.

"Your mother was asking your father to leave the house, isn't that true?"

"Yes."

"Your father was drunk, and she didn't want any trouble in the house, isn't that true?"

"Yes."

"Your father was accustomed to leaving for great periods of time, sometimes days, sometimes weeks, isn't that true?"

"Yes."

"He'd get upset; he would fight with the family; he would beat on the family; and somehow she would get him to leave for a while until he cooled off, isn't that true?"

"Yes."

"And isn't that what was occurring that day? Again, there was drinking; your father was drunk and she was telling him to leave the home, isn't that true?"

"Yes."

"Hadn't your mother previously suffered a heart attack after your father had assaulted her with a loaded gun?"

"Yes, she had two heart attacks."

"Didn't he fire the gun in the house to prove to her that it was loaded?"

"Yes."

"And he gave her a heart attack?"

"Yes."

"Your Honor, I object to that question. I think that would call for a medical opinion and not one coming from a lay person, as to the cause of a heart attack," stated Mr. Brenner, with his face becoming flushed.

In most circumstances, leading questions—*questions that suggest the answer*—are not allowed on direct examination of a witness—*the rules of evidence will not allow a lawyer to put words in his witness's mouth*—but on cross-examination, leading questions are permitted and are most effective.

"Overruled," declared the judge, expressing some irritation with Will's repeated objections to well structured cross-examination leading questions.

"Your father struck you that morning in the kitchen?"

"Yes."

"And where did he hit you?"

"In my face."

"And hadn't he struck your mother and tried to shove ice down her mouth?"

"Yes."

"Had your uncle Bill come down to the kitchen too?"

"Yes; he was trying to defend my ma, but dad slugged him too and it looked like my uncle was going to get a black eye."

"On past occasions, your father has smashed things in the house, hadn't he?"

"Yes."

"Hadn't he smashed the television?"

"Yes."

"Hadn't he smashed all the windows in the house?"

"Yes."

"Hadn't he set the house afire?"

"Yes."

"Hadn't he smashed vehicles into the side of the house?"

"Yes."

"Hadn't he threatened to kill himself and everyone in the house with guns?"

"Yes."

"Hadn't he threatened to kill your mother with a gun?"

"Yes."

"Didn't he point a knife at your mother on the morning in question, when this fight occurred in the kitchen?"

"Yes."

"And didn't he also threaten to commit suicide that morning?"

"Yes."

"When your mother fought back, her blows to your father were not at all hurtful to your father, were they?"

"No."

"Your father was seriously injured in a car accident many years ago, isn't that true?"

"Yes."

"Prior to that injury, was your father violent?"

"No."

"After his injuries?"

"Yes."

"In the years since his injury?"

"Yes."

"Aside from the heart attacks, had he ever caused physical injury to your mother?"

"Yes."

"In fact, wasn't there an occasion when he broke the stairway banister off and beat your mother with it, fracturing three ribs?"

"Yes."

"Wasn't there another occasion when he fractured her skull?"

"Yes."

"And he threw her out of the vehicle while driving down the highway, isn't that true?"

"Yes."

"Hadn't he said he could do anything he wanted and no one could stop him?"

"Yes."

"Hadn't he said that he could do anything and the police would not be able to do anything to stop him?"

"Yes."

"Didn't he make that statement to your mother on September 22nd?"

"Yes."

"Didn't you tell my investigator that your father wanted you to go outside and fight him?"

"Yes."

"When you arrived back at the house with your mother, wasn't your father so drunk that he didn't know how to open the door?"

"Yes."

"After entering the house, didn't your father try to shove ice down your mother's mouth?"

"Yes."

"Wasn't your mother's eye getting black?"

"Yes, she showed me."

"She showed you that it was black and blue inside of her mouth, didn't she?"

"Yes."

"Didn't she have to go to the bedroom and change her clothes, after your father had thrown ice water on her?"

"Yes."

"Didn't he threaten both you and her with guns on many occasions?"

"Yes."

"Didn't your father shoot at your mother on one occasion, when she and your uncle were driving away from the house?"

"Yes."

"Wasn't it a .308 Winchester rifle that he shot at her with?"

"Yes."

"The police were supposed to have picked up all his guns, isn't that true?"

"Yes."

"Didn't your father hide one rifle in the dog food bag?"

"Yes."

"Your father had been hospitalized because of his drinking and his crazy conduct, wasn't he?"

"Yes."

"He had been hospitalized in Tomah, Wisconsin, right?"

"Yes."

"He had been hospitalized at Newberry State Hospital, right?"

"Yes."

"He had been hospitalized in the psychiatric ward at Iron Town General Hospital, isn't that true?"

"Yes."

"Didn't he smash the windshield on your mother's car with a hammer, after you and she had returned to the house?"

"Yes."

"Didn't you tell my investigator that he was going to smash everything in the house?"

"Yes."

"He had previously smashed nearly all of the contents of your house, isn't that true?"

"Yes."

"Didn't you tell my investigator that you told your father that you were going to hit him with your baseball bat, if he started smashing the furniture?"

"Yes, I did."

"You had never challenged your father before that day, isn't that true?"

"Yes."

"But you saw fit to do so that day, isn't that true?"

"Yes, cuz I was sick and tired of it and I wasn't going to let him do it anymore."

"Didn't your father have a crazy look on his face that day?"

"Yes."

"It was scary, wasn't it?"

"Yes."

"In fact, didn't you threaten your father with a butcher knife when he tried to keep you from leaving the house, earlier that day?"

"Yes, he had a hammer in his hand and was saying that he was going to hit me with it."

"He hit you with that hammer, didn't he?"

"Yes, he hit me on my back and in the stomach with it."

"Didn't your mother and your uncle try to defend you against your father, after he had hit you with the hammer?"

"Yes, they began punching at him, but didn't really stop him."

"Didn't your father look at you with a mean look?"

"Yes."

Tears were streaming down Robert's face as he listened to David's questions and answered them, frequently looking at his mother, sitting at the defendant's table with her face buried in her hands and sobbing aloud. David could not end the cross-examination, however, until he was certain that he had a complete record for the trial. David knew that Will would be trying to rehabilitate Robert's testimony for Will's purposes, prior to trial.

"Your father had gotten hold of your mother and was shaking her, wasn't he? Didn't you tell my investigator that?"

"Yes."

"Didn't your father then release her and go into his bedroom and your mother followed him into the bedroom telling him to leave the house?"

"Yes."

"They were screaming at each other, isn't that true?"

"Yes."

"You heard your father tell your mother that he was thinking that he will kill her, your uncle, and you and then commit suicide, isn't that true?"

"Yes, but . . ."

"Isn't that true?"

"Objection, Your Honor," Will cried out to the court. "The witness should be permitted to answer the question."

"Well, Mr. Chartier," said Judge Kaufman, "the form of the question, where you are stating a fact and seeking assent has been going along rather well, but you need to give the witness a chance to fully respond."

"Thank you, Your Honor, I will certainly try to do that."

"You saw your father hit your mother in the bedroom and knock her to the floor, isn't that true?"

"Yes, she was pinned between the end of the bed and her oxygen tank."

"Your mother was not able to get up on her own, isn't that true?"

"Yes."

"Didn't you tell my investigator that you had to help your mother up?"

"Yes, my uncle had to hit my dad in order that I could help my ma get up."

"Did you see your uncle go upstairs and come down with a gun?"

"Yes, my ma was at the bedroom door, and my uncle was sort of behind her; my dad was screaming at them saying that he was going to kill us all and then commit suicide; he told my uncle that my uncle didn't have the guts to shoot him, my uncle turned around, stuffing the rifle under my ma's arm, and ran back up the stairs."

"I heard my ma tell my dad to get out of the god dammed house."

"You were in the kitchen at that time, isn't that true?"

"Yes."

"Did you hear your father say that he was going to take the gun from her and shoot both of you?"

"Yes."

"Yes, Ma said that he charged off the bed and tried taking the gun from her and was real close to her when she fired the gun."

"You then pushed your mother aside and went into the bedroom and checked on your father, right?"

"He must have staggered backwards cuz he landed on the bed. He was bleeding and coughing blood all over. It was running from his nose, too. My ma said to go call the ambulance, and I went and called 911."

"Now, Robert, earlier in the morning on that same day, you called the Michigan State Police when your father was threatening your mother with a knife, isn't that true?"

"Yes."

"And didn't they come to the house, around noon?"

"I don't know, I wasn't there at that time. I took off for a while on my bike."

"Now, Robert, you don't think that your mother wanted to kill your father, do you?"

"I object, Your Honor. It calls for a conclusion," Will raising his voice to the court.

"I'll take the witness's answer," the judge responded.

"Well, the times before, she never meant it and I think that she probably didn't want to pull the trigger this time, in my opinion, and I wish she hadn't."

"Now, after your mother told you to call the ambulance, you did so, isn't that true?"

"Yes."

"Your Honor, that will be all the questions I have for Master Robert Davis," David stated.

"Very well . . . Mr. Brenner, call your next witness," requested the judge.

"I would now call Dr. Donald Kreuger," Will stated.

Dr. Donald Kreuger was called by the people at 11:45 a.m., was sworn by the court, and direct examination began with Will Brenner questioning, "Doctor Kreuger, you are a medical examiner, is that right?"

"Yes."

"That's for the county of Pictured Rocks?"
"Yes."
"And for the record, will you state your entire name?"
"Donald Christian Kreuger."
"And doctor, were you on duty as a medical examiner on September 22, 1984?"
"Yes."
"Did you have an occasion to examine a body on that date?"
"Yes."
"What time did that examination occur?"
"8:05 p.m."
"Would you describe the person that you examined?"
"The body was an obese male, whose head was covered with blood; his oral cavity filled with blood, was not breathing, and had no heart sounds."
"Doctor, were you able to determine the cause of death?"
"Based on my external examination, I felt the obvious cause of death was a gunshot wound in the second intercostal space, just to the left of the sternum, by a small-caliber gunshot wound that I concluded entered the aorta, the trachea, accounting for his mouth being full of blood."
"Doctor, were you the person that also prepared and filed a certificate of death regarding Mr. John Davis?"
"Yes."
"Doctor, I show you a document and ask if you can identify it?"
"Yes, it is a certified copy of the death certificate that I completed, following my examination of the body that evening."
"Let the records show that I handed to the doctor for identification, the death certificate for John Davis."
"The people move for the admission into evidence, the death certificate of John Davis, as identified by the medical examiner."
"People's exhibit #1 will be received in evidence," declared Judge Kaufman.
"Thank you, Your Honor," Will stated.
"Doctor, showing you a copy of the certificate of death, does it appear to be a duplicate of the certified copy that was just entered into evidence by this court?"
"Yes."
"Does it identify the cause of death?"
"Yes."

"And what is that, please?"

"Hemorrhage of the ascending aorta."

"And, doctor, does it indicate the time of death?"

"Yes."

"And, what is that, please?"

"The hour of death was estimated at approximately 7:20 p.m., based on the history that I received and I pronounced dead at 8:05 p.m."

"Doctor, did you perform an autopsy on the body?"

"No, what I performed was only a simple gross autopsy."

"That's all the questions I have for you, doctor. Thank you."

"Mr. Chartier?" queried the judge.

"Thank you, Your Honor," David said.

"Good morning, doctor."

"Good morning."

"Doctor, what is a gross autopsy, as opposed to an autopsy?"

"An autopsy includes external examination, internal examination, and microscopic examination, whereas a gross autopsy is what you visibly see, from the exterior of the body."

"Doctor, did you go to the scene of the shooting?"

"No."

"So, did you give anyone orders to remove the body from the scene?"

"No."

"Did you perform some tests on the body?"

"Blood alcohol."

"Does that tell you how long a person has been dead?"

"No."

"Did you make any entry into the body other than with a needle to draw blood?"

"No."

"Did you do any rigor mortis studies on the body?"

"There wasn't any rigor mortis. I believe that death was sudden."

"From the examination of the body, can you tell the time of death in this case?"

"No, not accurately. I have to go by the history I received."

"After death, does the human body bleed?"

"There would be some gravitational flow of blood out of the wound until pressure reaches equalization beyond the wound where the blood is leaking out, the pressure within the blood vessels."

"But generally, the body does not bleed a great deal, after death, isn't that true?"

"True, but the weight of the lungs and the abdominal contents will generally push out a little more until the vessels collapse."

"You're not a pathologist, are you, doctor?"

"No, I am not."

"I have nothing further, doctor."

"Mr. Brenner, do you have any redirect?" inquired Judge Kaufman.

"No further questions, and the people move for a bind over on the charges brought before this court, Your Honor."

"Will the defense wish to present any testimony in this proceeding, Mr. Chartier?" asked the judge.

"I had contemplated no witnesses at the preliminary exam, Your Honor."

"Very well, the proofs are closed. We will take argument at 2:00 p.m., court is recessed and we will reconvene at 2:00 p.m."

"All rise!" declared the bailiff.

Judge Kaufman retired to his chamber.

David asked the sheriff to allow him to take Jean outside so that she could have a cigarette. He knew that she smoked Virginia Slims and that she must be half-crazy, not having had a cigarette since leaving the jail. They stood near the outside door of the courthouse and she had one of her "slims," while the sheriff watched from a distance of about twenty feet away.

It felt good to be out of the courtroom for a few minutes. Being a trial lawyer is very stressful at times, especially when your client is facing possible prison, if convicted. In spite of her frequent sobbing, David felt that Jean was holding up quite well. It is a harrowing experience being a defendant, with all the forces of government coming down on you. Even David, as her lawyer, could only imagine her stress and panic in realizing what was really happening.

At 2:00 p.m., the court reconvened.

"Continuing the case of the People of the State of Michigan v. Jean Davis, proofs have been closed and the people have made a motion to bind over. We will now proceed with argument from the defense, Mr. Chartier," declared Judge Kaufman.

"Thank you, Your Honor; I will try to be relatively brief in this matter. I understand the purpose of the preliminary examination very well, and the issues that are to be dealt with," David stated.

"Your Honor, the medical examiner testified concerning the cause of death and admitted that he is not a pathologist. He admitted that he does not have a pathology report and admitted that his tentative findings could be altered by scientific findings of a pathologist. Without definitive testimony as to the cause of death, the conduct of this defendant cannot be said to have caused the death of John Davis."

"The medical examiner's testimony merely speculates regarding the path of the bullet trajectory inside the body and the organs affected, after all, he never entered the body to confirm his suspicions and suppositions. I believe that the medical proofs offered by the prosecution are seriously lacking in identification of the injuries to the decedent and cause of death for purposes of this preliminary examination and fails to prove that a crime of murder was committed."

"The medical examiner never went to the scene and did not know the time of death, and even speculated that the person whose body he examined may not have died until just before his arrival at the hospital. There is no testimony that the person the doctor examined is one and the same person apparently shot at the Davis residence."

"There is no proof that there was not an intervening, superseding cause of death."

"Your Honor, for the reasons stated, I object to a bind over of this defendant on the charge of felony murder."

The court addressing the issue of bind over stated, "In this matter, the court considers the testimony submitted at preliminary examination. From that testimony, the court would find that there has been testimony introduced which proves and establishes, first, that a crime was committed as contained in the complaint and warrant and, secondly, that there is probable cause to believe that the defendant committed that crime."

"People's exhibit #1 was received in evidence and is a self-authenticating document as to the identification of the decedent and, from all the testimony taken in this courtroom this morning, the court finds that the person named in the death certificate is the same as in the complaint and warrant, to wit: John Davis."

"There is testimony that the defendant said in essence that she would have used any means to be free of him, or words to that effect, and the elements of the charge in the complaint and warrant have been made out on the open charge of murder, the degree of murder to be determined by a jury."

"Arraignment in the circuit court is set for October 24, 1984, in the circuit courtroom at 9:30 a.m. The defendant is remanded to the custody of the sheriff."

"Court is adjourned."

"All rise!"

Judge Kaufman retired to his chamber.

Jean was looking at David with that look that is a blend of anxiety and depression, questioning, without speaking, *"What's next?"* David asked her to stay seated and they would talk, as soon as everyone had left the courtroom. The sheriff, of course, remained in the courtroom next to the side door, as they had not yet arranged for her release under the bond agreement that had been agreed upon. David told Jean that it would be his next concern and that he would prepare whatever the court needed to secure her release, pending trial. With that said, he motioned to the sheriff that he could now return her to the jail.

David returned to his office and began drafting the pledge of real estate title, for twenty-five thousand ($25,000) dollars to the Pictured Rocks Circuit Court, subordinating his future interest in the Davis farm, giving the court a first position as a secured party, which would bear both the signatures of Jean and himself.

After he had completed drafting the document, Sandy typed it on her IBM Memory Typewriter, printed it, and David took the original and a copy of the documents to the jail and sat down with Jean to execute it in the presence of a notary public. *He had a notary public from the county clerk's office agree to walk over to the jail and notarize the document, as a favor to him*—and two witnesses—*both of whom were from the probate court, also as a favor to him.* David then recorded the pledge in the Office of the Register of Deeds of Pictured Rocks County.

He then obtained a certified copy of it and delivered it to the clerk of the circuit court. He was fortunate that the Honorable William F. Roode, judge of the circuit court, was in the courthouse and he was able to see him in his chambers. After showing him the certified copy of the recorded pledge, Judge Roode agreed to release Jean on the agreed bond by 5:00 p.m. that afternoon.

David went back to the jail and told Jean that she would be released on the bond by 5:00 p.m. and that she should come into his office the following day because he wanted to discuss the employing of expert witnesses and talk to her about the trial strategy that he had in mind. He said good-bye to her and noticed a change in her face, as she began thinking of leaving the jail and returning home. She was visibly pleased, and David swears that he could see a twinkle in her eyes as he left. She seemed more like a little farm girl than a woman who had killed her husband and was now facing trial for murder.

David left Jean, and as he drove back to the office, he had real mixed feelings about that day's events. David did not think that he seriously expected the judge not to bind Jean over for trial. He was hoping, however, that the judge might have bound her over on a lesser included offense of involuntary manslaughter, a maximum fifteen-year offense, instead of open murder . . . a life offense.

David was not able to think about that any more. He needed to contact the experts that would be required for trial—*witnesses who will raise a reasonable doubt as to the trajectory of the bullet on its way to the body of John Davis and hopefully Jean's state of mind, at the instant the shot was fired*—to counter the expected testimony of the Michigan State Police ballistics expert and the forensic examiner who he expected *would not testify favorably* regarding Jean's state of mind on the day of the shooting.

David had no idea who these experts might be, but he was thinking that he might call other attorneys who were members of the Michigan Trial Lawyers Association and, specifically, those who had tried murder cases in the past and might have a list of experts that they used in trial.

Chapter 7

A Search for Experts

(Dialing . . . 1-916-555-4700) . . . Ringing . . .

(Ringing . . .) "California State University," stated the operator, "May I help you?"

"Yes, would you please transfer me to the Criminal Justice School and I will speak with their receptionist to obtain the extension number that I need," David said.

(Ringing . . .) "Criminal Justice, may I help you?" said the operator.

"Yes, would you please give me the name and extension of the dean of the School for Criminalistics?" David requested.

Criminalistics is the forensic science of analyzing and interpreting evidence using the natural sciences. Forensic science pertains to all sciences applied to legal problems. Criminalists use the science of criminalistics to solve crimes. They examine and identify physical evidence to reconstruct a crime scene. Physical evidence can be a weapon, a piece of clothing, a bloodstain, drugs, or even a vapor in the air. Criminalists use this physical evidence to provide a link between a suspect and the victim. The transfer of clothing fibers or hair fibers between a suspect and the victim can provide just such a link. Fingerprints, bullets, and shoe impressions are other important links.

Physical evidence is collected from a crime scene that includes the victim's body and the surrounding area of the crime. Criminalists collect physical evidence at crime scenes and receive evidence at the laboratory, which had been collected at the crime scene by crime scene investigators. The proper collection of evidence is essential to prevent contamination and destruction of the evidence. Once the evidence is brought to the crime lab, criminalists conduct tests depending on the type of evidence. Criminalists are often called to court to provide expert testimony regarding their methods and findings.

Typical tasks include the following:

- *Examines, tests, and analyzes tissue samples, chemical substances, physical materials, and ballistics evidence, using recording, measuring, and testing equipment.*
- *Interprets laboratory findings and test results to identify and classify substances, materials, and other evidence collected at crime scene.*
- *Collects and preserves criminal evidence used to solve cases.*
- *Confers with ballistics, fingerprinting, handwriting, documents, electronics, medical, chemical, or metallurgical experts concerning evidence and its interpretation.*
- *Reconstructs crime scene to determine relationships among pieces of evidence.*
- *Prepares reports or presentations of findings, investigative methods, or laboratory techniques.*
- *Testifies as expert witness on evidence or laboratory techniques in trials or hearings.*

"Professor Paul C. Cachette, extension 5463, may I ring for you?" she inquired.

"Yes, please," David, replied.

(Ringing . . .) "Professor Cachette," the voice announced.

"Good morning, Professor, my name is David Chartier; I am an attorney from the Upper Peninsula of Michigan and am defending a murder case back here in Michigan," David said.

"Professor, I'm in need of a ballistics expert, can you help me?"

David was quite sure his voice sounded more like pleading than inquiring—hoping for an affirmative answer.

"I possibly can be of help to you, but I need to know more about the case, and what it is that you want me to do?" he asked.

"Well, I am defending a woman for the first-degree murder of her husband. He was drunk in the home, threatening to kill her, her brother, a minor son, and then commit suicide. My client's brother had stuffed a rifle under my client's arm, and she was trying to get her drunken husband to leave the house; he had violently assaulted my client numerous times during the day and she was just trying to get him to leave the house."

"He got up and was again sitting on the bed, while she was holding the rifle at her hip, five feet from the bed. He again threatened her saying that he was going to take the gun from her and kill her brother and the boy. She told him to leave the house, but he got to his feet and charged her. She says that he was real close to her when the shot was fired from her hip and that blood came to his mouth, as soon as she fired."

"The pathologist autopsy report states that the bullet entered the left upper chest and struck the second rib, and from there traveled with a downward trajectory *inside* the body, passing through the pericardium, posterior left atrim, left main stem bronchus, lodging in the seventh vertebral body."

"The ballistics expert for the Michigan State Police asserts that my client was at the threshold of the bedroom door, aiming *at a downward angle*, and fired while the decedent was seated on the bed, and that the distance from the muzzle of the gun and the shirt worn by the decedent was between eighteen inches to five feet."

"My private investigator, examining the scene, during the evening following the shooting, found a spot of blood at the threshold of the bedroom door, close to where the muzzle of the gun would have been."

"I specifically need to know if the downward trajectory *inside* the body of a .22-caliber bullet tells us anything about the trajectory of the bullet *on its way to the body*. I need to know if the ballistics evidence will support my client's story that her husband was on his feet, charging her, or if he was indeed seated on the bed when she fired the rifle."

"Professor Cachette, would you consider reconducting the ballistics tests, and *if* your testing supports my client's version of the facts, agree to come to Michigan to testify?"

"Yes, I think that it is an interesting case and I would certainly agree to conduct ballistics testing, but I would have to have the rifle, the shirt worn by the decedent, the Michigan State Police test patterns that they obtained from their testing. Are you going to be able to furnish them to me?"

"I believe so, Professor, I will work on getting a court order requiring them to release those items directly to me, and I will plan to visit you in Sacramento, when you're ready to do the testing."

"Please send me a letter outlining your consulting rates, including your travel and court appearance charges, and I will promptly pay those charges upon receipt of your invoice."

"Very good," Professor Cachette replied.

David hung up the telephone and felt grateful at having found a ballistics expert, with plenty of credentials, who is willing to conduct the ballistics testing and come to Michigan to testify, presuming his testimony will support Jean's version of the facts.

One down, two to go! David then wanted to try to find the psychiatrist that Mrs. Frances Hume had hired after pouring kerosene near her sleeping husband and lighting the house afire. David thought that his name was Dr. Carl M. Bergman, and when he dialed 411 Information for the Lansing area, the operator said that his number is 517-555-2000—*Lansing, Michigan, is about 351 miles from the city of Pictured Rocks, about a seven and a half hour drive by car.*

David dialed that number . . . (Ringing) . . .

"Dr. Bergman's office," a female voice announced.

"May I speak with Dr. Bergman?" David asked. "This is Attorney Chartier, from the Upper Peninsula."

"Please hold," she said.

. . . (Ringing) . . .

"This is Dr. Bergman, how can I help you, Mr. Chartier?" he questioned.

"Doctor, I am defending a woman in a first-degree spousal abuse murder case here in the Upper Peninsula and am in need of a psychiatric examination of her that will determine her state of mind, at the instant the shot was fired. I will be filing a notice of insanity, and she will be undergoing a forensic exam. I expect that they will find her competent to stand trial. Do you think that you could help me?" David asked.

"Well, I might be able to see her after her forensic exam. Call me to make an appointment as soon as you know when her forensic exam will be completed."

Two down and one to go! Much of David's time involved talking with people at the American Trial Lawyers Association, and the Michigan Trial Lawyers Association, trying to get a lead on a spousal abuse syndrome expert. He was given leads and followed up on most of them, but did not find any of them impressive. They did not have the credentials, had not published, and/or had no courtroom experience. Feeling a considerable degree of frustration, David talked to a friend of his, a trial attorney in Traverse City who had tried a couple of spousal abuse syndrome cases. His name is Attorney Bill Ryan, and after talking with him, he advised David that he had used a psychologist from Eastern Michigan University in Ypsilanti, Michigan, by the name of Ms. Camellia Storm, PhD.

He told David that she had an impressive background, had handled herself well in the courtroom, was very credible on direct examination, and was unshaken throughout the cross-examination. Hearing this glowing report about a prospective expert witness gave David some feeling of optimism, but he needed to talk with her. He could only hope that she might agree to see Jean.

David called her at her Ypsilanti office and, after introducing himself and telling her that Attorney Bill Ryan had recommended her, he told her about the case. He asked if she might see Jean and consider testifying if she found the spousal abuse syndrome to be involved, which influenced or controlled Jean's thinking at the time of the shooting.

"Yes, I will agree to see her, but I must warn you that I have very strict criteria that must be met before I will agree to testify in a case of this nature."

"I understand, Doctor, but if you will agree to see her, we can go on from there."

"When you're ready, call my office and make an appointment; by the way, what's her name?"

"Jean Davis, doctor."

"Very well, I'll watch for her name," she said.

David felt that he had a productive day, having located and spoken to three potential experts, having quite good credentials and who are willing to consider working with him to answer important technical forensic questions that could make the difference between a conviction and an acquittal.

Chapter 8

Discovery

A lawyer in the general practice of law does not often get involved in a murder case. Most attorneys never do. There are many aspects of the practice of law that compensate lawyers extremely well; very few become criminal defense attorneys.

Much of the time, the criminal defense lawyer finds himself or herself working with only small retainers, are appointed by the court at quite low rates, or doing the work pro bono—*for the public good*.

A lawyer in the Upper Peninsula embarks on the practice of law, never expecting to make the kind of money that one in metropolitan areas rightfully expect and usually receive. David came up to the U.P. to practice because he wanted a better quality of life for himself and his family than the metropolitan areas could provide.

David began drafting a "Notice of Intent to Claim Insanity as a Defense," alleging first that Jean was not competent to stand trial. Alternatively, David claimed that, at the time the shot was fired, Jean, although knowing the difference between right and wrong, was laboring under a mental illness and was unable to conform her conduct to the requirements of the law—*an irresistible impulse*—and thus was not guilty of the charged crime.

David prepared a motion for production of the statements, of res geastae witnesses—*[Latin: Things Done . . . An exception of the hearsay rule in American Jurisprudence, concerning spontaneous statements, made concurrent with an event, without deliberation, carrying a high degree of credibility, leaving little room for misunderstanding or misinterpretation]—* and for production of items of physical property, specifically:

a. the rifle,
b. spent shell casing,
c. bullet,
d. shirt worn by the decedent and
e. the ballistics test patterns made by the Michigan State Police ballistics expert.

He stayed at the office late each evening, researching the law, relative to these matters, and wrote a brief in support of the motion for production, filing each of his motions with the court and serving them upon the prosecuting attorney as well. He filed a notice of hearing relative to these motions for October 24, 1984, at 9:30 a.m., or such other date as may be ordered by the court.

David received a letter from the Center for Forensic Psychiatry in Ann Arbor, Michigan, on October 25, 1984, notifying him to have Jean appear at their facilities on November 7, 1984, to undergo examination for competency to stand trial and criminal responsibility, as ordered by Circuit Judge William F. Roode.

As a convenience to Jean, David was able to schedule her psychiatric exam with Dr. Carl M. Bergman in Lansing on November 8, 1984. He arranged lodging for her in Ann Arbor and in Lansing, to insure that she had a comfortable place to rest or to spend the night at each location, if needed. A friend of hers was going to drive and stay with her throughout the trip from the Upper Peninsula. David asked her to call him if anything went wrong on the trip when she returned home. He copied the preliminary examination transcript and sent it to Dr. Bergman so that he would have a chance to review it, prior to meeting with Jean.

On October 24, 1984, the court heard David's motion for the production of items of physical property. The judge issued an order directing the Michigan State Police to release those items to David and authorized his taking of them to the College of Criminology at California State University for further testing, by Professor Paul C. Cachette, over the objections of Will Brenner.

On November 9, 1984, David went to the Michigan State Police Post to pick up the rifle, shell casing, the bullet, shirt worn by John, and all of the ballistics test patterns. Sandy had made flight arrangements and had advised the airline security people that David would be taking an unloaded rifle on board as checked luggage.

California State University was beautiful. The temperature was in the 70s, and David sure appreciated getting out of the snow country for a few days. He was there on a very important mission, but could not help feeling happy, being in such pleasant surroundings.

When he was checking into his hotel room, David was given a message from Professor Cachette, requesting that he come to his laboratory at 10:00 a.m. the following morning.

It was near dinnertime and he called a friend who lived in Sacramento and invited him and his wife to dinner at the hotel. It was nice to see them and the dinner was great. After dinner, they suggested that they drive David around the area, seeing some of the city and countryside. They even drove past Folsom Prison, just twenty miles from Sacramento.

David could not help but think of Johnny Cash's 1968 performance there with his song "Johnny Cash at Folsom Prison." David liked that song when it came out and still enjoyed listening to it, on an "Oldies" station, from time to time.

The following morning, David went to the School of Criminology, specifically the Criminalistics Laboratory, and met Professor Paul C. Cachette. David carried with him the rifle, spent shell casing, bullet, shirt worn by the decedent, and the ballistics test patterns made by the Michigan State Police ballistics expert, as well as a copy of the autopsy report establishing the bullet trajectory inside the body of the decedent.

Professor Cachette explained his plan for doing the ballistic testing and started photographing all of the articles that David had brought to him and signed receipts for the evidence, being careful to maintain the chain of custody. David spent most of the day with him and at the end of the day; Dr. Cachette secured all of the items of evidence in an evidence safe in the laboratory. He told David that he needed to have possession of the items for two days and would then release them to David for the return trip to Michigan. David invited him to have dinner with him that evening at the hotel, but he declined, saying that he intended to return to the laboratory during the early evening hours to complete some of the tests. David bid him good night and told him that he would be back in the morning. That night, David stayed in his hotel room, thinking about the case and making notes that would become part of the "Defendant's Theory of the Case," which would eventually become part of the court's "Instruction to the Jury," after the closing of proofs and prior to the jury retiring to deliberate on their verdict.

Sleep did not come easily that night, David tossed and turned, found himself in a dream—*The trial was underway and he had no scientific data to combat the prosecutor's ballistic evidence. He was perspiring and the jury was announcing its verdict of guilty of first-degree murder. He awakened, wet with perspiration, fell back to sleep, only to find himself in the same dream, this time listening to the judge imposing a sentence of life imprisonment.* He couldn't just shut his mind off and go to sleep. He repeatedly fell asleep then moments later was awake, and this continued throughout the night.

It had never been David's nature to separate himself from an important case after leaving the office. Frequently, he would return to the office after having dinner with his family and work until midnight and beyond when getting close to trial. There is a lot for a trial attorney to do when preparing for trial *(e.g. frequently conversing with the client, studying the juror questionnaires, preparing for the voir dire of the jury, organizing exhibits, outlining the key questions for cross-examination of prosecution witnesses, preparation of opening statements to the jury, organizing and preparing to examine defense witnesses, preparing an outline of defendant's closing argument, drafting the defense theory of the case, preparing proposed instructions to the jury, writing a trial brief covering all anticipated issues, together with citations and authorities, and drafting of proposed forms of jury verdicts).* It is hardly a wonder why a trial lawyer gets very little sleep.

David awakened in the morning, felt that he had not had much rest, and after taking a shower, got dressed, went to the dining room for breakfast, and then went back to the laboratory to meet with Professor Cachette to get the results of his work.

"Good morning, Professor Cachette. Please don't ask me how I slept," David pleaded.

"Good morning, David, I'm sorry that you didn't sleep well, but I think that I have some good news for you," Dr. Cachette declared.

"Great, right now I could use some good news. I want to tell you about my night, but I'll wait until you share the good news."

"I test fired the rifle and compared the spent casing with the ones you brought with you from the Michigan State Police, and there is a perfect match of the casings and the bullets."

"Next, I performed a number of test firings of the rifle at different distances and a variety of angles and compared the patterns with the Michigan State Police patterns and the shirt worn by the decedent. My conclusions are that the distance from the muzzle of the rifle and the shirt worn by the decedent was greater than twelve inches but less than twenty-four inches, and the trajectory was slightly upward, at approximately thirty degrees up from level."

"Oh, Professor, you have made my day! You have given me objective scientific findings, corroborating my client's version of the shooting."

"Thank you, Professor Cachette, thank you."

"Professor, with a slight upward trajectory of the bullet on its way to the body, how can you explain the downward trajectory of the bullet on the inside of the body?"

"Well, a .22-caliber bullet is such a small caliber that once it strikes the skin or bone, it can easily take any direction it wants inside the body. The trajectory of the bullet on the inside of the body does not tell us anything with respect to the trajectory of the bullet on its way to the body. You simply cannot discern the outside trajectory of such a small-caliber bullet by looking at the trajectory of the bullet on the inside of the body."

"Professor, will you come to Michigan and testify at the time of trial and bring with you your test results and exhibits to be marked and introduced as evidence?"

"Yes."

"Professor, I am not going to request that you write me a report of your testing or your conclusions. I want you to have considerable latitude when you're testifying, not being boxed in by some data that may have appeared in a report. Just bring your exhibits and your notes to the courtroom."

"Of course I will, David, and I appreciate that I will have that latitude when I come for the trial. I will have my secretary send you my fees for the testing and my testimony, as well as my anticipated expenses. You can send me a check, as soon as you will know the date that I need to appear."

They then went through the process of transferring possession of the items that David had brought to the laboratory and the signing of the receipts, placing the items back in David's custody, to be taken back to Michigan.

"Again, thank you, Professor."

"You're welcome, David. Have a nice trip back to Michigan and stay in touch."

David felt good upon leaving the university, believing that with Professor Cachette's testimony at trial, he would raise substantial doubt as to the guilt of Jean. This testimony, combined with the testimony of Don White's discovery of the blood near the threshold of the bedroom, the testimony of a lab technician from the Pictured Rocks Memorial Hospital that the blood is human blood, and of the same type as that of the decedent, will surely bolster Jean's and Professor Cachette's testimony regarding distance and trajectory.

David loved being in California, but now, with Professor Cachette's findings, he could not wait to get home to tell Jean, who David knew was nervously waiting in silence for some word from him. He had a return flight the following morning and thought that he might just relax and rest up for his flight back to the Iron Town County Airport.

David had left his car at the airport and had a forty-five-minute drive to Pictured Rocks. It was November 16, 1984, and upon arriving back in Pictured Rocks, David went directly to the Michigan State Police Post and returned the items that he had taken to California and obtained signatures on the receipts for the items, insuring that the chain of custody was maintained. He thanked them but did not discuss the nature of the tests that Professor Cachette had performed, or the results.

David then returned to his office, called Jean, and asked her to stop in to see him, which she did about 4:30 p.m. that afternoon. David questioned her about her trip downstate and her appointments with the Center for Forensic Psychiatry and her appointment with Dr. Camellia Storm. She told David that she had felt that her visits with both of them went fairly well, but that she was very nervous about her interview in Ann Arbor. David then shared with her his trip to California and the findings of Professor Cachette. Jean's face lit up with a smile as he told her of the scientific testing that confirmed her version of the facts. He also told her that he would be in telephone contact with Dr. Camellia Storm within the next few days and will try to get her to commit to coming to the Upper Peninsula for the trial.

Dr. Camellia Storm seemed quite interested in testifying in Jean's defense at the time of trial. She indicated that this case was exactly the kind of case that met all of her criteria, leaving her comfortable with the prospect of appearing in court and testifying about the spousal abuse syndrome and its particular implications regarding Jean Davis.

David told Dr. Storm that he did not want a written report that could limit her testimony at the time of trial. Rather, he wanted her to have the greatest flexibility in describing the spousal abuse syndrome and relating it to Jean's state of mind, as of the instant in time when the shot was fired. Dr. Storm asked if David had any concerns regarding her fees and projected expenses, to which David replied that he would promptly pay her invoice upon receipt.

Next, David called Dr. Carl M. Bergman and thanked him for seeing Jean. Doctor Bergman said, "David . . . Jean was not insane, but was in dire fear for her life—*beyond terror*—when the shot was fired."

"Dr. Bergman, I am so pleased with your diagnosis and findings; I do not know what to say, besides thank you. I'll move to dismiss our claim of insanity and proceed to defend this case on the theory of self-defense," David declared.

"I do not want a written report, doctor, but I will contact you just as soon as I have a firm trial date."

"How much lead time do you need, doctor?"

"Try to give me at least two weeks' notice so that I can adjust my schedule."

"I will, doctor, and again, thank you."

As David hung up the telephone, he was shaking. It was hard to believe how well the self-defense issue was beginning to develop. Now he had to concentrate on the voir dire of the jury panel, and he was nervous about the notoriety of the Davis family and their dysfunctional lifestyle. He felt sure that some would put a lot of blame on Jean for not leaving the marriage earlier and for her own aggressive nature with John.

Chapter 9

Pretrial Motion Regarding Voir Dire

The court convened again on November 20, 1984, to hear David's motion, regarding the special procedures for the voir dire of the jury.

Jean was with David in the courtroom—*this time she was not shackled, nor wearing a jailhouse jumpsuit*—wearing an orange-sherbet-colored pantsuit; she looked nice. Moments before, she had been waiting for David in the hallway, outside the courtroom. When he arrived, she showed him a smile, as he reached the bottom of the stairwell and entered the basement hallway outside the courtroom. David was pleased to see her smile.

"Mr. Chartier, are you ready to proceed with your motion?" asked Judge Roode.

"Yes, Your Honor, I am," David stated.

"Are you ready to proceed, Mr. Brenner?" inquired the judge.

"Yes, I am," responded Will.

Will did not look or sound real interested being in court. His response to David's motion and brief did not really address the concerns that David had raised in the motion, nor did his brief challenge David's authorities cited in his brief. David felt that Will's response to his desire to voir dire the jurors alone and outside the presence of other potential jurors was weak and mainly stressed his concern in "wasting the court's time and unnecessarily prolonging the trial."

"Mr. Chartier, it is your motion, please proceed," stated Judge Roode.

"Thank you, Your Honor."

"May it please the court, pervasive and intense publicity has surrounded this case. That publicity, unfortunately, may intrude on the thought processes of the potential jurors and may lead to jurors having deep-seated prejudices for one or both parties in this case. The voir dire procedure is the method by which it is determined whether the jurors are able to fairly and impartially try this case.

"In Michigan, it has been stated by the Supreme Court that the purpose of voir dire examination is not only to determine if a challenge for cause exist, but also to allow the parties to intelligently exercise their peremptory challenges.

"The effectiveness of voir dire, as a means of selecting an impartial jury, is maximized, if questions are posed by the attorneys involved in the case. There are numerous reasons for this. Among the reasons are those held by numerous psychologists and sociologists, which are:

- since jurors look upon the judge as an important authority figure, they are reluctant to displease him, and therefore, will tend to respond to the judge's questions with less candor than if the questions were posed by counsel;
- lawyers, as advocates who have acquired a thorough working knowledge of the details of the case, are in a better position to determine what questions should be posed to jurors and are better equipped and more inclined to follow up initial responses with the type of probing and individualized questions needed, to explore and expose prejudices;
- the nonverbal communications of a prospective juror, such as displays of tension, evasion, or hostility, are revealed more completely when questions are posed by advocates and not by a neutral judge.

"Your Honor, I recognize that, under General Court Rules, the court has discretion whether to conduct the examination of prospective jurors itself or to allow the attorneys to conduct the examination. The defendant is not asking that her counsel be allowed to conduct the full examination, but that supplemental attorney voir dire should be permitted, especially on those issues that are embarrassing or controversial and may lead to the possibilities of a potential showing of prejudice.

"Numerous courts have recognized that, when there has been pretrial publicity around a case, the judge's examination may be ineffective. These courts have stated that it is best to allow the attorneys to conduct at least some voir dire themselves.

"Your Honor, I have cited numerous cases and authorities in my brief supporting this motion on file with the court and hereby move that those authorities be incorporated into the record, as though fully stated herein.

"Your Honor, the most frequently mentioned justification for not allowing attorney-conducted voir dire, is to save the time of the court. Although attorney-conducted voir dire may take a longer time in a case like this one, both sides in this case have expended a great deal of time and energy in preparation; all of that preparation would be futile if the juror's decision is based on bias and not on a fair weighing of the evidence.

"Any time that is taken in insuring a fair and impartial jury is time both the parties and the court should be willing to expend.

"At least one Federal Appeals court has taken the position that saving time is not a valid reason for not using a procedure that will insure a fair and impartial jury. The citation for that case is in my brief, Your Honor.

"Your Honor, that court took the position that a small amount of time would be involved when compared with the possibility of a new trial and that a slightly longer voir dire process is a small price to pay for use of the optimum method of insuring a fair and impartial jury.

"Your Honor, this is a unique case. Not only has there been publicity when the event occurred, but there has been extensive publicity around pretrial motions and procedures, and the news media is in the courtroom today. Further, the issue of a wife allegedly killing her husband is one that has extensive social ramifications.

"It is, in short, a touchy subject, and it is important that prospective jurors be able to express their feelings, beliefs, and thoughts on the subject without hesitation. Any procedure that puts the jurors at ease allows them to best communicate with the court, and the parties, is the one that should be used.

"Questioning potential jurors out of the presence of other prospective jurors is necessary to elicit candid responses from the prospective jurors and to minimize the impact of his or her bias on the entire jury panel.

"Additionally, counsel would be able to effectively exercise peremptory challenges if alternate juror seats have previously been designated.

"Your Honor, individual questioning, out of the presence of other potential jurors, serves the purpose of inducing the most candid responses from each juror and minimizes the impact of his or her bias on the entire jury panel.

"Jurors will respond more truthfully and extensively when questioned individually, out of the presence of others.

"In a group setting, a juror's response will affect the responses of others and will have an impact upon the other juror's interaction during deliberations.

"In addition, Your Honor, individual voir dire protects the privacy of the prospective juror by allowing him or her to give an answer without feeling that the information given will be known to everyone in the courtroom, including other jurors.

"Federal Courts have accepted the proposition that individual voir dire promotes candor.

"Your Honor, it is best that this court use its discretion in allowing in-depth voir dire examination concerning pretrial publicity and juror's personal experiences with alcoholism and spousal abuse to be done outside the presence of other jurors. This position also appears in the American Bar Association Standard (ABA) relating to Fair Trial and Free Press, Section 3.4 (A).

"In this case, Your Honor, there will be questions on serious and intimate issues, such as the juror's awareness and experience with spousal abuse and feelings about self-defense between spouses. If people give forthright answers on voir dire, there is a good possibility that they may be embarrassed by their answers if other jurors are present. Thus, for these reasons alone, this court should allow individual voir dire of the jurors out of the presence of other jurors.

"Lastly, Your Honor, under Michigan's system of empanelling the jury, more than twelve jurors may be selected for a case. I request that the court determine, prior to the selection of the jurors, which seats will be assigned to the alternate jurors and that the parties be so informed. The jurors that sit in those seats do not have to be told that they are alternates—*there will be no problem with their deliberating the verdict, if they are needed*—and by the use of this procedure, the parties will be able to most effectively use their peremptory challenge against a juror, not in a seat designated as an alternate.

"Thank you, Your Honor."

"Mr. Brenner, do you have objection to Mr. Chartier's motion?" queried the judge.

"Yes, Your Honor, I object to Mr. Chartier's motion to conduct the voir dire of the jury, in chambers, on the record, outside the presence of all other prospective jurors, on the ground that the trial would take much longer to complete and that the court time would be significantly lengthened," stated Will.

"Defendant's motion is granted as to the voir dire process, but is denied as to the treatment of the alternate jurors," declared Judge Roode.

"I am denying defendant's motion as to the alternate jurors, not on the basis of the prosecution's objection, but on the basis that Michigan has a Code of Criminal Procedure specifically speaking to the method of jury selection in criminal cases, including alternates, and it does not follow the Federal Rules and Procedures. We will seat fourteen jurors and at the conclusion of the case, draw two names prior to the jury's deliberation so that the remaining twelve will deliberate on the verdict."

David knew that the judge was technically correct in following the Michigan Rules of Criminal Procedure, but he thought that he would make the motion anyway to lay the groundwork for a basis for appeal, should he need it. In the trial court, David must argue what the law is, but in the Supreme Court, he can argue what the law should be. He does not know if he would ever need to argue the point in an appellate court, but he wanted the record to reflect that he had raised the issue by motion in the trial court. David must admit that he had begun to think that he might have a fair chance at conducting this trial, before an impartial jury, as well as having scientific evidence that could raise a reasonable doubt in the composite mind of the jury.

The law often refers to the reasonable man or woman, but does not say what a reasonable person looks like or how he or she acts or sounds. What is meant by that phrase, in the course of trial, is the composite thinking of the jury, as the reasonable man or woman. In civil cases, the jury will judge the conduct of the parties, their apprehensions and fears, using an objective standard, weighing what the reasonable man or woman would or would not do under a given circumstance, but when sitting as a juror in a criminal case, the subjective standard is used, whereas in a crime requiring specific intent, the mental apprehensions of the defendant, the specific thinking of the defendant will be the test to judge the conduct of the defendant, notwithstanding what the reasonable person might have been thinking or how the reasonable person might have reacted to a given set of facts.

Over the years, David had found, that when trying a case, his mind is alert and his adrenalin is flowing, but when leaving the courtroom and returning to his office, to his home, or to his hotel room, he becomes quite tired and does not want to talk about the case. He will continue to think of the case, the evidence, his trial strategy, and focus on what will become his moment of ultimate advocacy—*his closing argument to the jury.*

Some cases take a long time to try—*many will take numerous days and others might take numerous weeks*—and the stress and mental strain of staying at the top of his performance is a daunting challenge, sometimes a considerable burden.

David read somewhere that a recent survey had found that fifty percent of lawyers consider suicide at least once a month. Perhaps that is not true, but when one thinks of the stress of taking on every client's troubles and telling the client not to worry, it does seem plausible. David certainly did not contemplate suicide, as he had too much to do and he wanted to see Jean acquitted of first—and second-degree murder, at a minimum.

The title "Esquire" is reserved for attorneys-at-law. In feudal times, a squire carried the shield for the knight, got him mounted and dismounted. Attorneys-at-law carry the shield for the client, trying desperately, at times, to protect him or her from all harm. In reality, however, the lawyer can be the best advocate he can be, and that is all he can be. The lawyer never controls the outcome of the case. The control is with a judge, a magistrate, the jury, or perhaps some administrative officer. The lawyer is an advocate—*and has been trained to persuade the ultimate finders of the fact and the law*—and that is indeed the extent of a lawyer's control in any case in which he appears. The art of persuasion is a carefully honed talent, which when used correctly, forcibly, and convincingly, can indeed give an observer the inaccurate impression that the lawyer has controlled the outcome of the matter in litigation. The lawyer has not controlled the outcome, but the observer has just witnessed the awesome power of persuasion, in advocacy.

"Trial will commence on November 26, 1984, at 9:00 a.m. in the morning, with the voir dire of the jury, and continue until we have a jury selected with two alternates. One hundred and thirty-three jurors have been summoned to appear; I expect that jury selection will take a considerable number of days, however, I certainly do not expect you to exhaust the panel," the judge declared and further, "Following the selection of the jury, I expect that the pretrial instructions can be given to the jury by December 7, 1984, followed by opening statements of the parties."

"Does either of the parties have any further issues that need to be heard today?" asked Judge Roode.

"None from the prosecution," said Will.

"None from the defense," David said.

"Then, this court is adjourned," declared Judge Roode.

"All rise," the bailiff announced, as Judge Roode departed the courtroom.

Jean seemed to be somewhat numb to the happenings in the courtroom. David didn't know if she had trouble following his argument to the court or if she was just "spaced-out" with the entire court proceedings, her mind wandering, spinning, the discussions in her head drowning out all dialog and sounds in the courtroom. David thought that to have no control over what is happening to you is very frightening, even though the lawyer is working very hard for the client and advocating the client's innocence; still, the absolute powerlessness of the client in the proceedings is extremely unsettling.

Jean did not have a clue how to get out of her present circumstances and begin living her life again. She was absolutely helpless before the law. The faith one has in their trial attorney in these circumstances is remarkable. The relationship of criminal client and attorney is one of love-hate. He or she knows that they have to rely on their attorney to make the right decisions, to be vigilant, resourceful, credible, and persuasive. His advocacy must not only capture the attention of the jurors, stimulate their minds and their emotions, but also their compassion and desire for justice. The jury must believe in justice and have the courage to see that justice is done, even in the face of the prosecution's constant demands for conviction.

David had often asked juries to take a journey with him through the joys, fears, and disappointments of life, from the defendant's perspective, giving each juror a complete vision of the life of the defendant, often stained with the defendant's perception of his or her circumstances, beliefs, and perceived options and actions that brought them face-to-face with the law. For this, the client loves the trial attorney, in spite of the feeling of helplessness and despair in the face of such a momentous adversity. The human mind and spirit sometimes engages the client's sense of self-preservation and instills in the mind of the defendant the notion that he or she can think their way out of his or her problems or pretend that it isn't reality. In coming to grips with the reality of powerlessness, the client resents and hates his or her lawyer, who symbolizes the reality of the dilemma.

Chapter 10

Jury Selection

> *The Code of Criminal Procedure provides . . . that any person who is put on trial for an offense punishable by death or imprisonment for life, shall be allowed to challenge peremptorily twenty of the persons drawn to serve as jurors and no more, and the prosecuting attorney, on behalf of the people, shall be allowed to challenge peremptorily fifteen of such persons, and no more.*

Additionally, both the prosecution and the defense may challenge an unlimited number of jurors for cause. However, a juror's previous formation or expression of opinion, or impression, in reference to the circumstances upon which any criminal prosecution is based, or in reference to the guilt or innocence of the defendant, or a present opinion or impression in reference thereto, not being positive in character, or not being based on personal knowledge of the facts in the case, shall not be sufficient ground of challenge for principal cause to any person if otherwise legally qualified to serve as juror, provided that such potential juror shall declare on oath, that he or she believes that he or she can render an impartial verdict, based on the evidence.

If David challenged a prospective juror for cause, however, and the judge refuses to find sufficient cause to disqualify the juror, then he will have just made an enemy for life, and he had better use one of his peremptory challenges to get the juror off the jury panel.

Jurors resent being challenged, and once an attorney has done so, he had better have a peremptory challenge to use. If he has no peremptory challenges left, then no challenge for cause should be attempted, unless the attorney is certain that the judge will grant the challenge. It is a highly dangerous challenge and not recommended.

If the lawyer has one remaining peremptory challenge and there is a juror on the panel with whom he is not totally comfortable—*but it is only a gut feeling*—then the jury panel should be accepted . . . *as is* . . . and the lawyer should not risk getting a replacement juror who might be biased when all of the peremptory challenges have been used.

One hundred thirty-three potential jurors were in court, having been summoned the week prior—*to undergo voir dire examination by the prosecution, the defense, and the court*—to determine if a panel of fourteen could be selected to hear this case and render a fair and impartial verdict as to the guilt or innocence of Jean.

Jean was next to David in the courtroom, looking nice, but worried. One hundred thirty-three prospective jurors were also in that basement courtroom. *The majestic old courthouse had burned down in prior years, and the Pictured Rocks Circuit Court was located in the basement of the new courthouse annex, within which justice was to be dispensed; the liberty of defendants, through trial, was to be granted or denied.* There was no suitable jury room, nor was there an ingress and egress route for jurors to come and go from the court, without intermingling with the spectators attending the trial. The jury room was a furnace room located near the courtroom. The public was unable to enter the courtroom, pending the completion of the jury selection process, because there was no room left in which to be seated.

David had filed an objection to trying Jean's case in that dismal basement courtroom. Suggesting a change of venue for trial, the judge took the question under advisement, but never granted nor denied his motion, and trial preparations progressed, notwithstanding his objection.

Will Brenner was at the prosecution table, nearest to the jury box—*the prosecution having the burden of proof, is seated nearest the jury throughout the trial*—and was accompanied by the arresting officer. Will and David pleasantly greeted each other upon entering the courtroom and then took their respective places awaiting Judge William F. Roode's entrance into the courtroom.

The courtroom was abuzz with conversations among members of the prospective jury but stopped immediately upon the bailiff declaring: "Hear yea! Hear yea! The circuit court for Pictured Rocks County is now in session, the Honorable William F. Roode presiding; please be seated."

The courtroom was silent, except for the rustle of bodies and chairs, as the parties, the jury panel, and Judge Roode took their respective seats.

"Is the prosecution ready to proceed?" asked Judge Roode.

"The prosecution is ready, Your Honor," declared Will.

"Is the defense ready?" asked Judge Roode.

"Yes, the defense is ready," David declared.

The court, addressing the prospective jurors:

"It is a pleasure and privilege to welcome you as prospective jurors attending the circuit court for the county of Pictured Rocks. I know that jury service may be strange and new for some of you. The remarks which the court is about to make are intended as an introduction to the proceedings for which you have been called here. Jury duty is one of the most serious duties that members of a free society are to perform. Self-government could not exist without you.

"The jury is an important part of this court. In criminal cases, the Constitution of both the United States and of the State of Michigan provide for the right of trial by a jury of twelve impartial persons. It is an ancient tradition and part of our heritage that a person accused of a crime be afforded the opportunity to be judged not by one person, but by a group of twelve of his or her fellow citizens, selected to be impartial and fair.

"Each side in a trial is entitled to jurors who approach the case with open minds and agree to keep their minds open until a verdict is reached. Jurors must be as free as humanly possible from bias, prejudice, or sympathy and must not be influenced by things they may have read or heard about or persons they may know. Although you may be qualified as a juror, there may be something that could disqualify you in a particular case or make it harmful or prejudicial for you to serve.

"A trial begins with the selection of a jury. The purpose of this selection process is to obtain information about you so that a fair and impartial jury can hear this case.

"During this first step, the court and the attorneys will ask you questions. At some point during the questioning, we will adjourn and continue the questioning of each prospective juror in the privacy of my chambers, on the record, but outside the presence of other prospective jurors. The questions are designed to discover if you have any information concerning the case or any opinions that you cannot overlook or if you have had personal experiences in your individual lives that might cause you to favor or disfavor the state or the defendant or persons who may be witnesses.

"The questions which the court and attorneys will ask may probe deeply into your attitudes, beliefs, and experiences. Such questioning is required by law to assist the court and the attorneys in the selection of an impartial jury and is not an unreasonable prying into your private lives.

"If you do not hear or understand a question from either the court or one of the attorneys, you should say so. If you do understand the question, you should answer it truthfully and completely, and please do not hesitate to speak freely about any matter which you believe the court should know.

"The selection process in a trial is called the voir dire. During the voir dire, jurors may be excused by the court for cause; that is, the court makes a determination that there is a valid reason why a juror cannot or should not serve. In addition, the attorneys for each side have a legal right to excuse a limited number of jurors without giving any reason for doing so. There is no reason to feel bad or upset or to hold this ruling against anyone. You need not take such action personally. This is merely the procedure which has developed to allow both sides to find an impartial jury.

"You will now be asked to stand and swear to answer truthfully, fully, and honestly all questions asked of you as to your qualifications to serve as a juror in this case. Should you have religious beliefs against taking any oath, you may inform me that you wish to be permitted to affirm that you will answer all questions truthfully, fully, and honestly."

The clerk of the court questioned the prospective jurors, thus:

"You and each of you do solemnly swear or affirm that you will well and truly try the issues joined in the cause now here pending, and, unless discharged by the court, a true verdict render; and that you will do so solely on the evidence introduced and in accordance with the instructions of the court, so help you God?"

"I do," each member of the potential jurors answered.

The court, again addressing the prospective jurors:

"First, let me introduce myself and my staff. I am Judge William F. Roode; the clerk of the court is Mary Ann Dudley, and the court reporter is Jill Andrews.

"Next, I want to introduce the parties to the case and the attorneys. This is a criminal case involving the charge of open murder, which I will explain more fully later. This charge has been brought against Jean Davis. The defendant's attorney is David Chartier. The attorney for the State of Michigan is Wilfred Brenner."

A list of prosecution witnesses was read to the jury, including seven police officers, two of the decedent John Davis's siblings, the decedent's son Robert, and the pathologist who had performed the autopsy of the decedent.

The defendant's list of witnesses was also read to the prospective jurors.

Judge Roode continued addressing the prospective jurors:

"We expect that once a jury is selected, this trial will last about ten days. If you anticipate that the length of this case will cause you actual hardship, please let me know.

"From time to time we have prospective jurors who have health problems which prevents them from sitting as jurors. Is there anyone who has serious back problems, which would make them unable to sit down for two or three hours at a time?"

—*No response*—

"Is there anyone who has a serious hearing impairment?"

—*No response*—

Over the next ten days, excluding Saturdays and Sundays, each of the one hundred thirty-three prospective jurors were asked questions by both the prosecution and the defense attorneys, probing deeply into their thoughts, beliefs, prejudices, biases, and personal experiences, to determine which were able to be neutral jurors, capable of judging the guilt or innocence of Jean Davis, free of prejudice or bias.

Judge Roode excused many of the jurors for cause after hearing their answers to the questions that were asked of them. Many had formed opinions, read newspapers, and had talked to others claiming to know the facts; most stated that they would have difficulty setting aside those opinions or beliefs. Some were released because they indicated that they were quite familiar with the Davis family and had strong opinions about the lifestyle of both John and Jean Davis, favoring one side or the other.

Both David and Will had used most all of their peremptory challenges to excuse jurors that appeared to favor the opposition. Will eliminated jurors who previously had minor difficulties with the law or who appeared very adamant about holding the prosecution to a strict fulfillment of its burden of proof. David, on the other hand, excused prospective jurors who had been police officers, prison guards, former members of military police, family members of any type of enforcement officer, including DNR officers and teachers.

David felt that police officers or former police officers and their families were conditioned to be prosecution oriented, and would, deliberately or unwittingly, hold Jean to a high standard, shifting the burden of proof on her, to prove her innocence, where the prosecution had not proven her guilt, beyond a reasonable doubt.

—In the American legal system, the defendant does not have to prove anything, the burden of proof is always on the prosecution—

Throughout the years, David had previously tried cases where teachers sat in judgment of criminal defendants and found that a high percentage of them entertained a similar thought process as that of the police officers making their presence on the jury a highly risky affair for any defendant.

—David has found teachers to be extremely suspicious of any witness testifying for the defendant or of the defendant's testimony in his or her own defense. A defendant does not have to testify at all and is still to be presumed innocent until proven guilty beyond a reasonable doubt. He or she enjoys the privilege against self-incrimination under the Fifth and Fourteenth Amendments of the United States Constitution, as well as the Constitution of the State of Michigan—

The questioning of prospective jurors continued day after day until December 6, 1984. Will had exhausted his peremptory challenges and David had one remaining. There was one remaining prospective juror left of the one hundred thirty-three that had been summoned for jury service. This was a perplexing problem for David, as he had one member of the jury panel who was a teacher, but the remaining prospective juror was a very religious farmer who owned a farm very near the Davis farm, and David suspected that he had very strong opinions about the lifestyles of both

John and Jean Davis that, in David's mind, made him more dangerous than the school teacher.

"Well, Mr. Chartier, do you have any further challenges for cause?" asked Judge Roode.

"No further challenges for cause, Your Honor," David replied.

"You have one remaining peremptory challenge, Mr. Chartier, are you going to exercise it?" inquired Judge Roode.

After a long . . . long pause, David replied, "Your Honor, the defense accepts the jury, as is."

"Very well, we have a jury," stated Judge Roode.

"It is late in the day and tomorrow is Friday. We will reconvene in the morning at 9:00 a.m. I have additional instructions for the members of the jury, and we will hear opening statements to the jury by the prosecution and the defense and then adjourn for the weekend and begin with testimony on Monday morning at 9:00 a.m.," stated Judge Roode.

"Until tomorrow then, this court is adjourned," declared the judge.

"All rise," commanded the bailiff, as the judge left the courtroom for his chambers.

Throughout the jury selection process, David had been conferring with Jean, and she expressed her feelings about each prospective juror, ultimately agreeing with David's decisions whether a prospective juror was to be seated, or not. With respect to David's hesitance to use his only remaining challenge, Jean agreed that if the religious farmer were seated on the panel, it would have left her very worried, as she had once had an argument about religion with that farmer's wife and some strong words were exchanged between them.

The courtroom filled with spectators; the jury was in the jury room—*the furnace room*—on this first day of trial. Jean was again wearing a pantsuit—*this one was a light green color*—and she looked like she was holding up well under the intense stress of the jury selection process that occupied all of our thoughts and energies of the past several days, and today was to be another one of those tense days. The judge would be giving the jury additional instructions that are typical pretrial instructions, to set the ground rules giving the jury an outline of events and matters to expect, together with the court's expectations concerning their individual behavior as jurors, to be faithfully observed throughout the course of the trial. Will was at the prosecution table with a couple of the police officers that were involved in the arrest of Jean.

At precisely 9:00 a.m., the bailiff announced Judge Roode entering the courtroom.

Fourteen jurors also entered the courtroom and took the same seats in the jury box that they had sat in the day before. The jury was comprised of the following people:

Jerry Smith—a telephone company lineman
Judy Ackley—a stay-at-home wife of a farmer
Mary Anderson—a credit union employee
Sally Maki—a county road commission employee
Michael Carver—a radio station announcer
Gary Schmidt—a school custodian
Thomas Kinnunen—an iron miner
Bernie Rantinen—an unemployed miner
Gerald Smith—a high school teacher
Toby Andrews—a truck driver
Sally Forchette—a tailor
Mary Giddings—a bank teller
Jane Collins—a secretary
Eino Ruska—a bookkeeper for a paper mill

The judge, the lawyers, clients, and the spectators all took their seats after the jury was seated and Judge Roode commenced his further instructions to the jury.

"Ladies and gentlemen of the jury, you have been selected to sit in judgment upon a criminal charge made by the State of Michigan against one of your fellow citizens.

"Clerk, would you please read the oath to the jury?"

"Ladies and gentlemen of the jury, would you please stand for the oath and raise your right hand," requested the clerk.

The members of the jury doing so, the clerk read the oath, "Ladies and gentlemen of the jury, you shall well and truly try and true deliverance make, between the people of this state and the prisoner at the bar, whom you shall have in charge, according to the evidence and the laws of this state; so help you God." The affirmation in lieu of the oath is: "This I do under the pains and penalties of perjury."

Each of the jurors took the oath and two of them elected to make the affirmation, in lieu of an oath.

The jury again took their seats and Judge Roode continued, "Members of the jury, you will note that fourteen jurors have been drawn in this case. At the conclusion of all the evidence and after the charge by the court, there will be a drawing by lot in which two jurors will be eliminated from those present.

"Until the case is submitted to you at the conclusion of the court's final instructions, you must not discuss it with anyone, not even with members of your family or your fellow jurors. After it is submitted to you, you must discuss it only when the court so instructs you and only in the jury room and in the presence of all of your fellow jurors.

"It would be unfair for you to discuss the case among yourselves before you retire to consider the verdict. It would also be unfair to discuss the case with your family or friends, before a decision is rendered. Due process of law requires that a jury, acting only within the confines of a jury room, and considering only the evidence submitted in the case, render a verdict. You should explain this rule to your family and friends. When the trial is over, you are allowed to discuss the case with anyone you choose.

"In the course of the trial, the court may take one or more recesses during which you will be permitted to separate and go about your personal affairs. During these recesses, you are not allowed to discuss the case with anyone nor permit anyone to say anything to you or in your presence about the case. If anyone attempts to say anything to you or in your presence about this case, tell him or her that you are on the jury trying the case and ask him or her to stop. If they persist, leave them at once and report the matter to the court immediately upon your return to court.

"Your only information about this case should come to you while you are all present together, acting as a jury, in the presence of the court, the attorneys, and the defendant.

"You are not to visit the scene of the alleged crime. Should it be necessary for you to view the scene, you will be taken there as a group under the supervision of the court. Do not make any investigation of your own or conduct an experiment of any kind.

"Counsel and I are required by law to take up certain matters out of your hearing, and from time to time, the court will have to dispose of matters having nothing to do with the trial of this case. Do not concern yourself with these proceedings.

"The remarks which the court is about to make are intended as an outline of the trial of this case and of some legal principles you will need.

"I want to speak with you briefly about the function of the judge in a criminal trial and your function as jurors. The judge's responsibility is to conduct the trial of the case in an orderly, fair, and efficient manner, to rule upon questions of law arising in the course of the trial, and to instruct you as to the law which applies to the case. It is your duty to accept the law as the court will state it to you. None of my instructions reflects any opinion on my part about the facts of this case. As members of the jury, you alone must decide this case.

"The function of you, the jury, is to determine the facts. You are the sole and exclusive judge of the facts, and you alone determine the weight, the effect, and value of the evidence, as well as the credibility of the witnesses. You must consider and weigh the testimony of all witnesses who appear before you, and you alone are to determine whether to believe any witnesses and the extent to which any witness should be believed. It is your responsibility to consider any conflicts in testimony, which may arise during the course of the trial. Your decision as to any fact in the case is final.

"A trial follows long-established rules of evidence. Attorneys are trained on the rules of evidence and are required to make objections. The court is required to rule upon these matters according to the law, and the rulings do not reflect any personal opinion about the facts in this case. You should not give any weight to the court's rulings or to the number of rulings on either side.

"I may question some of the witnesses myself. The questions do not reflect any opinion on my part about the evidence or about the case. My only purpose will be to inquire about matters which counsel may not have fully explored.

"The questions which counsel put to witnesses are not themselves evidence. It is the answers of witnesses, which will provide evidence. You should not speculate that a fact may be true merely because one of the lawyers asks questions that assume or suggest that the fact is true.

"I am likely to give instructions during the trial, and will give you detailed instructions of law at the conclusion of the trial. You should consider all of my instructions as a connected series. Taken together, they constitute the law which you must follow."

Jean and David took the next recess opportunity to step into the upstairs outer hallway and went to the exit at the end of the hall, so that

Jean could smoke a cigarette. As she smoked, David felt the old craving for one too, but he took some deep breaths of the December air and soon the urge to smoke had passed. David had not smoked for twenty years, the tension that he felt in that courtroom was mounting, and he found himself thinking about smoking, feeling that he was on the brink of asking her for one.

Jean seemed intrigued with the judge's instructions to the jury. She had never heard a judge instructing a jury in a criminal case before. She had been in court for her deceased son's civil case but must have been oblivious to whatever the judge told the jury, as she was in such grief over the death of her son, and after having heart surgery, she was mostly numb as to her surroundings and to the events unfolding at that time. She had also been in court, after having been arrested for drunk driving, but appeared without counsel and disposed of that case with a guilty plea; there had been no need for a trial.

David and Jean returned to the courtroom, and moments thereafter, the bailiff was heard to say, "All rise!" as Judge Roode entered the courtroom.

Judge Roode declared, "Remain standing while the bailiff brings in the jury."

The jury was seated in the jury box, and the bailiff again declared, "The circuit court for the county of Pictured Rocks is again in session, please be seated."

"Ladies and gentlemen of the jury, I want to take an additional few minutes and tell you a little bit about trial procedure," Judge Roode stated.

"First, the prosecuting attorney makes an opening statement in which he outlines his theory of the case. The defense attorney may make an opening statement after the prosecutor makes his or may reserve it until later. These opening statements are not evidence and are only intended to assist you in understanding the viewpoints of the parties.

"Second, the evidence of trial is produced. The prosecuting attorney is allowed to present his evidence first. He may call witnesses to testify and he may offer exhibits such as documents or physical objects. The defense attorney has the right to cross-examine witnesses called by the prosecutor in order to test the truthfulness and accuracy of their testimony.

"Following the prosecutor's presentation of evidence, the defense attorney may, if he wishes, present evidence, but he is not obligated to do so. The law does not require a defendant to prove his or her innocence or to produce any evidence. The prosecutor also has a right to cross-examine witnesses called by the defense attorney in order to test the truthfulness and accuracy of their testimony. The prosecutor may also put witnesses on for rebuttal.

"After all the evidence has been presented, the attorneys for each side will have an opportunity to address arguments to you in support of their case. You are reminded that the statements of the attorneys in closing arguments, as in opening statements, are not evidence but are only intended to assist you in understanding the evidence and the theory of each party. You must base your decision only on evidence.

"It is important that you keep an open mind and not decide any issue in the case until the case has been submitted to you.

"At the conclusion of all the evidence and the arguments for both sides, I will instruct you in detail on the rules of law which apply to the case. You will then retire to the jury room to deliberate and decide what your verdict will be. A jury verdict must be unanimous; that is, it must be agreed upon by all and must reflect an individual decision of each of you.

"Now this is a criminal case. The Information in this case charges Jean Davis, with the crime of murdering her husband, John Davis, contrary to Michigan law. The defendant has pleaded not guilty to this Information. *[An Information is a formal charging document presented to a circuit court by the prosecution outlining the charge for which a criminal defendant is brought before a circuit court.]* You should clearly understand that the Information in this case is not evidence, but serves to inform the accused of the charges against her. An Information is presented in every criminal trial. You must not consider it as evidence of the guilt of the defendant or draw any inference of guilt because she has been charged.

"Basic to our system of criminal justice is the principle that a person accused of a crime is presumed to be innocent. This presumption of innocence starts at the very beginning of this case and continues throughout the trial and during your deliberations. Each one of you must be satisfied beyond a reasonable doubt, after deliberating, that the defendant is guilty before you can return a verdict of guilty. You must begin this trial with the presumption of innocence foremost in your minds.

"The fact that the defendant was arrested and is on trial is no evidence against her. There must be evidence introduced in this trial that convinces you of the defendant's guilt beyond a reasonable doubt. The law does not require this defendant to prove her innocence or to produce any evidence whatsoever.

"The burden of proving guilt is upon the prosecution throughout the entire course of the trial and at no time does the burden shift to the defendant. This burden of proof means that every element of the offense charged must be proven by evidence beyond a reasonable doubt.

"A reasonable doubt is a fair, honest doubt growing out of the evidence or lack of evidence in this case or growing out of any reasonable or legitimate inferences drawn from the evidence or lack of evidence. It is not merely an imaginary doubt, a flimsy, fanciful doubt or a doubt based on mere possibility of innocence of the defendant, or a doubt based on sympathy, but rather is a fair, honest doubt based on reason and common sense. It is a state of mind, which would cause you to hesitate in making an important decision in your personal life. By stating that the prosecution must prove guilt beyond a reasonable doubt, I mean there must be such evidence that causes you to have a firm conviction amounting to a moral certainty of the truth of the charges here made against this defendant.

"For reasons stated earlier in the trial, I must remind you not to read, listen to, or watch any news reports concerning this case while you are serving on this jury.

"We will break for lunch and return at one thirty this afternoon to begin opening statements of the attorneys and recess for the weekend, following the conclusion of the opening statements. I must remind the jury not to discuss this case with anyone and not to read, listen to, or watch any news reports concerning this case while you are serving on this jury."

"All rise," stated the bailiff.

"Please keep your seats until the jury has left the courtroom," stated Judge Roode.

There had been news articles in the *Iron Town Press* almost daily since Jean's arrest. The reporters are at every court hearing and are again at the courtroom for the commencement of the trial. David anticipates that they will be present throughout the trial and that the *Iron Town Press* will print a summary of each day's courtroom events, as well as reporting the events on the nightly TV 10 News.

The Pictured Rocks News publishes only once a week and it had been publishing weekly accounts of the motion hearings and court proceedings since the preliminary examination in the district court. There was not anyone in Pictured Rocks County who had not read or heard about this case.

A defense attorney must have clear, simple, and understandable objectives at the commencement of the trial. They should be:

Opening

—Tell the jury what testimony and exhibits that are going to be presenting to them throughout the trial—the things that the defense intends to prove through the evidence admitted by the court, raising a reasonable doubt as to the guilt of the defendant.

Trial

—Fulfill the promise by producing the evidence that the jury was led to expect either through the direct introduction of witnesses and exhibits for the defense and/or through vigorous cross-examination of the prosecution witnesses raising doubt as to the truthfulness, credibility, reliability and completeness of the prosecution's evidence.

Closing Argument / Summation

—Remind the jury that the promises have been fulfilled in providing the evidence that negates guilt or instills in the minds of the jury doubt as to whether the prosecution has proven each element of the charge, beyond a reasonable doubt.

David could see that the trial process was causing Jean much anxiety, and she looked tired and wore a depressed look on her face, as she had been looking at the newspaper reporters in the courtroom that morning. It was as if she was living a bad dream that would not end.

Every day that David had been with Jean in the courtroom, she seemed more and more depressed. David could not help wondering if she was going to hold up through the trial. David explained to Jean that the trial would start with the opening statements of counsel to the jury. He cautioned her not to become too distraught at the things that Mr. Brenner would be saying in his opening remarks, as it was his job to portray her as a person who had committed a very bad act, resulting in the loss of life of another human, without justification or excuse.

Chapter 11

Opening Statements

Once again, the standard courtroom procedure followed and Judge Roode stated "Ladies and gentlemen of the jury, we will now have opening remarks to the jury by the prosecution, followed by opening remarks by the defense, unless the defense reserves the right to address you, until the close of the prosecution's proofs."

The Prosecution's Opening Statement

"Mr. Brenner, are the people ready to proceed?"
"Yes, Your Honor; thank you."
"Mr. Chartier, is the defense ready to proceed?"
"Yes, the defense is ready, Your Honor."
"Mr. Brenner, you may proceed with you opening remarks."
"Thank you, Your Honor."

Will rose from his chair and walked to the podium, and facing the jury began: "Ladies and gentlemen of the jury, I want to thank you for your willingness to sit upon this jury in judgment of a fellow citizen. I know that you have had to adjust your daily routines, both at work and at home to be here, and we may be here for quite some time. The things that I tell you in this opening statement are things that I expect the evidence will prove."

Mr. Brenner outlined the people's theory of the case, as a compelling story of a deliberate murder committed by Jean Davis on September 22, 1984, following a "confrontation" with her husband John Davis. Will made a considerable point out of Jean pushing John out of the entranceway to the dining room, after which John went into the bedroom. He claims that Jean and her brother pushed the bedroom door open and began fighting with John.

Will did not mention that Jean had been a long time victim of John's abuse and death threats, that on the morning of September 22, 1984, John had threatened to cut Jean, while wielding a knife at her, had hit Jean a number of times and tried forcing ice down her throat when she would not drink with him. His theory fails to mention that young Robert Davis was a witness to his father sitting on the bed, of hearing his father threaten to kill his mother and himself, his mother standing at the threshold of the bedroom with his uncle Bill, approximately five feet from the bed, that she did not go and get a gun, but that one was pushed under her right arm by his uncle Bill, who then turned and abandoned her, while her husband was threatening to take the gun and shoot her, Bill, and Robert.

Being sick and tired of hearing his parents fight, Robert turned and walked to the kitchen, heard a shot, and ran back into the bedroom, passing his mother who was then holding a rifle at the threshold of the bedroom door, and saw his father lying on the bed, coughing blood.

Will failed to acknowledge Robert's account of the threats that his father had made of killing Jean and Robert and then committing suicide. Will's main theme is that Jean Davis killed John without any justification or excuse that John had done everything in his power to retreat from a confrontation initiated by Jean Davis and that John sat on the bed, quietly, until Jean shot him. Will further stated that Jean had made numerous acknowledgements to various persons and to the Michigan State Police that she had shot her husband. Will addressed the jury, "Ladies and gentlemen, this is a clear-cut case of first-degree murder against the defendant Jean Davis. Murdering her husband with intent, deliberation, and forethought, she provoked a family quarrel with her husband and shot her husband John Davis through the heart with a .22-caliber rifle bullet and now does not think that she should be prosecuted for this heinous, violent act.

"In spite of the fact that it was his home too, she demanded that he leave the home and when he refused, she took a rifle and shot him to death, without further provocation on his part. The arresting officer will testify that as he entered the home, she blurted out that he had hit her and she shot him. I believe that the evidence will show that she was standing at the threshold of the bedroom door and that she shot him as he was seated on his bed, five feet from her."

Will told the jury that he would bring them the testimony of the officers who heard the spontaneous admission by the defendant. He promised to present to the jury the Pictured Rocks County medical examiner and the pathologist who conducted the autopsy, who would identify the body of John Davis and render their opinions, as to the cause of his death. Further, He promised that he expected to present to them, through a police witness, photographs of the decedent in his stocking feet, slumped next to his bed, with blood all over his face, the bed, and the walls, where he had been coughing up blood in his last throws of life.

"The defendant wants you to believe that she was acting in self-defense," he stated. He told the jury that the ballistics evidence would show that the distance between the muzzle of the gun and the shirt worn by the decedent was greater than eighteen inches and up to five feet, that the trajectory of the bullet was downward, striking him in the upper chest and passing downward through is lungs and heart, as he continued sitting on his own bed."

Will stated to the jury that they would hear testimony from Jean and John's seventeen-year-old son that John had hit her earlier that day, but the evidence will demonstrate that their little morning spat had ended and at the time the shot was fired, he was sitting on his bed and was not a threat to her. "The evidence will show that she shot him with malice, premeditation, and deliberation," Will stated.

In his final words to the jury, he stated that at the conclusion of this trial they would be convinced that Jean Davis unlawfully killed her husband without provocation, and after premeditation and deliberation, with malice aforethought, and he asked that the jury return a unanimous verdict of guilty of first-degree murder. He then thanked the jury and returned to his seat.

The Opening Statement of the Defense

"Mr. Chartier, do you desire to make your opening statement at this time or reserve?" inquired Judge Roode.

"I will make my opening now, Your Honor." said David.

David glanced at Jean, sitting next to him. She was visibly shaking after listening to the short, but concise and firm opening remarks that Will had made to the jury. David next looked at the jury, as he rose from his chair and walked to the podium in front of the jury. He did not speak immediately, but smiled and studied their faces, giving them a few more moments for Will's words and their mental images to dissipate from their minds, taking a few breaths of new air in the process.

David began his opening remarks, "May it please the court, Mr. Brenner, ladies and gentlemen of the jury, as Mr. Brenner failed to explain to you, it is a great responsibility to serve on the jury trying the fate of one of your fellow citizens. It is an important role in our whole way of life in America, in our system of government in a democratic society, and to a society governed by the rule of law, not by the rule of men. It requires that each and every one of us sacrifice a little bit of our time and some of the things we would like to be doing.

"I am particularly concerned about this trial because of our coming right up to Christmas, and I know the pressures that are on people to try to get things ready for Christmas. So I really appreciate your being here, and I am hopeful that we will be able to present both sides of this case to you and afford you sufficient time to deliberate and reach a just verdict without the feeling the pressure of wanting to just go home and get things ready for Christmas. I really think that is a concern of some of you and it is understandable. But, at any rate, we will do our best to see that the trial progresses in an efficient way.

"In opening statements, the lawyers are expected to give you a 'bird's eye' view of the evidence that is to be presented to you from the witnesses and the exhibits admitted into evidence throughout the trial.

"Please remember, that the court's instructions to you included a caution that the evidence that will come to you, will be from the witness chair, not from the newspapers or television, not from rumors that you might have heard, but solely from the testimony of witnesses, and from exhibits that have been introduced and received in evidence in this case.

"During the voir dire, I asked each of you if you presumed Jean Davis innocent, and each one of you said yes, and that you promised to look at her throughout the trial as an innocent person with a shroud of innocence around her throughout the entire trial. Only after you deliberate and evaluate the proofs can you consider the possibility of removing the shroud of innocence.

"The burden of proof as to the criminal charge and to the defenses that are claimed, rest with the prosecution. As you recall, in terms of self-defense, this is not the burden of the defendant to prove beyond a reasonable doubt that her actions were in self-defense. It is the peoples' burden to prove beyond a reasonable doubt that, in the defendant's mind at the time, she did not act in self-defense.

"I want to stress this point, that as you hear the evidence, that you think of her state of mind, at the time. We cannot now look back and say, in fact that her actions might not have been necessary. That is not the test. The test is, what did she think, at that moment in time? What was her state of mind? What was her state of fright? What was her state of apprehension, at the time that she fired the rifle? Hers, not mine, not what you would have done, not what you would apprehend might have been her choices after cool reflection, but what do you believe was her mental state and the degree of her fright at the time?

"The things that I say to you in this opening statement are things that I expect the testimony will support. Now, as Mr. Brenner gave his opening statement, you may recall that I did not object and insist that he preface each sentence with the words *I intend that the evidence will show thus and thus.* He made the statement to begin his address to you by saying that *the things that he tells you in this opening statement are things that he expects to prove.* Again, now that I am addressing my opening remarks to you, I speak in the same fashion. The things that I talk to you about now are the things that I expect to prove. The comments of the lawyers are not evidence, as the court has told you, but are instead, intended to advocate our respective points of view, to convince you to view the proofs most favorably to our respective clients.

"I like to think of the role of the trial lawyer as being a person who is responsible to portray a drama, not to create one that did not exist, but to portray a real life drama that did in fact occur. Portray the drama of Jean Davis's life with its good and its bad aspects, the hopes and dreams, the disappointments and the grief, her sorrow, the fear, the pain, her love, her compassion and her ultimate relief.

"I want you to hear about Jean's early life as a child, what was her home life like as she was growing up on the farm, her relationships with members of her family, the absence of violence in her life, her dreams and aspirations for her future when she was young. Her first marriage was not a violent one, but one with great disappointment.

"She will tell you about meeting John Davis, their courtship and their marriage, their good years and the bad. She will describe to you his personality and nature in the early years, the events that gave them pleasure, the events that brought them pain and discouragement.

"She will tell you of John's accident, the nature of his injuries, and the change in his personality and nature, how John became despondent, suffered loss of self-esteem, turning to alcohol in his daily life, and the subsequent violence that she and her family suffered at his hands.

"She will tell you of her fear of John, about the his past acts of violence toward her, the destruction of property, the threats of death to her and their seventeen year old son Robert and his threats of suicide. She will tell you of her discussions with John's psychiatrists wherein—*and this goes to her state of mind*—her state of knowing what the risks were after she was advised that John would suffer a dangerous change of personality when intoxicated, and that he was capable of fulfilling his threats of death to his entire family and subsequent suicide.

"She will tell you about the death of their eight-year-old son who was killed when trying to get on an early morning school bus and was struck and killed by an eighteen-wheel truck and trailer, not stopping for the flashing lights of the school bus. This tragic event happened right in front of her, as she stood on the porch, watching, to insure his safe crossing and boarding of the bus. She will tell you how she suffered a heart attack because of witnessing the accident and having her baby die in her arms as she knelt on the shoulder of the highway with her dying son in her arms. She will tell you of her being taken to the Iron Town General Hospital by ambulance and having to undergo a double coronary bypass operation on the same day, all of this, while husband John was drunk in the house.

"She will tell you of repeated physical attacks and threats of death in the house, wherein she suffered additional heart attacks, brought on by her drunken husband. She will tell you that she knows that her life expectancy is not great and that her cardiologist has warned her that she may die if she is not able to get free of stress.

"She will tell you about the awarding of a judgment in the case involving her deceased son and how she used the monies to remodel the home, buy new furniture and appliances, and pay bills.

"She will tell you how she tried to protect the property during some of John's crazy behavior, pouring gasoline in the house and trying to burn down the house and barn, how he shot at the firemen who came to put out the fire.

"She will tell you of her making complaints to the police and to the prosecutor of John's violent assaults and injuries that she had received from him and how Mr. Brenner told her that there was nothing that he could do about it. She will tell you how John bragged that he could do anything he wanted and the police would not stop him. Proof of the past violent acts of John will be provided to you in the testimony of a number of witnesses, including the sheriff of this county, family members, and others.

"Michigan state troopers will testify that on July 5, 1983, they had gone to the Davis home in response to a complaint of assault on Mrs. Davis by her husband and that the matter was referred to the prosecutor, but that the prosecutor ordered the complaint closed. They will also testify that on August 11, 1983, they again went to the Davis residence regarding a complaint that her husband had beaten Mrs. Davis. The officer classified the complaint as a false complaint, without investigating the offense. On March 12, 1984, the officer will again testify that they had gone to the Davis residence regarding an assault by John Davis on Mrs. Davis with a loaded high-powered rifle. Again, the complaint was closed at the order of the prosecutor Mr. Brenner, who refused to issue a warrant against John Davis.

"As in most of the incidents, as the officer will testify, Mr. Davis did not resist the officers who surrounded the home with guns drawn and he allowed them into the house. John was heard to say to the officers that he would rather kill his own son, than one of the officers. The officers found three guns in the living room, loaded with rounds in the chambers, another in the corner of the bedroom, another in the corner of the bathroom and several others in the cabinet in the living room. Eleven loaded guns were removed from the residence that day. That was the day that Jean Davis suffered her third heart attack, resulting from the attacks by her husband.

"Sheriff David Cromby will deliver to this courtroom the guns that he has in his possession that were removed from the Davis residence, and will testify that he was at the Davis residence on January 5, 1984, on the complaint of Jean Davis that her husband was violent and attempted to burn the house down. The fire department was called to the scene, and the firefighters were threatened by John, who was upstairs with a gun, which he discharged in the direction of the fire truck. The officers got into the house and were able to take John without incident. The testimony will show that they took John Davis to a hospital for the treatment of the mentally ill and the complaint was closed without prosecution.

"Deputy Sheriff Grey will testify that he was present on the scene after the Davis's eight-year-old son was killed by a truck while trying to get on to the school bus. He will tell you that John Davis was very drunk and that he found him in the house loading a rifle and that he took the gun from Mr. Davis, fearing that he was about to kill the truck driver that had killed his son.

"Doctor Robert LaGale, a cardiologist will be here to testify that he first met Jean Davis who was suffering a heart attack, following the death of her son and about the surgery. He will describe bypass surgery and will testify about the subsequent heart attacks that she has had, following assaults by her husband. He will tell you about the warnings the he has given her regarding stress and will tell you of her short life expectancy."

"Objection, Your Honor," Mr. Brenner cried out to the court.

"I object to some of these pronouncements made by counsel. I feel they are irrelevant at this time, and I think they are highly prejudicial, especially the last comment, Your Honor."

"Well, proceed, Mr. Chartier, but your opening statement should be a preview of what you intend to show and what the defense theory of the case is and I would suggest that you stick with that," said Judge Roode.

"Thank you, Your Honor. I intend to show everything that I have said, Your Honor. Jean Davis will describe her husband's deep depression, and will tell you of her hopes that someday she could find help for John and that they might live a normal life. She will describe John's attacks upon her as becoming more and more desperate and violent and that she knew that he was very likely to kill her or cause her to die from another heart attack.

"She will tell you of her husband John leaving the family home in recent months for extended periods to live away from the family; and that upon leaving, he would take all the food from the family home and all the utensils from the kitchen, leaving them with nothing to eat nor kitchenware with which to eat it.

"Finally, she will tell you about September 22, 1984, that on that date John had wakened early, had begun drinking at 7:00 a.m. and rapidly became intoxicated, that she got in about an hour before that, having spent the evening with friends playing cards. She will tell you that they argued mostly about his unwillingness to look for some work that he might do and his violence when drinking. She pleaded with him to leave the house because she did not feel that she could continue to take the stress of more arguments and threats.

"She will tell you that John tried to jam ice down her throat when she refused to drink with him and punched her in the mouth. She will tell you of calling her son Robert and her brother Bill to come down to the kitchen about 10:00 a.m. that morning and that she looked to Robert and Bill for some protection from John.

"She will tell you of John's threats to kill her, her brother and her son Robert that morning and to commit suicide. She'll also tell you of his threats to destroy the house by fire and that she left the premises on two occasions that day, hoping that he would not be home when she returned and she would have a reprieve from the tension and the battering.

"Jean Davis, will describe the assaultive conduct that took place upon entering the home, in the late afternoon of September 22, 1984, how John immediately attacked her and her brother violently striking them with his fists and threatening to kill them and burn the house down. She had a deep fear that he was again going to start a fire while in the bedroom and that she entered the bedroom and asked that he leave the home, after which she was struck, knocked to the floor, pinned between the foot of the bed and her oxygen equipment. That her brother Bill had tried to defend her and that she was dazed by the blow from her husband, thought that this time she was going to die because of the anxiety and stress of the moment. She will then tell you that without her knowledge, her brother had gone upstairs and got a rifle and came back stuffing the rifle under her right arm and then turned and abandoned her while she faced her raging husband, threatening to kill her, her brother, son Robert, and destroy the home; this time, she believed he would do it. She will tell you that she remembers the gun being pushed under her arm and against her side, and demanding that he get up and leave the house. She recalls feeling very alone and fearful that he would get the gun and was in fear of dying and that when he got up, saying that he was going to take the gun away from her and kill her, he charged her and was reaching for the gun when the shot was fired.

"She will tell you that blood immediately came to his mouth and he staggered back and fell onto the bed and started coughing blood, but still felt terror that he was going to get back up and overpower her. You will also hear that she had not planned to shoot her husband and that she did not even know that the gun was loaded. She will recall telling Robert to call the ambulance and that she was still afraid to try to assist or render aid for fear that he would grab her and that he was still capable of hurting her if she got any closer to him. She will admit exclaiming, 'No more beatings, No more beatings,' and later feeling despair over the realization of what had happened.

"You will hear testimony from Mr. Don White, the investigator that I hired in this case. He is a retired Michigan State Police detective who is now a private detective. He will tell you that he has investigated many murder cases during his career as a state police detective and that I asked him to help in investigating this case. He will tell you of his inspection of the home on the night of September 22, 1984, and into the early morning hours of the following day. He will identify a blood sample that he discovered and retrieved from a throw rug at the threshold of the bedroom doorway and of his interviews with Robert Davis and of a server at a tavern who had spoken with Jean Davis about abuse and injuries that she had previously suffered at the hands of John.

"You will hear from Dr. Paul Cachette, from Sacramento, California. He is a professor of criminalistics who assisted me in making some of the ballistics tests that determine distance—*how far the decedent was from the muzzle of the gun at the moment it was fired*—as well as testimony regarding the trajectory of the bullet on its way to the body of John Davis.

"Dr. Carl M. Bergman, a clinical psychologist from Lansing, studied Jean Davis. He will tell you of his background, of the testing and interviews that he had with Jean Davis and of his conclusion that she did not intend to kill her husband, but that she was in unimaginable fear, *beyond terror*, at the time that the shot was fired."

"Objection, Your Honor, again I must object. Let the good doctor testify for himself," Will cried out.

"Well, objection overruled," stated Judge Roode.

David continued, "Lastly, you will hear from Dr. Camellia Storm, another clinical psychologist. Dr. Storm, as you will find from the testimony, is involved in psychotherapy with children and adults, psychological consultation and supervision in research in the area of domestic violence, as well as with community consultation in the area of domestic violence."

"Objection, Your Honor, This is really argument; this is improper opening statement and is argumentative," Will stated.

"Your Honor, I am stating what I intend to prove, what the evidence will show," David replied.

"Well, proceed, Mr. Chartier, with your statement, but limit it to a statement of theory in an outline of what you expect the testimony will show with respect to that, without precise detail of the testimony of that witness," stated Judge Roode.

"Thank you, Your Honor. Dr. Storm, I believe, will explain to you why it is not possible or why it is extremely difficult, in the minds of some women, to leave their battered situation. I think that throughout this trial, this will be one of your most critical concerns. But, I want you to listen very carefully to Dr. Storm when she talks on this point.

"Ladies and gentlemen of the jury, Mrs. Davis will not try to paint herself as being without fault in her marriage. She will admit that she has made many mistakes in her marriage and that recently she has been more provocative toward John. But, I believe she will state that she was trying to get John to begin to realize the seriousness of his problems, and that she had always hoped somehow, somewhere, he could be helped.

"She will tell you that she still deeply loves John, even though she had to do what she did. I think that you will find from her testimony that she did not premeditate nor deliberate the killing of her husband. I think that the evidence will show that she did not intend to kill him, but that she acted in self-defense and in defense of her minor son Robert, to stop him, not to kill him, and that she was hopeful that he would just leave the home on that day.

"She will tell you that she was in immediate fear of dying, when he charged off the bed at her and knew that he would have killed her, her brother, her son and destroyed the house, if he would have been able to reach the gun. I believe that you will find from her testimony that although justified in her act of self-defense in that instant of desperation, abandoned, beyond terror, that the discharge of the gun was not even contemplated by her.

"I remind you that as you hear the proofs in this case, that you must look to her state of mind and try to understand the degree of the threat, as it appeared to her, at the moment, and that her action was necessary to save her life, that of her brother's, and the life of her son.

"I believe that the court will instruct you, as I indicated, that once the issue of self-defense is raised, then it becomes the burden of the prosecution to prove beyond a reasonable doubt that her actions *were not in defense* of herself and/or her son. In addition, I believe that when all is said and done, you will find from the evidence that the prosecution has failed completely in satisfying this burden of proof, and that your verdict of not guilty on the charges of first—or second-degree murder should be returned to this court."

"Thank you," David stated, as he completed his opening statement to the jury.

"Court will recess for approximately ten minutes," declared the judge.

"All rise," declared the bailiff, as Judge Roode retired to his chambers and the jury was allowed to go to the jury room.

David turned around and saw that the courtroom was filled with spectators, news reporters, and John's family. David's wife Ann was in the courtroom and smiled at David, as if saying that he had done a good job on his opening remarks to the jury.

Jean was anxious to leave the courtroom and have one of her Virginia Slims, so they exited the side door of the courtroom to do just that. She looked at David and appeared pleased with his opening statements. The spectators and reporters left the courtroom by a different door leading to the front of the annex, while Jean, David, and the sheriff stood near the back of the building. David again felt the urge to smoke one of Jean's cigarettes, but again took deep breaths of the fresh air instead of doing so. It only seemed that a minute had passed and David and Jean returned to the courtroom, on the suggestion of the sheriff. The full ten-minute break was over.

Chapter 12

The Prosecution's Case

"All rise," declared the bailiff, as Judge Roode entered the courtroom and the jury was filing into the rows of the jury box and taking their seats.

"Please be seated, the circuit court for the county of Pictured Rocks is now in session," the bailiff called out once more.

"Call your first witness, Mr. Brenner," commanded Judge Roode.

Will Brenner called witness after witness, attempting to show that Jean Davis was the instigator of the fight that occurred between her and John on September 22, 1984, that she had been equally at fault in most all of the complaints that she had made in the past, regarding John's aggressive assaults. David felt that Will was indirectly trying to defend himself for not effectively dealing with her complaints in the past, as well as convicting her for causing the death of John, which he classed as deliberate murder. His officer witnesses testified as to the *res gestae*[1] statements that Jean had made to the officers coming to the home, right after the shooting, admitting that she had shot her husband.

Will Brenner took the testimony of the medical examiner, as well as the pathologist who had performed the autopsy, identifying the trajectory of the bullet after entering the body of John Davis, both of whom, under David's effective cross-examination, could not speculate about the trajectory of the bullet on its way to the body of John. Will took the testimony of the state police ballistics expert, Roger Benny, who described his ballistics testing of the rifle, comparison of the bullet and its casing, and stating that in his opinion, the trajectory was downward and that the distance between the muzzle of the gun and the shirt worn by John was greater than eighteen inches but less *than five* feet. Upon cross-examination, however, he admitted that sometimes the inside trajectory of a small-caliber bullet might not match the outside trajectory of the bullet on its way to the body.

Robert testified that Jean pushed his dad out of the way to gain entrance to the dining room, that his dad had retreated into the bedroom and attempted to close the door. He stated further that Jean pushed the door open and began fighting with him, wanting him to leave his home. He further testified that his uncle Bill Bakum went up the stairs and obtained a rifle, and after coming back down the stairs, tried to threaten his dad to get him to leave the house until he sobered up, but became scared when his dad did not frighten, turned around and left, after placing the rifle under his mother's arm and then abandoned her to face her raging, threatening husband. After turning away from the bedroom and walking toward the kitchen, Robert said that he heard a shot, turned, and ran to the bedroom doorway, seeing his mother holding a rifle, and his father lying across the bed, blood on his face, coughing up blood all over the bed and the walls.

David knew, based on the testimony of the prosecution witnesses, that Will Brenner was going to argue in his final argument, that Jean killed John Davis without any justification or excuse, that John had done everything within his power to retreat from the confrontation initiated by Jean and remained seated on the bed, while Jean shot him. Jean had admitted shooting him to numerous people, whose testimony would be offered in evidence, before this jury. Will had taken testimony from twelve witnesses, including John Davis's blood relatives who all portrayed Jean as the assaultive wife, starting many of the fights.

David objected to their statements as being hearsay even though they claimed that John told it to them. They were not statements that would meet the definition of a dying declaration[2] and thus could not be considered trustworthy and violated Jean's right to confrontation and cross-examination of the person from whom they claimed to have heard it. Judge Roode sustained David's objection and instructed the jury to disregard the alleged statements and to give them no weight in their deliberations. *The judge did not have to determine if John believed that he was facing death, because the alleged statements did not pertain to the cause or circumstances of what John might have believed to be his impending death.*

They, instead, were alleged statements that John had made, concerning Jean's alleged assaultive nature.

After five days of the prosecution witnesses' testimony, Will Brenner rested the prosecution's case, and Judge Roode adjourned the case until Monday, December 17, 1984. David moved, outside the presence of the jury, for a directed verdict of acquittal for the defense, at the end of the prosecution's case in chief.

"Mr. Chartier, I will be taking your motion under advisement and will rule on it Monday morning, prior to your commencing your proofs. Until then, this court will be adjourned," stated Judge Roode.

As the jury filed back into the courtroom, Judge Roode announced:

"Ladies and gentlemen of the jury, I have had to take up some matters in this case, outside your presence, and have decided to release you a little early today, but will want you in the courtroom at 8:30 a.m., Monday morning."

"Court is adjourned until Monday, at 8:30 a.m.," declared Judge Roode.

David felt sure that the judge would be seriously reviewing his notes regarding the testimony given by the prosecution witnesses over the past seven days to see if there was evidence, which would support a verdict of first or second-degree murder. David felt that he might have successfully defended Jean as to the charges of first—and second-degree murder, but was worried that without a witness seeing John charging her, together with the testimony of the distance and downward trajectory of the bullet, the judge might deny the motion until David had concluded taking testimony of the defense witnesses.

"Jean, are you all right?" David asked, before leaving the courtroom, noticing that she had been extremely quiet and tense and had a sustained worried look on her face.

"Jean, I know that you are very tired and scared, but I think that the case is going along just fine. Even if we do not get a directed verdict, we have a strong defense, and I will renew my motion at the conclusion of the testimony of the defense witnesses, but before the case is submitted to the jury," David remarked, trying to put her immediate fears at ease.

As Jean was getting into her car, preparing to drive back home, David said to her, "Jean, I think that you're doing just fine, even though you did devour part of your paper cup and part of your pencil during today's proceedings," trying to get her to lighten up just a little. It appeared to have worked some, as Jean smiled at David before leaving.

David returned to his office and sat at his desk looking at the stacks of mail that needed attention, as well as the telephone call slips of clients' calls. David could see that he would be working all weekend to return correspondence and calls. When a lawyer takes on the defense of a capital murder case, other clients do not stop in their desire to discuss their own matters with their attorney, even though he is working full time in defending a criminal trial.

David felt that he should go home, spend time with his family for the rest of the evening, and return to the office on Saturday to work on the numerous other legal matters that were on his desk calling out for attention.

Jean was in the parking lot waiting for David as he drove up to the courthouse. She was looking around at the spectators who were arriving to observe the continuation of the trial, as David greeted her and they made their way to the courtroom.

"Good morning, Mr. Brenner and Mr. Chartier. Before we allow the jury into the courtroom, I want to address Mr. Chartier's timely motion for directed verdict, made pursuant to Michigan Court Rules," stated Judge Roode.

"The motion has given me some unrest. I have given it serious consideration, and I must admit, I was very close to ruling in the defendant's favor, but I am now satisfied that the jury could find, from the prosecution's evidence, that the shooting may have been a deliberate act on the part of the defendant, without just provocation or excuse, as there is no witness to the actual firing of the gun nor the position of the deceased, at the moment the shot was fired. It is a question of fact for the jury. Therefore, I am denying Mr. Chartier's motion at this time, but I will again entertain the motion at the conclusion of the case, prior to submitting the case to the jury. Motion denied," stated Judge Roode.

CHAPTER 13

The Case is with the Defense

"You may call your first witness, Mr. Chartier," announced Judge Roode.

"Thank you, Your Honor; I call to the stand David Cromby, sheriff of Pictured Rocks County," David announced.

As Sheriff Cromby prepared to take the witness stand, he turned to face the clerk of the court and swore under oath to tell the truth, nothing but the truth, so help him God, and then sat in the witness chair.

"Would you state your full name, please?" questioned David.

"David Michael Cromby," replied the witness.

"Where are you employed?"

"I'm the Pictured Rocks County Sheriff."

"How long have you been with the sheriff department?"

"Since 1975."

"Prior to being elected sheriff, you were an under-sheriff and before that, a deputy, is that right?"

"Yes, sir."

"Sheriff Cromby, do you recall how many occasions you went to the Davis residence in response to complaints of violence directed toward Jean Davis by her now deceased husband John?"

"I do not know the exact number, but I am sure there were at least three."

"Do you recall any of them specifically?"

"I can recall the last incident, but may I refer to our complaint report?"

"Did you bring any of those complaints with you today?"

"Yes, I did."

"Can you tell me the complaint number that you are referring to, and its date?"

"The last incident was our complaint number 312444, dated March 10, 1984."

"Now, what caused you to go to the Davis residence on that occasion?"

"I was notified through my department that several officers were at the Davis residence due to a family disturbance and there was a shooting involved. At the time of receiving the call, I believe that John Davis was in the house with a high-powered rifle with the officers at the scene. I went there too, as a backup."

"How many officers were on the scene, if you know?"

"Four, according to my report."

"Now, you had been called there by whom?"

"I got it, I believe, over my radio in my patrol car."

"What did you observe upon your arrival at the scene?"

"Okay, when I arrived at the scene, the officers had already gone into the house and were talking to John Davis."

"Did you remove anything from the house?"

"Yes, I had asked John to give me all of the guns in the house, and he gave me several of his long guns, rifles, and shotguns."

"Where were those guns located?"

"Some were in a gun cabinet in the living room, some were in the bedroom, and I believe that I took one gun out the trailer, which was located on the Davis property."

"Were any of the guns loaded?"

"They were all loaded."

"Do you continue to maintain possession of those guns?"

"Yes"

"Did you ask Mr. Davis if there were any other guns?"

"Yes, I did, and he said that there were no other guns on the premises."

"What was the disposition of the case?"

"The case was closed without an arrest."

"Do you have another incident report with you?"

"Yes, I do."

"It is complaint number 204311, dated May 5, 1984."

"Did this involve a report of violence?"

"Yes."

"Who was the complainant?"

"Jean Davis."

"Can you tell us about that incident?"

"As I recall, it was a domestic quarrel between Mr. and Mrs. Davis. We arrived at the residence and found that John Davis passed out. The report reads that he was conscious but seemed stupefied and was very intoxicated."

"Did Jean complain about John assaulting her?"

"Yes, she did, and we advised her to call us if there were any further trouble, as we would remain in the area."

"You did not arrest John?"

"Not at that time, but we were called back there within twenty minutes, and we then took John into custody because he had apparently woke up and started assaulting Mrs. Davis again and broke his son's arm, but neither Mrs. Davis nor their son wanted to press charges."

"Did you have another report of a different incident?"

"Yes, I was called to assist the Michigan State Police on January 3, 1984."

"In looking at your report, I'm just trying to refresh your recollection; does it not state that the complainant was Jean Davis?"

"Yes.

"Apparently, John had become violent and tried to burn the house down."

"What did he do, if you know?"

"He had ripped a piece of plywood off the stairway in the living room, put it on the living room floor, poured oil on it, and lit it afire."

"Was the fire department called?"

"Yes, it was, but John would not let them on the property."

"Was there a gun involved in keeping the fire department off the property?"

"Yes, the fire chief told me that he had fired the gun from an upstairs window, and John was taken into custody and transported to a mental hospital in the town Newberry."

"What reputation, if any, are you aware of in the county of Pictured Rocks concerning John Davis, for violence and destructiveness?"

"Well, he had a reputation of violence and destruction."

"So, is it fair to say that he indeed has a reputation, a general reputation, in the community for violence and destructiveness?"

"Yes, sir."

"Thank you. I have no further questions, Your Honor," David stated.

"Mr. Brenner, you may cross-examine the witness," Judge Roode said.

"Thank you, Your Honor," responded Will.

"Sheriff, do you know if Jean Davis had a reputation in the community?" asked Will Brenner.

"Objection, Your Honor. The general reputation of Jean Davis is not at issue," David cried out.

"I would agree. Mr. Chartier's objection is sustained," declared Judge Roode.

"That is all the questions that I have." stated Mr. Brenner.

Mr. Brenner, obviously, did not want to cross-examine the sheriff, and had David not subpoenaed him, he would not have called him at all. David believed that Will was not pleased to have, in evidence, corroborating testimony from a law enforcement witness concerning John's dangerous and assaultive propensities. David felt that the testimony of the sheriff was important testimony from which a jury could then infer the state of mind of Jean, as she was again faced with John's credible threats of death and suicide.

Call your next witness, Mr. Chartier," Judge Roode stated.

"Thank you, Your Honor. I call Private Investigator Don White to the stand," David announced.

Don White came forward and raised his right hand, as he faced the clerk of the court, preparing to take an oath to tell the truth.

"Do you swear to tell the truth, nothing but the truth, so help you God?" inquired the clerk of the court.

"Yes, I do," responded Mr. White.

"Mr. White, would you please tell the jury where you live and a little of your background and training?" asked David.

"Yes, I live in the city of Pictured Rocks and I was a trooper for five years and then a detective for the Michigan State Police. My total service time with the state police was twenty-five years and seven months, and I retired at the age of fifty-two and came to the Upper Peninsula to live. I went to school to become an auctioneer and also got my private investigator license," Don stated.

"In your experience as a detective for the Michigan State Police, did you have occasions to investigate murder cases?"

"Yes, quite a few over the years."

"Where were you primarily stationed?"

"At the Redford Post, northwest of Detroit."

"Now, Mr. White, did I hire you to assist me in an alleged murder investigation, in September of this year?" David inquired.

"Yes, indeed, I went to the Davis residence at your request, located in the farming area west of the city of Pictured Rocks, and was met there by young Robert Davis and yourself. You had told me that there was a shooting at the Davis home and that Mr. John Davis had been shot and killed, the police had previously examined the scene and had left."

"What, if anything, did you do at the Davis residence?"

"After gaining entrance to the home, I interviewed young Robert Davis, and he told me that his mother had shot his dad in their bedroom earlier that evening. He said that his dad had been beating his mother up throughout the day and that his mother was really bruised and scared and he believed that she shot him in self-defense. He described his dad as being extremely intoxicated and that he had been threatening to kill him and his mother and then was going to commit suicide."

"Did you examine the scene where the shooting was reported to have occurred?"

"Yes, I did. It was in Mr. and Mrs. Davis's bedroom on the first floor of the house. I went into the bedroom, photographed the room and the blood-soaked bed, the blood splatters on the walls adjacent to the bed, and found blood at the threshold of the bedroom door, where Mrs. Davis was reported to have been standing with a rifle, before the shooting, according to Robert. I photographed the blood at the threshold and took a sample of the blood and the throw rug, upon which the blood was located, and placed it into a clean plastic baggie and marked the outside with the date, time, and location from which it was taken."

"Did you do anything else while in the Davis residence?"

"Yes, photographed and measured the inside of the first floor of the house and prepared a rough sketch of the first floor, including the bedroom."

"What, if anything, did you do with the blood sample?"

"I took it to the laboratory at the Pictured Rocks Memorial Hospital and asked them to type the blood and determine if it was human blood and of the same type as John Davis's blood."

"Did they do that for you?"

"Yes, they did and they said . . ."

"Objection, Your Honor, Mr. Chartier is calling for hearsay testimony, as to what was told, if anything, to Mr. White, concerning the testing of the blood sample by the laboratory technician," stated Will.

"I sustain the prosecution's objection. Mr. Chartier, if you are going to get that evidence in, you will need to get it in through the testimony of the laboratory people," ruled Judge Roode.

"Thank you, Your Honor, I intend to do that."

"Mr. White, did you get a receipt from the laboratory technician for the blood sample that you delivered to them?"

"Yes, I did, and when they had completed their testing, they returned the sample to me and I gave them a receipt to insure the chain of custody."

"Did you bring that sample with you to court today?"

"Yes, I did. I have it right here."

Mr. White handed David the baggie containing the blood sample, and David asked that it be marked defendant's exhibit A and requested that it be entered into evidence.

"Is there any objection from the prosecution, Mr. Brenner?" asked Judge Roode.

"I would like to voir dire the witness, if I could, Your Honor?" requested Will.

"Your Honor, Mr. Brenner may now cross-examine this witness," stated David.

"Mr. White, it has been a long time since you were involved in gathering and preserving evidence isn't that true?" asked Will.

"No, in fact, I have been hired by insurance companies within the past year and have investigated cases of suspected arson, collecting and preserving evidence," stated Don.

"Now, Mr. White, are there animals and poultry at the Davis farm?" inquired, Will.

"Yes, there are some dogs and some chickens there," responded Don.

"Do you know if any of the dogs or chickens are allowed into the house?" inquired Will.

"Well, it is a farming area. They could perhaps have on some occasion gotten into the house, but I do not know that," answered Don.

"Now, Mr. White, you are not sure that the blood sample is not that of a dog or a chicken, are you?"

"Well, Mr. Brenner, the hospital laboratory technicians determined that it was human blood, of the same type as John Davis," Don responded.

"Objection, Your Honor, the court has already ruled that Mr. White's answer was hearsay and I ask that it be stricken from the record," demanded Mr. Brenner.

"Well, Mr. Brenner, your sure did it that time, you opened the door inviting Mr. White's answer to your question, and I am afraid that I will have to let his answer stay," ruled Judge Roode.

"No further questions," stated Will, as he slammed down his yellow pad and took his seat.

"It is now 11:45 a.m., and I think that I will be adjourning for lunch; please be back into the courtroom by 1:30 p.m."

"All rise! This court will be in recess until 1:30 p.m., please remain in your seats until the judge and the jury have left the courtroom," announced the bailiff.

During the break, David took Jean to lunch at the Red Cedar Restaurant in town, ordering homemade soup and a sandwich. David and she briefly went over her testimony, and he told Jean that he would be putting her on the stand next. Perhaps he should have waited until after the lunch hour to tell Jean that she would be taking the witness stand as soon as the court is again in session, as she only ate half of her sandwich and half of her soup. David could sense that her appetite had suddenly left her and she looked somewhat pale.

"Mr. Chartier, you may call your next witness," said Judge Roode.

"Thank you, I would call Mrs. Jean Davis to the stand," David stated.

Jean got up from her chair and walked to the witness seat and raised her right hand.

"Do you swear to tell the truth, nothing but the truth, so help you God?" the clerk of the court said, administering the oath.

"Yes, I do," Jean stated.

"Mrs. Davis, may I call you Jean?" David asked.

"Yes, that would be fine," she answered.

"Jean, I would like you to tell the ladies and gentlemen of the jury about your early life," said David.

"What was your home life like as you were growing up on the farm?" asked David.

"It was nice; my home was not a violent one. I was a happy girl, did well in grade school, but did not do well in high school. I had good relations with my family and the normal relationships in school. I had girlfriends and boyfriends. In the tenth grade, my boyfriend and I got married. He was a couple years older than I was and I was pregnant.

That marriage was not violent, but after a couple of years, we divorced. Right after that, I met John, went steady for quite a while, and then got married."

"Please tell us about your early life with John," said David.

"We were in love and our lives were quite happy for a long time. We lived in Milwaukee for a couple of years and later moved to Pictured Rocks County, taking up residence at the old Davis farm, west of Pictured Rocks. We had a lot of fun, we both worked hard, and we had three boys. Life was good. John was an ironworker and took a great deal of pride in that fact."

"How and when did that change?"

"John had a very bad car accident some years ago and he had very serious injuries, preventing him from returning to his job. He became depressed because he could not do much of anything anymore, both of his arms had been broken, both legs were broken, and he had severe head injuries. His personality changed after the accident, becoming despondent, suffered loss of self-esteem, turned to alcohol—*drinking every day and through the nights, becoming intoxicated and violent.* My children and I suffered at his hands. In recent years, he had beaten me many times and had been threatening my son Robert and me, always followed with additional threats of suicide. John's psychiatrists told me that John was suffering a dangerous change of personality when intoxicated and that he was capable of fulfilling his threats of death to his entire family and subsequent suicide."

"Mrs. Davis, you said that you and John had three boys. We have talked to your son Robert, but you have not mentioned the other two, can you tell us about the two other boys?"

"Norman is our eldest boy. He is living in Iron Town right now and has a good job. He just recently was engaged to a nice girl, and I think that they will be married soon. Our youngest boy was killed when trying to get on an early morning school bus and was hit by an eighteen-wheel truck and trailer, not stopping for the flashing lights of the school bus. This happened right in front of me, as I stood on the porch, watching, to insure he would be OK. I saw the truck coming. I thought that it was coming too fast to stop for the bus, and I realized that it was not even trying to stop, and I turned to see my baby hit by the truck and thrown way up into the air, landing on the shoulder of the road in front of the school bus. I could hardly believe what I had just seen and I ran to the side of the road and picked him up; he looked at me and died in my arms. I had a heart attack as a result of witnessing the accident as I knelt on the shoulder of the highway with my dying son in my arms."

"Did you go to the hospital?"

"Yes, I was taken to the Iron Town General Hospital by ambulance and had to undergo a double coronary bypass operation on the same day, all of this, while my husband John was drunk on his ass, in the house."

"Mrs. Davis, was this the only heart attack you had ever experienced?"

"No, John punched me and dragged me by my hair many times, broke my ribs, fractured my skull, blackened both my eyes, and as a result of repeated physical attacks and threats of death in the house, I suffered additional heart attacks that were brought on by my drunken husband. I know that my life expectancy is not great and that my cardiologist has warned me that I may die if I am not able to get free of stress."

"Did you file a lawsuit, as a result of the death of your little boy?"

"Yes, I did, and John and I were awarded a judgment in the case. John and I bought the old seventy-seven-acre Davis farm where we were living, used a great deal of the monies to remodel the home, buy a new car, tractor, furniture, and appliances, and we paid bills. We lost a lot of money in the casinos, too.

"I tried to protect the property, but John was getting very destructive, pouring gasoline in the house and trying to burn down the house and barn, and shooting at the firemen who came to put out the fire."

"Mrs. Davis, had you complained to the authorities?"

"Yes, I made a couple of complaints to the police and to the prosecutor of John's violence, assaults, and injuries that I had received from him, and Mr. Brenner told me that there was nothing that he could do about it. John bragged that he could do anything he wanted and the police would not stop him. The Michigan State troopers came to the farm on July 5, 1983, in response to a complaint of assault, and the matter was referred to the prosecutor, but the prosecutor ordered the complaint closed. On August 11, 1983, they again came to the house regarding my complaint that my husband had beaten me. The officer classified the complaint as a false complaint, without investigating the offense. On March 12, 1984, the officer came to the house regarding an assault by John Davis on me with a loaded high-powered rifle. The officer later told me that the complaint was closed at the order of the prosecutor, Mr. Brenner, who refused to issue a warrant against John."

"How did John react to the officers coming into the house?"

"As in most of the incidents, John did not resist the officers who surrounded the home with guns drawn and he allowed them into the house. John said to the officers that he would rather kill his own son, than one of the officers. The officers found three guns in the living room, loaded with rounds in the chambers, another in the corner of the bedroom, another in the corner of the bathroom, and several others in the cabinet in the living room. Eleven loaded guns were taken from the house that day. That was the day that I suffered my third heart attack, resulting from the attacks by my husband."

"Had your husband ever been treated for mental illness?"

"Yes. On January 5, 1984, Sheriff David Cromby took him to a hospital for the treatment of the mentally ill, on my complaint that he was violent and attempted to burn the house down. My complaint was closed by the prosecutor, without prosecution."

"Are you able to testify about other occurrences of threats and/or assaults by John?"

"Yes, Deputy Sheriff Grey was present on the scene after our eight-year-old son was killed by a truck while trying to get on to the school bus. He later told me that John was very drunk and that he found him in the house loading a rifle, but took the gun from him, fearing that he was about to kill the truck driver that had killed our son."

"Mrs. Davis, did you ever entertain hope that the domestic situation would ever change?"

"Yes, I did. I had hoped and prayed that someday I could find help for John and that we might live a normal life, but John's attacks upon me became more and more desperate and violent, and I knew that he was very likely to kill me or cause me to die from another heart attack. Whenever he would leave the house for extended periods, I would hope that he might be getting help from someone, but he would take all the food from the house and all the utensils from the kitchen, leaving us with nothing to eat nor kitchenware."

"Mrs. Davis, will you tell the jury about September 22, 1984?"

"On that date, John had awakened early and had begun drinking at seven a.m. and rapidly became intoxicated. We argued mostly about his unwillingness to look for some work and his violence when drinking. I pleaded with him to leave the house because I did not feel that I could continue to take the stress of more arguments and threats.

"John tried to jam ice down my throat when I refused to drink with him and punched me in the mouth. I called my son Robert to come down to the kitchen about ten o'clock that morning, and that I looked to Robert for some protection from John."

"Did the threats continue?"

"Yes, he threatened to kill me, my brother Bill, and our son Robert that morning and to commit suicide. He also threatened to set the house on fire, and I left the house on two occasions that day, hoping that he would not be home when I returned and I would have a break from the tension and his punches."

"When you, your brother, and Robert returned to the house, late in the afternoon on September 22, 1984, was there an altercation that took place upon your entering the home?"

"Yes. John had the door locked and Robert and I had to use an extra key that we had always kept hidden in the shed. When we entered, John got upset and was again gesturing with a knife, threatening to kill both Robert, my brother, and me. He had that look that I had seen so often when he was about to go into a rage, a strange look that I had gotten familiar with over the years, just before he would beat me. Robert, my brother, and I pushed past him and got into the living room, but he turned and went into the bedroom. I was hoping to reason with him; I entered the bedroom, and as soon as he saw me, he got up from the bed where he had been sitting and punched me right in my jaw, and I fell behind the bed and could not get back up on my own. My brother Bill came into the bedroom to help me and had to fight with my husband while Robert came and helped me get up. I did not realize it, but my brother went upstairs to his bedroom and got a rifle and brought it down the stairs, stuffing it under my arm and then turned and left me standing there alone. I felt trapped; both my brother and Robert had left the room and I was there alone. John got to his feet and said he would take the gun from me, kill us all, and then commit suicide. I was never so scared in all my life, there was no time to turn and run; he charged, was almost on top of me, reaching for the gun, the gun went off, blood came to his mouth, and he staggered backward, falling back on the bed. I was afraid to go near him, I knew he was not dead and was still feeling terror that he would still get up and grab me."

"Did anyone call for an ambulance?"

"Yes, I told Robert to call the ambulance."

"How did you feel after knowing that John had died?"

"I did not plan to shoot my husband and was not certain that the gun was even loaded. I recall telling Robert to call the ambulance, but I was still afraid to try to assist or render aid for fear that he would grab me and that he would hurt me if I got any closer to him. I admit feeling relief that I would not have to take a beating that night and I kept saying 'No more beatings—No more beatings,' but later feeling terrible after realizing what had happened."

"No further questions," David concluded, hoping that Jean had said enough to place some credible doubts in the minds of each of the jurors and stay focused during Will's cross-examination.

"Counsel, we are going to take a break at this time," said Judge Roode.

During the break, Jean and David again went to the rear of the building to have a cigarette and take a moment to talk about her testimony. David told her that he felt that her direct testimony went fine, but he was now concerned about how she would hold up on cross-examination. David told her to tell the truth and not let Mr. Brenner put words in her mouth, to listen carefully to his question and think about each question before answering it. He told her that most all of his questions would call for a yes or no answer, but if she needed to give a further explanation, she should turn to the judge and ask him if she could be allowed to give a complete answer to the question. He told her not to get into a debate with him, not to reply to his answers out of anger or fear. David advised her to look at the jury when answering his questions. David told her that if he tries to push her into answering quickly, she should take her time and answer the questions directly and not to appear evasive.

"Mrs. Davis, will you take the stand again? I remind you that you are still under oath," Judge Roode said.

"Mr. Brenner, you may cross-examine the witness," said Judge Roode.

"Thank you, Your Honor," replied Will Brenner, looking in David's direction with a look of a tiger, preparing to jump on its prey, tearing and ripping, excited for the kill.

"Mrs. Davis, before your husband's auto accident, you and he spent considerable time in bars drinking throughout the weekends, isn't that true?" Will asked.

"We went out on Friday and Saturday nights, but it wasn't all weekend, we didn't go out on Sundays, as a rule," replied Jean.

"But you and he would get drunk together, isn't that true?"

"Sometimes we would both get drunk, but most of the time he would and I would not, I had to drive the car home," Jean replied.

"There were times when you would beat on him when you were fighting in the bars, isn't that true?"

"Before his accident, no. After he had healed enough following the accident, we tried going out together, but he was always looking to argue and fight with me, and yes, I did hit him back sometimes. That was before he threatened to kill me. After that, I was afraid to hit him back."

"Well, at that point in time, he had never seriously hurt you, did he?"

"Yes, he did; he broke three of my ribs, gave me black eyes, knocked out one of my teeth, and gave me two heart attacks. Once, I was riding home with him from the Moose Lodge, in Pictured Rocks, and asked him to let me drive, because he was drunk, driving all over the road; he pushed me out of the car while driving fifty miles an hour down the highway, I hit my head hard on the pavement; I must have lain on the side of the road for quite a while, because he never stopped, or if he did, he just left me lying next to the guardrails; when I woke up, I had to walk three miles back into town to the hospital. I had blood running down my face, my skull was fractured."

"Your Honor! I would like her answer to my last question stricken from the record," Will cried out.

"I oppose Mr. Brenner's motion to strike," David stated.

"Mr. Brenner, you asked the question whether or not her husband had ever hurt her; she answered the question. I'm afraid you're going to have to live with her answer, motion to strike denied," ruled Judge Roode.

Boy... Will had shot himself in the foot with that question. Spending a little time with Jean during the last break was the right thing to do. She was not allowing Will to intimidate her, while keeping eye contact with the jurors, thought David.

"You had previously testified that your heart attack was brought on when witnessing the death of your eight-year-old son, isn't that true?"

"That was my first heart attack, the next two were brought on by John beating me," answered Jean.

David looked at the jury. A number of the jurors seemed uneasy with Will's questioning of Jean, asking for answers that were only producing what she had said in direct testimony. David felt that Will was having a difficult time in cross-examining Jean and that he would be much better off if he just sat down.

"Now, you testified that on the early evening of September 22, 1984, your husband had hit you while you were in the bedroom and knocked you to the floor. Why didn't you just leave the bedroom after your son Robert helped you up and then went into the kitchen?"

"My brother Bill had put a gun under my arm and it further enraged John. I still wanted him to leave the house, until he sobered up. John said he was going to take the gun from me, saying that he was going to shoot me, my brother, and our son Robert. There was no time to turn and leave. I knew that I was going to die right then. He was not afraid of me, even though I then had a rifle. Bill and Robert had left and there was no one there to help me."

"So you stood in the doorway of the bedroom and he was sitting on the bed when you raised the rifle and shot him, isn't that really the truth?"

"No, it is not the truth. He was on his feet, charging at me, reaching for the gun, but I never raised the gun."

"You pulled the trigger of that gun and you killed your husband, isn't that the truth?"

"I don't remember pulling the trigger, but I must have. I was so scared, I didn't want to die."

"You told the officers that you had shot him and that you were not going to be beaten again, isn't that true?"

"Yes, I did. I was just happy to be alive, knowing that he could no longer beat me."

"Then you did indeed kill your husband, didn't you?"

"Yes, I guess I did."

"Where did that rifle come from? Weren't all the guns previously picked up by the sheriff, or perhaps it was your gun?"

"No, it was not my gun. I do not own a gun, do not know how to load one, or where the safety is located on the gun. Robert told me that John had a gun hidden in the dog food bag, and that is why the police did not find it."

"Now, Mrs. Davis, I understand that you and John never actually farmed that land, but tell me, did you have chickens or pets?"

"Yes, we have a few chickens and a female dog and three young pups."

"Had the female dog given birth to the pups before September 22, 1984?"

"Yes, the pups were born in August."

"You are not sure that the blood that your investigator found at the threshold of the bedroom doorway didn't come from that female dog, are you?"

"It was John's blood. I saw it come out of his mouth before he staggered back and fell on the bed."

"I have no more questions of this witness, Your Honor," Will Brenner stated.

"Any redirect, Mr. Chartier?" asked Judge Roode.

"None, Your Honor," replied David.

David breathed a sigh of relief. Jean did really well during Will's cross-examination, answering his questions directly, keeping eye contact with the jury, and not allowing her emotions to take away from the direct answers she knew she had to give to the questions asked. David felt very proud of her.

"Mr. Chartier, you may call your next witness," announced Judge Roode.

Testimony of Robert LaGale, MD

"Thank you, Your Honor; the defense calls Doctor Robert LaGale, M,D. to the stand, please," David announced.

The witness was called by the clerk and was sworn.

"Would you state your full name please?" David requested.

"Robert LaGale, MD."

"Where do you live, Dr. LaGale?"

"In Iron Town, Michigan."

"Are you a medical doctor?"

"Yes, I am."

"Where were you educated, doctor?"

"I went to high school at the Otsego High School in Bowling Green, Wisconsin, graduated from Michigan State University with a bachelor of science, and went to University of Michigan Medical School, University of Pittsburg for internship and residency, and the University of Pittsburg for cardiology fellowship."

"Doctor, are you licensed to practice medicine in the state of Michigan?"

"Yes, I have been licensed since 1977."

"Are you certified in any particular field of medicine?"

"I am board certified in internal medicine and am board certified in cardiovascular disease."

"Doctor, what is cardiovascular disease?"

"It is the study and treatment of diseases of the heart and vascular system."

"What does vascular mean, doctor?"

"It means blood, the transmission of blood throughout the body."

"Do you have a medical practice, doctor?"

"Yes, I do; my office is at the Iron Town Medical Center, in the city of Iron Town, Michigan."

"Are you on the staff of any hospitals, doctor?"

"Yes, I am on the staff of the Iron Town General Hospital and several others throughout the U.P."

"Doctor, in connection with your practice, have you had an occasion to examine and treat the defendant in this case, Mrs. Jean Davis?"

"Yes, I have."

"I saw her on October 1, 1983. She had suffered an acute inferior myocardial infarction in upon witnessing the death of her young son and she was having continuing chest discomfort, and she was referred to me for a cardiology evaluation."

"What is the condition that you have mentioned, acute inferior myocardial infarction?"

"In lay terms, it is a heart attack, an occlusion of an artery leading to damage of the heart muscle."

"Doctor, when you first saw Mrs. Davis, what did your examination include?"

"I took a history, performed a physical examination, and reviewed her X-rays, electrocardiogram."

"Is a history an important part of the exam, doctor?"

"Your Honor, I object to Mr. Chartier's question regarding the doctor's examination and diagnoses of Mrs. Davis, on the grounds of relevancy," Will stated in an abrupt manner.

"Well, may I inquire, Mr. Chartier, do you claim that her medical diagnosis has relevancy in this case," inquired Judge Roode.

"Your Honor, the medical condition of Jean Davis is important and crucial to understanding her state of mind on the date in question. Her physical condition, deteriorated health, the early and progressive condition of her diseased heart, and Mrs. Davis's knowledge of the state of her health is a crucial issue in determining her state of mind or apprehension of impending death, at the moment that we allege that she was in fear of dying when the shot was fired."

"All right, I can understand and agree that testimony concerning her medical condition and what knowledge she had of it can be relevant concerning her state of her mind at the time of the incident. Now, I think that this witness may be examined as to what diagnosis he made and as to what effect this would have on her state of mind and as to what he informed her concerning her condition and as to what effect that might have on her state of mind," stated Judge Roode.

"Thank you, Your Honor," David responded.

"Doctor, what did your examination of Mrs. Davis include?" asked David.

"As I mentioned before, history, physical examination, review of her X-rays, and EKG—electrocardiogram," Dr. LaGale replied.

"Following the exam, did you make a medical diagnosis?"

"Yes, I did."

"What did you diagnose, if anything, doctor?"

"Well, the medical term for it would be arteriosclerotic heart disease with a recent inferior wall myocardial infarction and ongoing angiopectoris."

"Doctor—*showing the doctor a model of the human heart*—would you say that this model is an accurate representation of the human heart?"

"Yes, it is. It is enlarged somewhat and I have one just like it in my office."

"Would this aid help you in explaining to the jury the nature of her condition and your diagnosis?"

"Yes, I think it might."

"Would you hold it, doctor, as you explain the nature of Mrs. Davis's medical condition?"

"Okay. Well, we performed a cardio-catheterization of Mrs. Davis because she was having continuing chest pains after her myocardial infarction, which usually means there is still some obstruction of the coronary arteries. On the catheterization, we determined that she had a weak heart muscle with an enlarged heart, with no movement on the under surface, the inferior wall of the heart, where she had the heart attack, and very poor motion over the rest of the heart. The contractual force of the heart was about half of what a normal heart would be. It was very weak and slow. She had a very severe narrowing in the circumflex coronary artery in the front of the heart—*gesturing to the jury the location of the circumflex coronary artery*—coming around in the A.V. groove and then proceeds down to the inferior wall of the heart. She had a 90 percent narrowing here and a severe 80 percent narrowing of the diagonal branch, left anterior descending artery, and a milder 40 to 50 percent narrowing of the left anterior descending artery."

"Doctor, how can you distinguish the arteries from the veins on this model?"

"The veins are colored blue and the arteries are red."

"Doctor, is there a circulatory system for the heart separate from the—"

"Objection, Your Honor, that is leading," Will cried out.

"Overruled," declared the judge.

"Please answer the question, doctor?" David requested.

"Well, the blockage in the arteries is actually bypassed. A vein is taken out of the leg, and that vein is used to bypass the blockage in the artery. It is sewed into the aorta above the coronary arteries, and then brought down beyond the blockage. She had two bypasses performed."

"And, this was accomplished by you?"

"No, I do not perform that surgery. That is done by a cardiovascular surgeon, in this case Bruce Hunt, MD."

"Do you follow her as her cardiologist?"

"Right, exactly."

"Now, doctor, have you had an opportunity to determine, since that surgery, how those arteries bypasses are functioning?"

"Yes. Initially, she did well, but then again she began to have chest discomfort, and we brought her back for repeat catheterization and found one of the two bypasses had occluded so only one was working. That happens not infrequently; usually one out of five bypasses will occlude."

"When you say occlude, what do you mean?"

"Well, I mean it just blocks off, fills with clot, and the blood flow ceases."

"So, of the two coronary bypasses that she had, only one is functioning?"

"Correct, and she was not felt to be a candidate for a repeat operation. That is quite a lot to put a person through just for one additional bypass."

"Have you had subsequent opportunities to see Mrs. Davis?"

"Yes, I have been seeing her regularly since I initially saw her, again giving her medication and gradually increasing doses to help alleviate her symptoms of chest pain."

"And has she had subsequent occurrences of heart attacks?"

"Yes, she required admission to Iron Town General Hospital in March of this year for prolonged chest discomfort, which did prove to be another small myocardial infarction; she was in the hospital for nine days on that occasion."

"Doctor, patients experiencing the type of heart condition that you have described in Mrs. Davis's case, what, if anything, have you advised them as to stress problems?"

"I tell them to avoid stressful situations at all times."

"Doctor, have you had an occasion to talk with Mrs. Davis about stress in her life?"

"Yes, I have."

"What have you been concerned about with regard to stress in her life?"

"I recommended that she avoid all stress, physical and mental or emotional, if possible. Physical stress increases the heart rate, increases the blood pressure, and puts extra workload on the heart. If the heart is already compromised with a compromised circulation that could cause further angina episodes or infarctions."

"What is meant by a heart attack?"

"It is actual death of an area of the heart muscle and that turns to scar tissue and is permanent damage to the heart."

"Does it ever begin to function again?"

"No, it doesn't; it is lost forever."

"Did you talk to Mrs. Davis about this?"

"Yes."

"What did you tell her?"

"I told her to avoid all stress, physical, mental, and emotional."

"Did you tell her of possible consequences if she failed to minimize her stress?"

"Yes, I did. I told her that she is likely to die if she failed to avoid stress of any kind."

"What did you tell her, if anything, about her life expectancy?"

"Objection," Will cried out, saying that he failed to see the relevancy.

"Overruled," stated Judge Roode.

"You can answer the question, doctor," David said.

"Right after the surgery, I told her that she had a fifty-fifty chance of living five years. That was in 1983 and we now know that only one of the bypasses was functioning."

"Did you have an occasion to talk to Mrs. Davis regarding stress in her home life?"

"The first heart attack followed her witnessing the death of her minor son. In March of this year, she had another one due to the stress at home where the police had told—"

"Objection; I object to the hearsay," Will stated, addressing the court.

"Well, overruled," ruled Judge Roode.

"Continue, doctor," David said, addressing the witness.

"Well, I admit my information was from the patient and her family. But, when I saw her in March, she told me that the police had told her to leave the home and stay away for a while."

"Again, Your Honor, that is really hearsay. It is double hearsay," Will stated.

"The objection is again overruled. This is not testimony that is being used to prove the truth of the facts stated, but this has to do with the state of mind of the defendant and is entirely different," stated Judge Roode.

"Thank you, Your Honor," David said.

"Please continue, doctor," David stated.

"Well, as I was about to say, in March she showed me bruises and was very upset about her husband hitting her and threatening to kill her and their minor son. She was fearful that her husband would assault and beat her again, that she could not survive another beating."

"Thank you, doctor; I have no other questions of this witness," said David.

"Mr. Brenner, do you wish to cross-examine this witness?" inquired Judge Roode.

"Yes, thank you, Your Honor," Will replied.

"Doctor, have you testified in court before for Mr. Chartier?"

"Not in court. I have done a deposition for him before in a civil case, not a criminal case."

"Was the case resulting out of the incident involving Jean Davis's son?"

"Yes, it was."

"Have you ever testified for Mr. Chartier since that time?"

"To the best of my knowledge, no, but it is possible. I give a lot of depositions, you understand, and a lot of cases for people with heart disease, and it's possible I could have testified for a number of lawyers, and I testify frequently."

"Doctor, what is stress?"

"Stress is relative. Stress for one person may not be stress for another, and there are many different definitions for it. But, in my practice, I usually count it as something that quickens the pulse, raises the blood pressure, or causes some physical sign of emotional strain."

"How does one avoid stress?"

"Oh, it can sometimes be avoided through medication, sometimes mental process, psychiatric help, and avoidance of certain situations."

"Have you ever recommended to Mrs. Davis that she avoid certain situations to avoid stress?"

"Yes, I have."

"And what have you recommended to her?"

"Well, I recommended that she avoid any kind of heavy labor; she could only do very light housework, minimal physical activity. I also told her to avoid mental stress as much as possible, anything that in the past has caused her problems."

"What causes a buildup of cholesterol?"

"There are a number of factors involved; there is no one single factor. It has to do with the family history of coronary disease, diet, smoking, history, lifestyle, a number of factors."

"Could the fact that she smokes and drinks bring an onset of her condition, this angina?"

"Yes. It contributes, it all contributes."

"Is her diagnosis basically of narrowing of the coronary arteries?"

"Well, she is a little different in that she also has what we call cardiomyopathy, which is a generalized weakness of the heart muscle out of proportion of the degree of narrowing of the coronary arteries. Therefore, she probably has a couple of processes going on. She has basic weakness of the heart muscle."

"Would you say that Mrs. Davis is one of the most seriously diagnosed patients that you are treating?"

"She would probably be in the top 10 percent of the most seriously diagnosed patients that I am treating."

"That is all of the questions that I have," announced Will.

"Any redirect, Mr. Chartier?" asked Judge Roode.

"Yes. Thank you, Your Honor," David responded.

"Doctor, did you know Mrs. Davis to be living in a battered-wife situation?"

"She told me this, yes."

"In fact, did not her admission in March of 1984 involve a serious incident in which she was assaulted?"

"She and a family member told me that her husband had been discharging a firearm around the house."

"And, doctor, would this be a situation in your opinion sufficient to create stress and bring on a heart attack?"

"I would think so."

"Doctor, can a generally stressful situation cause this defendant, because of her medical condition, to fear for her life?"

"Certainly. A stressful situation could well bring on an episode of angina causing her to believe that she was in a very threatening situation, including the fear of death. In Mrs. Davis's situation, mental stress played a greater part in producing her angina than her smoking or drinking or even physical activity. It seems that her emotional state was much more important in her case than in others I have had, in precipitating her angina spells, yes."

"I have no further questions," David stated.

"Mr. Brenner?" asked the judge.

"No further questions, Your Honor," replied Will.

"Mr. Chartier, you may call your next witness," said Judge Roode.

"Thank you, Your Honor; I now call Mr. Berry Southern to the stand," David announced.

"Would you state your full name, please?"

"Barry Southern."

"Where do you reside?"

"I reside in Pictured Rocks, Michigan."

"Are you employed?"

"Yes, I am; I am the lab director at the Pictured Rocks Memorial Hospital."

"Would you please give me a brief statement as to your educational background?"

"I have a bachelor's degree with a major in chemistry and biology from Northern Michigan University, a master's degree in biology, and I am a registered medical technologist."

"What is involved in becoming a registered medical technologist?"

"You have to have a bachelor's degree in a science from an accredited university and do a one year internship at an accredited hospital."

"What type of work do you do as a registered medical technologist?"

"Most of the work I do is blood testing."

"How long have you been employed in that capacity at the Pictured Rocks Memorial Hospital?"

"It will be nine years in July."

"On how many occasions have you had the opportunity to test and determine the nature and type of blood?"

"Probably infinite. I do not recall, but thousands, I suppose."

"Did you have an occasion last night to come to the hospital, at my request?"

"Yes."

"And, did you meet with myself, Mr. Don White, and Dr. Cachette?"

"I did."

"For what purpose did we meet?"

"When I got there, Mr. White arrived with two pieces of carpet and I was asked to determine whether there might be blood on some of the spots on the carpet."

"Did you make such a determination?"

"Yes, I did."

"Let me show you this—*showing the witness a piece of carpet*—do you recognize it?"

"Yes, it is one of the pieces that I tested last night."

"How do you know that?"

"I signed my initials to it and dated it. I can see my initials on it now."

"Could you tell me if the blood on the carpet was human blood, as opposed to animal blood or chicken blood?"

"Yes, it was human blood."

"Did I show you a copy of an autopsy report on one John Davis?"

"Yes."

"Did you review that report?"

"Yes."

"Did you notice the blood type that was listed for John Davis?"

"Yes, it was A+."

"And did you type the blood sample that you found on the carpet sample that we brought to you last night?"

"Yes, I did."

"The blood sample that I tested was A+."

"Did you review your prior medical records relative to Mrs. Jean Davis, pursuant to a signed release that I provided to you last night?"

"Yes, I did."

"Mr. Southern, would you please tell me the blood type of Mrs. Davis?"

"Yes; she has O+ blood."

"Your Honor, I would like to have these blood samples marked as exhibits for the defense."

"Any objections, Mr. Brenner?" asked Judge Roode.

"I would like to ask the witness a couple of questions first, Your Honor," Mr. Brenner stated.

"Mr. Southern, did you do any DNA testing of the blood to determine if it was that of John Davis?" inquired Will.

"No, we do not do DNA testing."

"So, you are not able to tell me positively if the blood on the carpet is that of John Davis; isn't that true?"

"Yes, that is true."

"Your Honor, that is all of the questions that I have for this witness, and I do object to the receipt of those proposed exhibits into evidence in this case, for lack of positive identification."

"The exhibits will be received into evidence and it will be up to the jury as to the weight that they will give to that evidence," stated Judge Roode.

"Mr. Chartier, you may call your next witness to the stand," declared the judge.

"Thank you, Your Honor; I now call Deputy Sheriff Grey to the stand," David announced.

After the witness sworn, David commenced his questioning of the witness.

"Would you please state your full name?" asked David.

"Henry J. Grey," replied deputy Grey.

"Are you employed?"

"Yes; I am employed by the Pictured Rocks Sheriff Department."

"How long have you been a Sheriff Deputy?"

"About twenty years."

"Deputy, do you know where the Davis residence is located?"

"Yes, I do."

"Are you acquainted with Mrs. Davis?"

"Yes."

"Do you recognize her sitting at the defense table?"

"Yes, I do."

"Are you acquainted with John Davis?"

"Yes."

"Do you recall going to the Davis residence in the earlier morning hours of October 1, 1983?"

"Yes, I do."

"What was the occasion for you to go to the Davis residence on that date?"

"Well, the sheriff received a call that there was a fatal accident on the highway in front of the Davis residence."

"Who was involved, if you know?"

"Mrs. Davis's small boy."

"Did you see Mrs. Davis at the scene?"

"Yes, I did."

"What did you observe, if anything?"

"Mrs. Davis was lying over her boy and was screaming and hollering, but then fell over and was unconscious lying in the road, next to her dead son."

"Did you see Mr. Davis outside?"

"No, I didn't."

"What else, if anything, was happening at the scene?"

"The ambulance had arrived and a second ambulance was called; Mrs. Davis was put into the first ambulance and left for the Pictured Rocks Memorial Hospital; the body of the young boy was sent in the second ambulance."

"I went into the house and saw John Davis loading a rifle, and he appeared intoxicated to me. I told him to give the gun to me and that I wasn't going to let him leave the house with a loaded rifle. I figured that he was intending to shoot the truck driver."

"How long have you known John Davis?"

"About twenty years."

"Do you think that you knew him well?"

"Yes, I did."

"Do you know whether or not he had a general reputation in the community for destruction and violence?"

"He was violent."

"Do you know whether or not he had a general reputation in the community?"

"Yes."

"What was that reputation?"

"He had a reputation in the community for being a violent person."

"Thank you, Deputy Grey. Mr. Brenner, you may cross-examine this witness," Davis said.

"Deputy Grey, how do you know that Mr. Davis had a general reputation in the community for violence?" Will asked.

"Because I have talked to his neighbors and others in the area of the Davis farm, and everyone I talked with described him as a violent man," Deputy Grey replied.

"I have no further questions, Your Honor," stated Will.

"Any redirect, Mr. Chartier?" asked Judge Roode.

"Yes, Your Honor," David stated.

"Deputy Grey, do your duties at the sheriff department ever place you in charge of the security of prisoners?"

"Yes."

"Did you ever have an occasion to have Mr. John Davis as one of your prisoners?"

"Yes."

"Was he ever violent while in your custody?"

"No."

"I have no further questions of this witness, Your Honor."

"Your Honor, if it pleases the court, I would like to call as my next witness, State Trooper Dale Carbon," David stated.

"Proceed," stated Judge Roode.

After Trooper Carbon was sworn, David began with his questioning of the trooper.

"Trooper Carbon, are you acquainted with John Davis and Mrs. Davis, seated here at the defendant's table?"

"Yes, I am acquainted with her and I was acquainted with him, while he was alive," responded Trooper Carbon.

"Did you ever go to the Davis residence in response to a complaint received at the Michigan State Police Post in Pictured Rocks?"

"Yes, I have been there numerous times, in response to complaints."

"Has Mr. Davis ever threatened you?"

"Yes, he did on a number of occasions; the most recent occasion was on the twenty-second of September, 1984, he threatened to kill me."

"At what time did that occur?"

"Around noon. I was there in response to a telephone complaint received from Mrs. Davis. John had been threatening his family with a knife and was threatening suicide."

"The back door was locked and I called out to John to let me in. I could hear John moving around in the kitchen. He asked who I was and I identified myself and told him that I would like to talk with him. He said that he had a 12-gauge shotgun and would blow me away. I persisted in asking him to let me in and he finally did. He was very intoxicated."

"What did you then do, if anything?"

"I called the post and learned that Mrs. Davis and the boy had left the home and were safe with one of Mrs. Davis's uncles, living on Downers Lane. I then talked with John for about twenty minutes and tried to calm him down. Further, I told him not to try driving any of the vehicles and that he should lie down and try to sleep off his drunken condition. Not finding any firearms, I left the home."

"Did you have an occasion to go to the Davis home before the twenty-second of September, 1984?"

"Yes, I did. I believe it was a couple of years before that."

"On that earlier occasion, why were you at the Davis residence?"

"We had received a report that John was attempting to burn the house down and burn up vehicles on the property."

"What, if anything, did you observe when you responded to that call?"

"When I was about four miles from the scene, I could observe smoke coming from the vicinity of the Davis home and an adjacent building; I called the AuTrain Township Volunteer Fire Department and they arrived shortly thereafter. I was then advised that John had left the premises and was headed north across a field on foot."

"What, if anything else, did you do?"

"I drove my patrol car around to the north end of the forty and found John hiding in a pile of brush. I placed him under arrest and put him in the back of the patrol car. He told me that he torched the house because he was mad at his family. He was very intoxicated and smelled of kerosene, and I took him to the Pictured Rocks County Jail."

"How long have you been dealing with these problems with the Davises?"

"About seven years."

"Are you aware of John Davis having a general reputation in the community as to force and violence?"

"Yes, I am."

"What is that general reputation?"

"He has general reputation in the community for violence and destructiveness, and every time I have been called out there, his assaultive behavior and his offenses have accelerated both in intensity and frequency."

"Do you know if that reputation is generally known in the community?"

"I would say, yes."

"Have you had occasions to talk with other people and come to the conclusion that he does have a general reputation in the community for violence and destructiveness?"

"Yes."

"Thank you, Your Honor. I would have no further questions of this witness," David stated.

"Mr. Brenner, do you wish to cross-examine?" inquired Judge Roode.

Mr. Brenner paused for a long time, while he discussed the State trooper's testimony with the arresting trooper sitting next to him at prosecution's table. I could not mistake the silent contempt he was conveying to Trooper Carbon as he looked in his direction, with the piercing glare of a mongoose, stalking a cobra. In Will's mind, Trooper Carbon was the snake.

"No questions," stated Will, as he threw his yellow pad and pen onto his table, expressing his displeasure with the testimony of Trooper Carbon.

Testimony of Professor Paul C. Cachette

"Mr. Chartier, call your next witness," commanded Judge Roode.

"Thank you, Your Honor. I now call Professor Paul C. Cachette to the stand," David announced.

After Dr. Cachette had taken the oath, David commenced his questioning of him.

"Would you please state your full name?" asked David.

"My name is Paul J. Cachette," stated the witness.

"Where do you live, Mr. Cachette?" asked David.

"I reside in Sacramento, California."

"Are you employed?"

"Yes, I am. I am a professor at the California State University, Department of Criminal Justice."

"What is your educational background, Doctor?"

"I have a bachelor of science in criminalistics and forensic science from the University of California-Berkley. I also have a doctorate in the same field from the University of California-Berkley."

"Doctor, what is involved in your work at the university?"

"Well, essentially, I am involved in teaching a number of criminalistics and criminal justice courses. These include basic as well as advanced criminal investigation, criminal identification, introduction to physical evidence, firearms examination, drug and narcotic analysis, forensic microscopy, and things of that nature."

"Where do they ultimately work?"

"They work at police departments in most cases, but some go into the field of forensic science and criminalistics work in crime labs, local and state crime labs, usually in California, but sometimes across the country."

"Are you associated with any law enforcement agencies?"

"I am a reserve officer for the city of Sacramento, in California."

"Have you taught at any other universities?"

"Yes, I have. I have taught at the community college level in California, the University of New Mexico, and have taught at medical and legal seminars throughout California on death investigation."

"Doctor, did you have an occasion to be contacted by myself involving the investigation of ballistics in this case?"

"Yes, I did."

"When did that occur?"

"In October of this year."

"And was there an occasion when I visited you in your laboratory at California State University?"

"Yes, you did. I believe that it was in November of this year."

"Doctor, do you recognize this?" asked David, as he showed the witness a .22-caliber rifle.

"Yes, I do."

"Does that look like the weapon that I brought to your laboratory in California?"

"Yes, it does."

"Did you have an occasion to test fire that weapon?"

"Yes, I did. I fired that weapon several times."

"What was your purpose in doing so?"

"One purpose was to obtain a test-fired bullet for comparison purposes with the questioned bullet that was submitted to me at about the same time. Another purpose was to determine gunshot residue patterns at relatively close distances."

"Let the record show that Dr. Cachette has been referring to people's exhibit no. 2," declared David.

"Dr. Cachette, I show you what has been marked as people's no. 15. Would you examine its contents please?"

"Doctor, do you recall ever seeing that projectile?"

"Yes, I do. I made a comparison of that projectile with test bullets fired from the rifle in question."

"And did you come to any conclusion, doctor?"

"I concluded that this projectile had been fired from that particular weapon," gesturing to the rifle marked as people's no. 2.

"Thank you. Doctor, I now show you what has been marked as people's exhibit no. 11. Can you tell me what that is, please?"

"It is a .22-caliber Winchester Super X expended cartridge case."

"Did you ever see that prior to coming to court today?"

"Yes, I did. I compared that with the test-fired cartridge cases."

"Did you come to any conclusion regarding the same?"

"Yes, I did. I concluded that the question cartridge case was consistent with having been fired from the exhibit 2 weapon."

"Doctor, did you perform a sodium rhodizonate test?"

"Yes, I did. I did a sodium rhodizonate in my distance determination."

"And did you examine the T-shirt that I'm now handing to you?"

"I examined that T-shirt, yes."

"Do you recognize it as the T-shirt that I brought to your laboratory in Sacramento?"

"Yes, I examined that T-shirt."

"How do you recognize that shirt as the one you examined in California?"

"My initials and the date of my examination are on the bag containing the shirt, and it appears to be the same shirt that I examined. Additionally, I have close photographs of all the pieces of evidence that I examined."

"Doctor, were you able to examine, last night, the ballistics evidence that has been marked and submitted in this trial by Mr. Brenner, on behalf of the State Police?"

"I was able to examine a photographic print that had been used to pick up gunshot residue off of that T-shirt, then lifted up and sprayed with chemicals."

"And, what is that test called?"

"A Griess Test. The test was originally developed by Griess but was later modified by Walker in 1937 specifically for gunshot residue."

"And, were you able to examine this evidence last night?"

"Yes."

"Do you recognize people's exhibit no. 23, which are the ballistic patterns resulting from the State Police ballistics testing?"

"Yes, I do."

"And what, if anything, did you do with regard to exhibit no. 23 when you examined it at the sheriff station last night?"

"Were you under supervision when you examined it?"

"Yes, I was. There were several deputies in the room, as I examined it."

What, if anything, did you do?"

"I examined the state police patterns under a low-powered microscope, initially. Then I prepared a plastic overlay of the color, spots of color showed up on this particular item," showing his overlay work product, obtained from the examination.

Defendant's proposed defense exhibit was marked for identification.

"Doctor, what was the purpose in making this examination?"

"The purpose of making this examination in essence was to attempt to determine if any particular pattern could be discerned on the basis of the Griess-Walker test that was done. In other words, until last night I had not seen people's exhibit no. 23. And, in situations of this nature, in order to determine the distance and the angle that a weapon was fired from, one has to observe some sort of pattern, whether it is brought up chemically or whether you can see it with the naked eye or under a low-power microscope."

"Doctor, I want to show you the work product that you created last night during your examination of the ballistics evidence at the sheriff station. Is this the overlay you prepared last night?"

"Yes it is. It is a simple plastic overlay on which I outlined the markings that are on people's no. 23, and I just simply laid out the plastic sheet over and outlined the markings that are on it. I then put dots with a blue pen wherever I saw the blue reaction here on the Griess-Walker test."

"When this was done, we see a mirror image of people's no. 23. If we reverse it, it gives us some indication of the gunshot residue pattern that was produced. There is a roughly elliptically shaped pattern, indicating both distance and angle of trajectory, relative to the muzzle of the gun and the shirt worn by John Davis when the shot was fired."

"Doctor, from your independent study and the examination of the State Police ballistics testing, have you arrived at a conclusion, based on scientific principles, both as to distance and angle of trajectory?"

"Yes, I have."

"And, Doctor, what would your opinion be?"

"I estimated the distance between the muzzle of the gun and the shirt worn by John Davis to be between twelve and twenty-four inches when the shot was fired."

"Doctor, would you have an opinion as to the angle at which the gun must have been held, at the instant the shot was fired?"

"Yes, it is my opinion that the gun was fired in an upward and to the left direction."

"Doctor, how many times have you been involved in ballistics comparisons involving both distance and trajectory determinations?"

"I believe in excess of two hundred times. I have testified in court hundreds of times and most of those times were for the prosecution. At the present time, I am a consultant and I have testified in numerous cases for the defense."

"Doctor, is your professional witness fee the same, regardless of the outcome of the case?"

"Yes, of course."

"Dr. Cachette, have you examined the autopsy report in this case?"

"Yes, I have."

"Did you note that the trajectory of the .22-caliber bullet had a downward trajectory on the inside of the decedent's body, according to the pathologist?" asked David.

"Yes, I did."

"Tell me, doctor, does the trajectory of a small-caliber bullet like the .22-caliber bullet in this case tell us anything about what might have been the outside trajectory of the bullet, on its way to the body of the decedent?"

"No, not at all. With a small caliber, once the bullet enters the body, the bullet can go in any direction. We saw that in the assassination attempt on President Ronald Regan, where the small-caliber bullet hit a rib and took a downward trajectory on the inside of the body. From the autopsy report, it indicates that here, too, the bullet hit the second rib of John Davis and thereafter traveled on a downward trajectory inside the body. A .22-caliber bullet fired at an upward angle can take a downward trajectory once it enters the body especially if it strikes a rib on an angle."

"Your Honor, the direct examination of this witness is now complete and Mr. Brenner can cross-examine, should he choose to do so," David stated.

"Mr. Brenner, you may cross-examine," Judge Roode said.

"Thank you, Your Honor," Will replied.

"Dr. Cachette, what kind of a doctor are you?" inquired Will.

"I am a doctor of criminology in criminalistics."

"Are you a medical doctor?"

"No, I am not. I am a doctor in criminology."

"Is that as PhD?"

"It is a professional doctorate, similar to a medical doctor, a doctor of dentistry, or veterinary medicine."

"Did you have to write a thesis?"

"Yes, I did, at the University of California-Berkley.

"How many years of schooling did it take to obtain your doctorate?"

"Three years graduate work and approximately seven years to finish my dissertation."

"That is all the questions that I have," stated Will.

"Any redirect, Mr. Chartier," inquired the judge.

"None, Your Honor," replied David.

"We are going to take a recess for twenty minutes," declared Judge Roode.

David wanted to talk to Jean during the recess and again went to the back door of the annex where he knew that she would be smoking one or two of her Virginia Slims. He asked Jean for one of her cigarettes, and while she and David smoked, he told her that he was quite pleased with the testimony of Dr. Paul Cachette, and she said that she was, as well. Jean looked like she was feeling more confident, as the trial unfolded in front of her. She told David that she was surprised at the extent of trial preparation he had done and seemed pleased at the progress of the trial. It seemed only a moment and they were returning to the courtroom.

"Please be seated, court is back in session," again the bailiff announced.

"Mr. Chartier, call your next witness," the court commanded.

"Thank you, Your Honor. I call to the stand Dr. Carl M. Bergman," David announced.

Dr. Bergman was dressed quite conservatively with a dark grey suit, white shirt, with a bow tie, and he wore stylish eyeglasses. David was pleased about that, as probably most of the jurors had never seen a psychologist, nor heard one talk about the psychological aspects of spousal abuse. Everyone in the courtroom was about to learn a great deal about the dysfunction, thought David.

"Doctor, would you state your full name, please," David requested.

"Dr. Carl M. Bergman."

"Where do you reside?"

"In Lansing."

"Where were you educated?"

"I received a bachelor's degree in psychology at Dayton College in Dayton, Ohio, a master's degree in psychology at Ohio State, and a doctor of philosophy at the University of Kansas, and a second doctor of philosophy degree in psychology at the University of Pittsburgh. I did an internship in clinical psychology at the University of Pittsburgh, Western Psychiatric Institute, and I did a second internship in clinical psychology at the University of Michigan, School of Medicine, Department of Psychology, in Ann Arbor, Michigan."

"In what year did you get your doctor's degree?"

"1972."

"What professional experience have you had in the field of psychology, Doctor?"

"Just after receiving my doctor's degree, I was employed for approximately five years at the counseling center at Michigan State University. Then I was employed in the Department of Psychiatry at the College of Human and Osteopathic Medicine at Michigan State University. Since 1982, I have been in the private practice of clinical psychology in Lansing, Michigan, and hold an appointment as a clinical associate professor at the University of Michigan."

"Have you been involved in consulting, doctor?"

"Yes, I have."

"Can you tell the members of the jury what might be involved in that work?"

"What is involved in being a consultant is going to various agencies, clinics, hospitals, or persons and using the discipline of psychology to help them to either understand better the kinds of patients that they might be working with or to help them develop more effective programs or to use the science of psychology in any one of a number of ways for the benefit of the people with whom I'm consulting."

"With what agencies have you consulted?"

"I was a consultant for many years with the Genesee County Community Mental Health Center. I was a factory resource person for the Family Life Referral Clinic Center at Michigan State University. I was a consultant for approximately three years at the Gastroneurolic Clinic Center of Michigan State University. I was a consultant for about six years to the state of Michigan Department of Vocational Development, and I have also served as a consultant to the Forensic Psychology Institute in Southfield, Michigan."

"Doctor, what areas of psychology are you involved in?"

"Psychotherapy, psychological testing, neuropsychological testing, clinical psychology training, and forensic psychology."

"Have you ever had any publications, doctor?"

"Yes, I have."

"Could you tell me the nature of the publications?"

"One publication is entitled *The State versus a Battered Woman*. It is a case study, which was published. Another publication is entitled *Supervision of Co-Therapy Teams*, which is, at present, in press in a journal entitled *Psychotherapy and Practice*, which is published by the Psychological Association."

"Doctor, did you have an occasion to see and study Mrs. Jean Davis?"

"Yes, I did."

"Do you recognize Jean Davis in this courtroom?"

"Yes, she is seated at the defense table."

"When did you see Jean Davis?"

"On November 9, 1984."

"Where did you see her?"

"I saw her in my office in Lansing. I was with her for three to four hours. In addition to that, I reviewed all of the reports from the Pictured Rocks County Sheriff Department and the State Police. I also listened to two tape recordings of defense counsel interviewing Mrs. Davis shortly after the incident."

"As a result of your study, Doctor, have you formed any opinions with regard to Mrs. Davis's state of mind?"

"Yes, I have."

"Doctor, you know that this case involves a shooting in which it is alleged that Mrs. Davis killed her husband and is currently on trial for the crime of murder. Are you aware of that?"

"Yes, I am."

"Would you have any opinion as to the state of Jean Davis's emotions when the shot was fired?"

"At that moment in time, I would surmise that she was in deep fear, *beyond terror*, at the time the shot was fired, profound fear."

"Doctor, why would you use the term 'profound fear'?"

"There had been a long seven-year history of extraordinary brutal and violent actions directed at Mrs. Davis by her deceased husband. In addition to that, she has had a various heart condition, already having suffered two heart attacks, one of which occurred just after a time when Mr. Davis had held a loaded rifle on her with the safety off, which precipitated one attack. She was afraid that would occur again. Another reason to account for her fear is that she had been brutally assaulted earlier that same day and threatened with a knife by her drunken husband. He was threatening suicide, which meant to her that he would have nothing to lose, should he kill her. When she was trying to encourage him to leave the house, her brother, who was also staying at that residence without her knowledge, placed a loaded rifle under her arm, which enraged him further, and he said that he was going to kill her and their minor son. She was holding it at her hip at the bedroom doorway as he charged her, saying that he was about to take the gun from her and kill them all and then commit suicide. As he charged her, the shot was fired, striking him in the chest and causing his death."

"Doctor, would you have an opinion, based on your study, as to why Mrs. Davis did not leave her husband?"

"The first ten years or so of their marriage was a very good marriage for both of them. It was a very good marital relationship. They had a very happy life together and felt respect for one another. However, at the time of her husband's automobile accident, things went very badly downhill. He became increasingly more brutal to her, very angry, physically abusive, while constantly drinking alcohol."

"Would you continue, doctor?"

"Mrs. Davis experienced John as becoming increasingly more violent, more belligerent, and more brutal toward her. Nevertheless, she always felt that sometime or someday, he would get the kind of help that he needed to understand what was happening to him. She was also afraid of what would happen to him if she left him. There were many times when she would encourage him to leave, which he would sometimes do, for several days or weeks at a time. Other times she would leave the house, which occurred even on the day of the shooting. The major reason why she did not leave or divorce him was her loyalty, her love of him, her concern whether he could make it on his own, her hope that things would someday, somehow get better, if he would only get help to stop drinking and get help with his anger issues."

"Doctor, do you have an opinion as to whether or not Jean had the psychological capacity to hurt her husband?"

"Yes, I have."

"Would you please state that opinion, doctor?"

"No, she did not have the psychological capacity to harm him. She told me that she could easily have hurt him by hitting him in his legs, which were very vulnerable and fragile because of his severe automobile crash injuries, yet, she never did that. She could not plan to do that; she could not plan to hurt him, even in the worst of times."

"Do you have an opinion, doctor, as to whether or not Jean was afraid of her husband?"

"Yes, she was."

"How, if at all, would she control him, if you have an opinion?"

"She tried to talk to him. That is one way she tried to control him. She would on occasion talk back to him, encouraging him to leave the home until he felt less angry. She tried to either leave the room or leave the house when she could, simply to get away from him, feeling that he would eventually calm down and sober up."

"Doctor, do you have an opinion as to whether or not she is a violent person?"

"No, she is not."

"Doctor, do you have an opinion as to whether or not Mrs. Davis is the kind of person that would have planned to murder?"

"No, she is not."

"Hypothetically, Doctor, if Mrs. Davis had indeed pulled the trigger, could she have intended to kill?"

"I doubt very much that at the time she would have pulled the trigger that she had the intent to kill. I think that she had intent, but it was a very different intent."

"And, Doctor, what would that intent be, in your opinion, based on your study of Mrs. Davis?"

"In my opinion, her intent was to stop him from potentially killing her. Her initial intent would have been to save herself by escaping. When he came off the bed, she thought that she would have a chance to escape, but he got up quickly and was threatening to take the gun from her and kill her, her brother, and their son. There was no time to turn and run. He was a mad bull charging her, as she held the rifle at her hip. Her brother and her son had abandoned her at the bedroom door, holding a gun that she did not even know if it was loaded. Any opportunity that she had to escape instantly faded into the past, as he was within two feet from her."

"Thank you, doctor. The prosecution may cross-examine this witness," David stated.

David breathed a sigh of relief at the conclusion of Dr. Bergman's direct testimony, having not personally met him prior to his coming to court. His direct testimony was very credible, and David doubted that Will would be able to discredit either his credentials or his findings and opinions. David knew, after looking at Jean, that she probably felt that she had a new lease on life after hearing that Dr. Bergman understood what she had lived through for so many years.

"Doctor, you testified that you examined Mrs. Davis in your office. Tell me, doctor, did Attorney Chartier accompany her to your office?" asked Will Brenner.

"No, he was not there. She had a friend with her who had driven her from the Upper Peninsula."

"Now, this study of yours took three to four hours. All of these opinions you have given are based on that study?"

"Yes."

"What does your study consist of?"

"I spent approximately three hours interviewing her, performed and/or administered several psychological tests, and spent a good deal of time reviewing police reports, as well as tape recordings of interviews between Mr. Chartier and the defendant."

"And she told you everything that you are telling us today?"

"Yes."

"What tests did you perform?"

"A Minnesota Multiphasic Personality Inventory."

"What does that test determine?"

"That test gives us various scales which, eventually when a psychologist integrates the results, gives us a certain kind of personality profile or a profile of an individual psychological state."

"What other test did you conduct?"

"A test called the Rorschach Ink Blot Test, which is the test we call a projective test."

"Okay, what does that test tell us about a person's personality?"

"By the manner in which a person responds to various ink blots, the way they integrate with what they see and what their associations are to the ink blots, it tells us a good deal about their personality structure."

"What other tests did you conduct?"

"The sentence completion test, where she was given the beginning of sentences which would have certain kinds of meanings to her and she has to fill in the rest of the sentence."

"And how did she do on that test?"

"In none of these tests is it a matter of how she did, because we look at them all together. That test, particularly, was very interesting because at the time she took it, she was stressed. In fact, during much of the time she was taking the tests, she had to administer medication to herself, what were, I believe, nitroglycerin tablets."

"Now, all of these opinions where you say that she had no plan to murder her husband are based on your interview with her?"

"Yes."

"And that, where she had no intent to kill when she pulled the trigger—and she admitted pulling the trigger?"

"No, she didn't. I said *if* she had pulled the trigger. I relied most heavily in my evaluation of her on the extensive interview that I had with her. For a psychologist, that is still our very best tool."

"Is psychology, a precise science or an imprecise science?"

"Psychology is a very broad science, ranging from the study of the brain, a very precise science, and the study of the principles of behavior, also a precise science, to other areas of psychology and clinical psychology, which is in the middle of the spectrum."

"The clinician bases a lot of his opinions upon the facts he receives?"

"Yes, as well as a clinician's knowledge of principles of behavior, principles of personality development, psychopathology, and the whole underlying core or body of knowledge of the science of psychology. So, it becomes much more than simply an intuitive judgment."

"Doctor, one of your opinions was as to her state of mind, which you described as a deep fear, a profound fear, beyond terror. Was that based on what she told you?"

"Yes, together with the testing, reading of the police reports, and Mr. Chartier's taped interviews with her."

"That is all the questions that I have, doctor. Thank you," announced Will.

"No redirect," David announced to the court.

David felt that he might be trying this case beyond Christmas. After all, there seemed so much more testimony to bring to the jury. David had tried long trials before. Most of the long ones, however, were civil cases, malpractice cases, products liability cases, auto negligence cases with extensive medical issues. He had tried a products case against a major automobile manufacturer that lasted five weeks, a case against a major oil company that lasted four weeks, and a case against a major snowmobile manufacturer that lasted about a month.

During the next recess, David could see that the stress was getting to Jean. As she smoked her cigarette, her hands were shaking. David tried to engage her in light conversation, but she was not receptive to that. She wanted out of the stressful thoughts that seemed to be pounding in her brain. Again, it appeared to David that she was trying to think her way clear of the trial, a fruitless endeavor, powerless to control the judicial process. David thought of an old legal maxim which goes like this: "The wheels of justice grind slowly, but exceedingly small."

David repeated this maxim to Jean and told her that they were in this ordeal together and that they were here for the long haul. He told her that they had better get comfortable with the proceedings as the wheels grind, and at some point, the trial would be over and it was important not to lose hope.

"Mr. Chartier, call your next witness," commanded Judge Roode.

"Thank you, Your Honor. I now call Camellia Storm, PhD to the stand," David announced.

"Would you please state your full name?" asked David.

"Camellia S. Storm."

"You're a doctor?"

"Yes, I have a PhD in clinical psychology."

"Dr. Storm, where do you reside?"

"In Ypsilanti, Michigan."

"Are you employed?"

"Yes, I presently am in private practice in clinical psychology."

"What is involved in clinical psychology?"

"It is an area in which I engage in a number of activities, including psychotherapy, which is the treatment of people who have various kinds of emotional or behavioral problems. It includes research and testing of people who have emotional problems."

"Dr. Storm, where were you educated?"

"I went to school in Hudson, Michigan. I went to college at the University of Michigan in Ann Arbor, Michigan, graduate school at Columbia University in New York, and I did my doctoral internship at the University of California, at Berkley. I received my doctorate degree in 1970."

"Doctor, would you please outline for the jury your professional experience?"

"I was originally employed at the Midfield Mental Health Center, after completing my internship. I worked there for ten years. I was involved in testing, individual counseling of adults and children. I did consultations with a program for emotionally impaired children, court counseling, which involves written reports for the court in cases of family violence. Originally, I worked with police officers and prosecuting attorneys to develop programs to help families who were involved in violent relationships."

"Are you associated with anyone else in your current practice?"

"A social worker and I are in joint private practice."

"Doctor, have you received any awards or honors in conjunction with your studies or your work?"

"In the area of family violence, I was appointed by the legislature to a special joint legislative subcommittee on spouse abuse in 1975, a group of citizens from a variety of professions studying the problem of family violence in Michigan. We made some suggestions and recommendations about the kinds of laws that might be helpful in allowing us to effectively work with violent families.

"As a result of that work, one of the pieces of legislation that came out of this effort was setting up what is now called the State of Michigan Domestic Violence Prevention and Treatment Board. I was recently appointed by Governor Jacobs in 1980 and remain on that board today. During the last several years, I have worked extensively with prosecutors from around the state and have been awarded the Liberty Bell Award for outstanding contributions to the law, by a non-attorney as well as for the equal application of the law because of my work with both victims and assailants."

"What presentations, if any, involving family violence, have you been involved with, doctor?"

"I have been involved in doing workshops for approximately five years, travelling around the state, as well as throughout the country, giving people information and helping them understand family violence, specifically in the area of treating men who have been violent toward their spouses. I have spoken at many colleges and universities, as well as the National District Attorneys' Association meeting on Mackinaw Island."

"Have you written any papers, doctor?"

"I have written many papers on the subject of the spousal abuse syndrome. I wrote a paper on the profile of male assailants who batter women. It's presently in press and is going to be published in book form to join several other books that I have published on related topics."

"Have you testified in court before?"

"Yes, I have testified many times in Michigan as well as numerous times in California, Texas, Illinois, Indiana, New York, and Boston. In three cases, prosecutors, when providing information to juries in murder cases, brought me into court to talk to the jury regarding the spousal abuse syndrome. I have also testified for the defense, on numerous occasions, where both husbands and wives or girlfriends had killed their spouses."

"Doctor, what is your experience in dealing with violent relationships in a home setting?"

"I have seen, over the course of ten years, at least five hundred battered women in therapy at mental health centers as well as in my private practice. Each of those cases involved violence in the home. In addition, as I mentioned earlier, I have had the opportunity to work with police, prosecutors, and judges in instituting programs that have been very effective in helping to control the violence so that we can help people establish a healthy and positive relationship."

"I object, Your Honor," cried out Will Brenner. "I object to these questions of the witness, unless they are relevant to this case. I think that voir dire is to qualify this witness and then get on with testimony concerning this particular case."

"Well, the objection is overruled," ruled Judge Roode.

"Thank you, Your Honor," David responded.

"Again, doctor, why is it necessary to explain family violent relationships?"

"Most of us, when we look at any situation, bring our experiences and our own understanding of relationships to a situation. For example, we see something or hear about something that happens in a violent relationship, and we think that we might understand it because we know that we may have done a similar kind of thing, say a battered woman may leave a relationship, and then come back. We see that as an indication that she loves the man. While it is understandable that we interpret relationships in this way, in the area of violent relationships we are in a position where things do not mean the same thing as they do in relationships where violence does not exist. In fact, we may come to a great many wrong conclusions and inaccurate interpretations in trying to understand them that way.

"Unfortunately, many people believe that women provoke violent assaults on themselves, that they ask for it, that they need to be beaten. These kinds of beliefs and attitudes on the part, particularly of people who are asked for help, have often led to their refusing to help or failing to help in ways that are effective, because they do not understand."

"What we have in a violent relationship is a woman who doesn't understand what is happening to her, a man who cannot admit, even to himself, who he is and what he is doing in a society that doesn't understand either of them or their relationship. Virtually, nothing in violent relationships is what it appears to be. That is why we need to explain the meaning of them."

"Doctor, is there a difference between a battering relationship and one in which just some hitting might occur once or twice?"

"Your Honor, again, and I do not like to keep objecting, but again the relevancy that testimony and this case, I fail to see," the prosecutor once again yelled out.

"Well, the objection is overruled. She may answer the question," stated Judge Roode.

"Doctor, I'll ask the question again. Is there a difference between a battering relationship and one in which just some hitting might occur once or twice?"

"Yes, there is. Almost anyone is capable on an individual occasion of becoming so pressured that they lash out, and I think it is critically important that you understand that there is a difference between a man who develops a long-term pattern of very severe abuse as opposed to someone who hits. The differences are as follows:

- First of all, a man who lashes out on a single occasion or maybe on one or two occasions maintains a sense that he is responsible for that action. The man who batters, on the other hand, will see it as the other person's responsibility. He does not see himself as responsible.

- Another difference is that the man who may lash out on one occasion or another usually finds some way to control himself over a period. He knows that he is angry; he knows that he is upset before that hitting occurs. He may start to leave the situation prior to the time when any attack occurs.
- The man who develops a pattern of repeated violence, on the other hand, is someone who may not necessarily know that he is angry until the assault is well underway. He does not understand what his feelings are, where the situation is going, and therefore, he beats her. A man who is likely to lose control will often warn the woman and allow her to leave before there is any hitting. He may tell her that if she does not stop certain behavior, he is going to plaster her, but allows her to get out of the situation.
- The man who is violent, however, is strongly invested in keeping her there and, in fact, may become even more provoked if she tries to leave.
- One last thing is that the man who loses control on one or two occasions is one who keeps the same rules from one day to the next, whereas, a man who becomes a batterer is not predictable in what he will become enraged about. There is complete inconsistency in what upsets him because it has to do with, not what is going on outside himself, but what is happening *inside* himself."

"Doctor, is there a psychological profile of a man who becomes a batterer in a marriage?"

"Yes, there is. There are two patterns, and some of the characteristics are the same characteristics that have occurred in this particular case.

—One is the man who is never violent outside the home. He may be seen, in fact, as exceptionally nice, kind, thoughtful by all his neighbors, and people that he knows outside the home and still be very violent within the home.

- The other pattern is a man whose violence spills over in a number of areas. He may be in trouble for fighting in bars, he may have assaulted one of his neighbors, and he may be someone who has a drunk driving or whatever. However, those are two general patterns.

- But, within that, we see some specific kinds of characteristics among men who batter women. First, they are usually men who have a background of having been beaten themselves. In addition to that, they are someone who is terribly dependent on their wife. They highly value that relationship and that the wife is the only person with whom they feel comfortable. Because they are so dependent on her, they are invested in keeping her no matter what. If she attempts to leave, they will become very upset, potentially violent because they are so terrified of being by themselves. Another part of the syndrome or personality pattern of violent men is that they often go through serious periods of depression. When they think about themselves and what they are doing, they feel remorseful. They do not want to be destructive to their family, but does not know how to change the pattern, so they become even more depressed. They often view themselves as the victim, having been provoked, pushed into violent behavior, often trying to get some sympathy, trying to get some understanding."

"Counsel, it is three-thirty in the afternoon and I noticed a number of people yawning. We have had a long day and I think that we will call it a day and let the jury go home a little bit early today, and Mr. Chartier can continue his examination of this witness in the morning," stated Judge Roode. "Court is adjourned."

David thought to himself, that he had a long way to go, but was pleased that the judge adjourned early. He felt tired, but at the same time felt that Dr. Storm's testimony was being well received by the jury. Looking at the jury, over the past couple of days, gave David a feeling that many of them were following the testimony well and that they were learning much from Dr. Storm's testimony. The teacher on the jury, however, was giving David concern; he would not make eye contact with David and throughout the conduct of the defense witnesses' testimony, he seemed removed. David found himself hoping that he might be removed from the jury panel when the alternates are selected at the end of the trial and before the jury deliberates.

"Jean, how do you feel about Dr. Storm's testimony so far?" David inquired.

"Mr. Chartier, I am so surprised that she knows so much about John and me from my brief meeting with her in Ypsilanti. It is just like she can see right through us," Jean said.

"Jean, I am sorry that I am not spending more time with you, explaining how I foresee the case unfolding before the jury, but I really have to work on questions for the balance of the Dr. Storm's testimony," stated David.

David walked Jean out of the courthouse and said good-bye to her in the parking lot, reminding her to be on time for tomorrow's court proceedings. He then went to the office, placed his feet on his desk, closed his eyes, and slept for twenty minutes, awakening to the words of Sandy, saying that he ought to check some of his mail and return some of his calls, as clients were asking for him to give their cases some attention too. In long trials, it is common to find the trial lawyer exhausted by the middle of the case, feeling like he just wants to go home and sleep for a week. David thought back to his law school days, splash some cold water on your face and on the back of your neck and get to it. Gee, that sure brought back David's memories of his daily routine when he was working full time at an aerospace company in Ann Arbor and driving the Ford Expressway to law school in Detroit after work. David recalled returning home from law school at eleven o'clock at night and sleeping for twenty minutes after eating supper, getting up, splashing cold water on his face and on the back of his neck, and then studying until two o'clock in the morning, returning to bed, and getting up again at six thirty to go to work.

David was hoping and praying that the jury was not getting tired of hearing the testimony of Dr. Camellia Storm; she had so much to say about the spousal abuse syndrome that was relevant in this case, and her testimony had been a real education for David, as well as the judge and jury. He could not stop now; he had to finish taking her testimony and finish with a very strong connection with the defense of Jean.

"Mr. Chartier, you may continue with the testimony of Dr. Storm, if you wish," Judge Roode stated.

"Thank you, Your Honor," said David.

"You are still under oath, Dr. Storm," Judge Roode declared, as Dr. Storm was again taking the witness chair.

"Dr. Storm, as you might recall, you were giving testimony yesterday concerning the spousal abuse syndrome and relating that syndrome to this particular case," David began.

"Doctor, has your research found that alcohol plays any role in family violence and do you find that it did in the instant case?" David asked.

"Yes. Some people think that alcohol causes family violence, but what we know now is that people, who have a possibility of becoming violent, are more likely to become violent when they are drinking than when they are sober. It is a facilitator; it makes it more likely to happen, but it does not cause violence."

"Doctor, is there a psychological profile of the woman who becomes involved in a violent relationship?" David inquired.

"Not prior to the time when the violence begins. It used to be believed . . ."

"Objection, Your Honor. Again, I must object to this. We are talking about psychological profiles, and again I regret having to object, but we are dealing with this specific case and not generalities and not statistics and not research studies. And I would ask that this kind of testimony be not permitted by this witness," said Will, with a strained look on his face.

"Your Honor, in voir dire of the jury, I was permitted to ask each and every member of the jury as to whether or not they believe psychologists can give us some insight as to how a person might react in different relationships. Each one of the jurors answered that question in the affirmative. It's a subject that is a science, Your Honor, based on the science of psychology," David responded.

"I'll overrule the objection, and you may proceed, Mr. Chartier."

"Thank you, Your Honor."

"Dr. Storm, again—is there a psychological profile of a woman who becomes involved in a violent relationship?"

"Not prior to the time the violence begins. We used to believe that it would happen to certain types of women, women who had certain types of problems. What we now understand is that it can happen to virtually any woman. What we do also know is that there are certain characteristics that develop in the battered woman because of the violent victimization. She is someone who is likely to have a very low self-esteem because of being beaten. She is someone who is likely to develop a sense of tremendous dependency on the man who batters her because of the damage that is done to her personality functioning as a result of being beaten.

"She may feel terribly, terribly guilty and ashamed about what is happening to her. Sometimes, women for years do not tell anyone else what is happening to them because they feel guilty and responsible," Dr. Storm stated.

"Thank you. Are you able to describe a battering relationship, doctor?" David inquired.

"Yes. There is a kind of cycle that occurs in battering relationships, and it has four parts to it. The first part is what we call the tension-building phase. During that time, there may not be any attack going on, but the level of tension in the house and in the relationship is steadily building. That is the first phase. During that time, often both people continue to believe that the problem somehow has been settled or solved and wouldn't happen again.

"The second part of the battering relationship is what we call the acute battering incident that is the actual assault. The assault may last anywhere from two to twenty-four hours in a given situation, and it is very difficult to intervene at that time or to help in any way, except by the use of something such as a police officer coming in and taking charge of the situation. After the incident, there is a period of time when the couple is most amenable to help from the outside. Those are the times when the police have been called or they have consulted a mental health clinic or a psychologist. In addition, for that period, if we can work on things that are contributing to the problem, in other words, we work specifically on the sense that he is responsible for his behavior, rather than her being responsible for it. If we can work at that time, sometimes we are able to change the whole course of what is going to happen in the future. That is a phase that I call a reintegration phase, right after the assault.

"Following that is the period that some people call the warm, loving period. I have been inclined to call it the calm euphoric period, and that is mainly characterized by a sense of the two people agreeing that somehow they have resolved it, it's all been settled, everything is going to be all right. They do not want anyone involved from the outside. At that point in time, the woman might, either because she believes everything is settled or because she is being pressured or threatened by the man, she might want to withdraw any charges that have been made to the police or with the prosecutor.

"After the calm or euphoric phase, it circles back again to the tension-building phase, another acute battering incident, another reintegration phase, and another calm phase. Now, initially, that whole cycle may occur over a period of one or two years. The cycle will start happening closer and closer together. In very severe situations, we may see it happening within a twenty-four hour period. Also over a period of years, the assaults are likely to build in the intensity that we see in the present case."

"Thank you, doctor. Doctor, an outsider's response to a violent relationship is often asking the question, 'Why doesn't she just leave the relationship'?"

"In some of the early phases of her relationship, for example, if the violence has not moved above the level of strong verbal or lower continuum of physical violence, the woman may not leave because she may not have an income, she may have no way to support her children. She may have no other place that she can go and live. It may be very difficult for her to leave on those bases, and that is something that may keep her there at that point in time.

"In addition, she may have some religious beliefs against divorce or against breaking up the family and maintain the sense that somehow they will be able to solve the problem. As the assaults get worse, other kinds of things start to play into her difficulty in leaving that situation.

"First of all, because of what had been done to her, she is likely to have a very difficult time adjusting to being single and being out on her own. One of the most critical things that we see is that there is serious damage to the person's ability to be independent. The ability to be out on her own is damaged because of the violence to which she has been subjected. The man may react by being exceptionally kind, caring, almost courting her for a period of time, motivated by his desire to get control of her again, to get her to come back.

"The fact that the man is asking nicely for her to come back does not mean that she can say no and still be safe. Beyond that, there are also serious incidents of violence that will likely occur if she tries to leave. She may not be able to hide. We have had many reported occurrences of the man continuing to pursue, continuing to harass, and continuing to assault women for months and even years after the completion of the divorce. He may become more violent if he realizes that she is really going to separate from him. Many of the killings that occur of women and of families have occurred after a separation. It may be a few weeks, months, or even years after the separation. When people ask why she has not left the relationship, they usually fail to understand that leaving is enormously difficult because of the potential effects to follow, as in this present case."

"Thank you, doctor. Doctor, do women generally provoke the beatings?" David inquired.

"No, but again, it may look like that. What we need to understand about provocation is what effect it has on the person who is potentially assaultive, not because of what we might, apart from that situation, think of as a provocative act. Because the assaultive man needs the interaction; because he needs to have the kind of conflict going on in order to avoid feeling bad within himself, he will provoke an incident, and if the woman tries to just be quiet or simply leave, that is likely to result in his being angry or even increasing the likelihood of his assaulting her. He needs her to be there. On the other hand, an aggressive reaction from her might sometimes stop his assault.

"We have numerous accounts of women who begged, pleaded, did everything that they could to talk the man down, to get him to stop being angry, to somehow intervene in the conflict, and over the years, it never worked. I have a description from a woman who describes herself as having done that and finally he had her cornered after years of this. She turned around, looked at him, and said that if he took one step closer . . ."

"Your Honor, I'm going to object to that as being hearsay, and I again have to make the statement that it is irrelevant to the issue at hand."

"The objection is overruled. This is illustrative of a claimed principle," ruled Judge Roode.

Dr. Storm continued, "She turned on him and told him that if he took one step closer, she was going to kill him. She was about one-third his size, she had no weapon, she had no way of following through on her threat and after an eight-year history of the assaultive pattern and those cycles, it was the first time that he had ever stopped an assault.

"What happens in this kind of situation is that once it works, it is likely to happen again in the next situation; its effectiveness will begin to wear off over a period of time, and she develops a pattern of being very nasty or aggressive toward him, causing an outsider to think that she is just as bad as him and in fact she is provoking him. If you are in a position where you are potentially a victim of someone who can physically overpower you, the only possibility that you have for protecting yourself, unless you have a weapon, is what you say verbally and how you respond to that person verbally."

"Doctor, can women prevent beatings by just being good or doing what they are told?" inquired David.

"No. The critical feature of the battering relationship again is that the man, because of his own background of victimization, is someone who gets out of control and violent. She may have some things, some maneuvers that she can use periodically to either delay the situation or to keep the situation within some bounds, but once he reaches that trigger point, there is nothing she can do to stop it."

"Doctor, what would be the similarities, if any, that might be found between battered women and other victims of terror, and are those similarities, if any, apparent in this case?" asked David.

"There are numerous of these characteristics, and I am not going to go through all of them, but I would like for you to be aware of and to understand some of them, because I think it is important for you to know what you might expect from a victim of violence is not really true. First, victims of violence often feel guilty and ashamed of what has happened to them. They feel somehow responsible, that they should have somehow prevented it. This was even true of people who were victimized in concentration camps, because it was a way for them to have some sense that it was somehow under their control, even by the fact that they didn't do something they should have done, and that was somehow psychologically more comforting to them.

"Another characteristic is that there is very little emotion related to very severe beatings. What happened in concentration camps and in other brainwashing situations is that people who were severely and brutally beaten did not even have retaliatory dreams to the most severe assaults. One of the most astounding characteristics of people who were part of the liberating forces is that the people describe the most horrible and inhuman brutality in a very flat tone. They were not emotionally distressed or upset about it.

"The same kind of characteristic happens with severely battered women. A battered woman may describe a severely violent incident to you, and it may sound like the kind of tone that she would use if she were listing her groceries. There is not the kind of emotion attached to it that we are often led to believe would be attached to it from watching television. This is a critical characteristic because it is one of the things that has resulted from so many people listening to her and maybe not believing her or suggesting or thinking that somehow the beatings or the assault must not be important to her, because if it was, she would look and act really upset.

"It is simply not true. We do not develop emotional reactions to the most violent beatings. In connection with that and at the same time, people may react emotionally to things that seem terribly insignificant by comparison. Many of the people that were in concentration camps will describe comments by the guards that were insulting and be very indignant about them, and at the same time have this characteristic of being very flat emotionally in talking about severe brutality and beatings.

"Battered women also can show this kind of behavior. They may seem terribly offended about something that seems by comparison very insignificant to us. Mental health professionals recognize this as hysteria. It is a product of a certain form of violent victimization that often leads one to feel that the emotional or psychological abuse in those situations was somehow worse than the physical abuse.

"I think the most unusual characteristic about this is the difference between what we would expect people to feel about their captors and what is actually the case, in terms of the feelings of the victims. Most of us would expect a great deal of rage, a great deal of anger toward the person, if not even hatred. This is not true.

"In another setting, what we call the Stockholm syndrome, when people are victims of hostage taking, or kidnapping, in some way, within about seventy-two hours, they develop very positive feelings toward the hostage taker to such an extent that they will actually defeat the efforts of police who attempt to rescue them.

"When we see those kinds of feelings among victims of family violence, what we are likely to believe is that she loves him and that is why she stays, rather than understanding that people can have those kinds of positive feelings toward those who are very brutal toward them."

During the morning break, David left the courtroom with Jean and headed toward the outside door on the first floor of the annex, so she could have a cigarette. David knew that the testimony of Dr. Camellia Storm would be lengthy but was so pleased that to this point, Judge Roode had been allowing the testimony over the periodic objections of Will Brenner. David believed that Judge Roode was finding her testimony interesting and relevant and was going to continue to give her a lot of leeway, so long as she kept relating her testimony to the present case.

"Doctor, when is a battered woman likely to seek help or go to the authorities?" inquired David.

"The typical time for her to do that is immediately after an assault or sometimes during an assault. She will reach out perhaps to any number of people, neighbors, family, the local community health clinic or psychologist, or she may contact the police or potentially the prosecutor, as the defendant did in this case."

"Doctor, is the legal system helpful in these relationships?" inquired David.

"In some areas, now it is very helpful. What we have done over a period of years is that we worked very hard to help people in those positions to understand the nature of these relationships so that they can help effectively. I am not saying that people in positions to help do not want to help, but that they do not know how to help. They do not know how to understand the relationship and, therefore, do not understand the critical importance of certain kinds of actions, particularly from the legal system."

"Doctor, what happens when she does not get help?"

"If she goes and tries to get help, as a last resort, and the help is not there, she feels guilty, more ashamed, more alone, and more isolated. The effects on the man, however, will depend on who has been called. If the police have been called, oftentimes he initially starts out being frightened that the police are going to arrest him. However, with numerous contacts with the police in which he has not been arrested, he has not received any kind of consequences or statement that his behavior is unacceptable, as in the present case, he may develop a sense of satisfaction about the contacts with the police. He may feel that he is able to frighten them or he is able to outsmart them. That may be part of the incentive, so the fear goes away for him of having the police called in. And, also, he may develop a sense that that the police are his buddies, and he may begin to use their contacts and their lack of responses as part of his verbal abuse of her in that relationship. In other words, the police are on my side too and they are not going to help you, as the decedent is purported to have said to this defendant."

"Doctor, what is the man's perception of the woman's ability to harm him?"

"Eventually, if she has been using retaliatory threats, but with no means to carry out those threats, she is bluffing and it becomes apparent to the man that she is bluffing. The first time she says something like that, he backs off, and he is surprised; he is shocked. It may stop an attack, but when she does it a second or third time, the effect has worn off. So, she does not have the intention of carrying out her threats; she knows it and now he knows it too."

"Doctor, when there has been a long history of severe violence in a relationship, an incident which may appear to an outside observer to be just one more attack and it turns out to be a homicide, what should the woman have seen, as danger signals, if any?"

"Situations that will seem to her as life-threatening will be based on her past history. If there is a separation or a discussion of separation between them, that will increase her sense of danger. It is a very threatening situation for her. In addition, there are certain kinds of things that may be characteristic of him when he is especially violent. In other words, he may assault her in ways that an outsider who had never been there would be very distressed about, but it may not mean a life threat to her because certain aspects of that assault are not characteristic of the most out-of-control situations that she has experienced in the past.

"Characteristics which may be seemingly insignificant to those on the outside, a look in his eye, an expression on his face, a certain thought pattern that he goes through in that situation, those things become associated with life threats that will increase her sense and her perception that she is in serious danger at that point in time. Jean saw that in the way her husband looked at her when threatening to kill her and her son as he came up from the bed grasping for the rifle. Additionally, a situation might become a homicide out of chance factors. Something that has been ordinarily available to her, such as a telephone, suddenly is dead. If something happens that is very new, until she knows the meaning of that or the effect of that for her, she will see that as more threatening.

"In addition, sometimes there are resources or people who might be available to her, if she has gone through an assault in the past, someone has in some way rescued her, and that same quality of assault is happening again, but that other person is not available to her at that time. She will be in a position of greater threat because she believes she would not have been able to control the last one without help. You may understand her behavior as an effort on her part to stay as safe as she possibly can in a situation where total safety is not possible."

"Doctor, you have told us with regard to the woman's perception of her ability to harm her husband that she really does not believe that she would be able to kill him, and that she believes that she would die if she tried. What is the man's perception of her ability to harm him?" asked David.

"Initially, when some of the first attacks are made, he will back off; he will feel threatened or be concerned about that. As time goes on, he takes her threats as less of concern to him and he gets to the point of believing that she is psychologically and emotionally incapable of harming him, and he ends up in a position where he will do something, such as hand her a loaded gun and taunt her into using it. He believes that she is incapable of that, and following that thought, he will not react to it in a way that puts him back in control. He may be overtly contemptuous of her ability to do anything to harm him.

"If the woman is consistently being assaulted for doing something that the man does not like, she will begin feeling very uncomfortable, anxious, or fearful or will experience *terror*, even if she thinks of doing what the man does not like, even though the person is nowhere around. Thus, she will start to do certain kinds of things and behave in certain ways because she wants to avoid that very painful feeling inside herself that is the result of a long-term history of being assaulted. Once a life-threatening assault has occurred to a woman, and a verbal threat is later made to her, that becomes much more threatening than it would be if that person had never hit anyone, and if she felt that she could be killed by the man when he says he will kill her, it results in *terror*, because of that past history. Even if there is a period of time when things are rather settled, the *living terror* does not go away. All of the man's behavior becomes meaningful to her and she becomes aware of when that person is a life threat to her.

"She is staying in that relationship out of the instinct to survive. She might have been told that if she leaves, he will kill her. Other people trying to help her get out of the relationship sometimes are also in danger, whether they be friends, family, therapists, psychologists, lawyers, and even police officers.

"To give you a further analogy, animals have a way to establish dominance and submission relationships in nature. Among animals, we have a pattern in which there are fights, there are battles to establish who is the dominate animal. In the context of those fights, the animal that is losing can make a submission response. It is an instinctual response to save the animal's life so it can establish which animal is dominant and which is submissive without running the risk of an animal having to die. Therefore, there is an instinctual response to submit in the context of severe threat and that battle.

"A battered woman's behavior is that she is trying to submit to that environment. She is trying to adapt to it in some way so that she might stay safe. Now, with animals, there is an equally strong counter-instinct where the animal that is winning the fight, once that submission response is emitted, cannot complete the kill, that animal backs off. With the battering relationship, however, is that the counter-instinct does not exist because of his history of victimization, and what has happened to him, perhaps in childhood. She may be trying to submit in the situation, but she is not in a position to do so or to stop the assault because his counter response does not work in that situation.

"What happens when a violent relationship reaches the point of life threat is that there is a kind of survival bond set up between the two people by the man's violence. She is in a position where she cannot safely stay because the violence will continue, but she cannot leave because the violence will get worse and she believes he will kill her. And, indeed, that may happen. Thus, she is locked into that relationship by his violence. She is unable to leave because of the terror that is induced in her. The man, however, believes that he will die if she leaves. However, if she leaves, he becomes terribly depressed and becomes suicidal. If he cannot push all his anger outward toward her, it all comes down on himself, and his own sense of self-hatred, results in his becoming suicidal-depressed. In his troubled mind, he sees her as killing him. He might well decide to kill her if she leaves, and in his thinking, it is self-defense because she does not care about him, she has left him, and therefore she is killing him. He kills her, and usually afterwards, kills himself. In my opinion, this is the exact point at which Jean and John Davis were on the evening of September 22, 1984."

"Doctor, what are terror-induced responses?" asked David.

"Terror-induced submission responses do not reflect the woman's personality; they reflect her situation. These are not terribly variable among women who have been victimized at this level. There is a sense of loving the batterer. In other words, you will be in a situation probably of hearing horrible brutality, life-threatening conduct, and you will hear from the wife that she still loves him. That is characteristic of terror-induced submission response. It is part of the pattern. It does not mean that she liked the beating, but it is characteristic of a violent relationship.

"The man holds the power of life and death over her. This tends to be much stronger in situations where she feels very isolated. If she is not in a position where she feels that she can get some help, he may say that he has an in with the police, and she may well believe that. In the present case, John Davis is reported to have told her that he could do anything to Jean Davis and the police would not do anything to him.

"Another example of terror-induced submission is that the battered woman focuses her life on the batterer in the sense that he is the center of her existence because she is trying to avoid being killed. The more she does for him, the more she is likely to be victimized by him. If she says that she will solve a problem, but fails, he is likely to be angrier with her and becomes the focus of his resentment because she made the effort, but failed. She may not even allow herself to think of leaving, putting it out of her mind, for fear of being killed, which is especially baffling to people who, when looking at a violent relationship, consider leaving as the most obvious solution. The reason she cannot think about it is then she would recognize the horror of how entrapped she was, and human beings cannot live with life threat on a twenty-four-hour-a-day basis, so she covers the terror over by attributing it to other factors.

"If she is involved in a situation where she cannot leave and cannot stay, to keep from becoming depressed to the point of suicide, she will continue to hope that someone, some way, from somewhere, will come along to help her. The reason for that hope does not have anything to do with his behavior, but the need for all humans to hope. She has to hope; otherwise, if she gives that up, she will be in a position where she has no way out; there is no exit. There is no possibility for her, so she will continue to hope, no matter what.

"She will have an uncanny or almost supernatural awareness of the batterer. She will recognize a certain sense coming over him, a certain expression on his face, a look in his eyes she recognizes that her life is going to be threatened again and that she is in for a beating. Over the years, if she has been beaten while he has had a certain look on his face, it becomes etched in her psyche. She begins to develop a feeling that she can read his mind. Her life depends on her ability to predict somehow, some way, that the person is going to be critically threatening to her, if she is going to have any possibility whatsoever of reacting or trying to escape.

"Uncanny awareness of feelings, actions, or gestures they see as threatening, others would think of as silly. Believe it. Their lives depend on knowing those kinds of things about that particular individual because of the history of life-threatening assaults.

"Battered women are inhibited against killing the batterer. It is the fear that he would not die and that somehow he would survive long enough to kill them, before he died. This is a very powerful inhibition to begin a counterattack. The woman is convinced in her mind that she will die.

"For the battered woman to kill her batterer, she must be in a situation where she is in some way trapped. She must be in a state of mind where she sees a counterattack as the only possible way for her to survive. The only thing that will overcome her inhibition to kill is if she believes that she is going to die, and that she is trapped, and in her state of mind, it is the only possible way to survive. Where she has previously sought help from the police or the prosecutor and has received no help that leads her to understand that no help will be coming and that she is trapped.

"In addition, it may be a matter of whether she would have time to call the police, but if the police have not been helpful in the past, that course will seem fruitless to her. She may be entrapped, cornered in a bedroom, or finding that he is about to instantly overpower her. At that point, it is a reflex, and the defensive attack occurs. It may be a single response like a knife slash, a gunshot, or it may be a pattern of responses, that once started, she has no way to stop.

"In my opinion, after studying all of the police reports and studying testing and interviewing Mrs. Davis, we have in her, someone who knows more than any potential homicide victim about the potential killer. She had to; her life depended on it. We have someone who has a more powerful inhibition against responding to that assault than any other homicide victim. We have a person who believes that she will die if she tries to kill that person, that somehow he will kill her before he dies. When this kind of response happens, we are dealing with the purest form of self-defense killing that exists in human behavior; it is based entirely on instinct."

"Thank you, doctor," David stated.

"Doctor, have you read the letter written to Jean Davis by the prosecutor of Pictured Rocks County, dated March 24, 1984?" David asked.

"Yes, Mr. Chartier, I have read it," responded Dr. Storm.

"What did that letter tell Mrs. Davis?" inquired David.

"The letter basically says that Mr. Brenner feels that he is unable to prosecute on a complaint that was filed by Jean Davis, regarding an assault on her by her husband John Davis."

"Did it refer to an assault on March 10, 1984?"

"Yes, it does."

"Doctor, based on your experience with battered women and violent relationships, would you have an opinion as to the psychological effects that such a letter would have on a battered woman?"

"In the context of being severely threatened, this letter would tell her that the legal system was not going to help her. She would feel more alone and more abandoned."

"Doctor, assuming that the battered woman has a severe heart condition and that her doctors have told her that further stress is likely to cause a fatal heart attack, would you have an opinion as to the psychological effects of her knowing of that condition?"

"Yes, I would."

"Doctor, what would that opinion be?"

"Such information would greatly increase her sense of life threat in the relationship."

"Doctor, would you also assume that the batterer has threatened to commit suicide, do you have an opinion as to the psychological effect on the battered wife of such suicide threats by the batterer?"

"Yes, I do."

"Doctor, what is that opinion?"

"When a batterer threatens suicide, it takes away one of her kinds of support, in her own thinking. She believes that he would have a great deal to lose by doing that. When he begins threatening suicide, it is very frightening and greatly increases her sense of threat because there is a sense that he has nothing to lose and he is more likely to go ahead and kill her."

"Thank you, doctor," David stated.

"Mr. Brenner, you may cross-examine," David stated.

"Thank you," Will replied.

"Doctor, were you at the Davis residence on September 22, 1984?" asked Will.

"No, sir," replied Dr. Storm.

"And, doctor, are you married?"

"Yes, sir."

"Doctor, have you personally experienced any spouse abuse in your marital relationship?"

"No, I haven't."

"In your upbringing?"

"No, I have not."

"Your knowledge of spouse abuse is based on your educational background?"

"That is partly true. I would also say my experience."

"What experience is that?"

"The experience that I have in terms of extensive clinical interviewing and the research experience that I have in dealing with the legal system and attempting to help people who are involved in violent relationships."

"What types of input do you receive, except questioning or the interview with the battered spouse?"

"Well, if it is at all possible, I would interview the violent man. I would gather information from any other source where possible. I would gather information from police officers who may have been called to the scene. I would gather information from the prosecuting attorney. I would read the police reports and any statements made by the battered woman. I would review medical reports in order to assess and research the medical effects of some of the beatings, if medical help was sought or received."

"Doctor, have you ever conducted studies of abuse committed by women upon men?"

"I have had some experience with that; there has been a total of three male clients that I have seen over the course of the last eight years in which a woman was the aggressor in the situation and the man was the victim."

"But, is it fair to say that the predominance of your expertise deals with the wife being the abused party?"

"That is true."

"Is clinical psychology a precise science?"

"Clinical psychology is a science that deals in a number of areas; we do not have the kind of measurement techniques, such as a thermometer so that you can tell with absolute precision what the temperature is in a room. Psychology deals with averages, looks at patterns, and depicts those kinds of patterns."

"What you're saying is that clinical psychology is not as precise as biochemistry?"

"Yes."

"But, it is probably a little more precise than say anthropology?"

"I am not sure that I can answer that. I'm sorry."

"That is all the questions that I have."

"Any redirect, Mr. Chartier?" inquired Judge Roode.

"Yes, thank you, Your Honor," David stated.

"Dr. Storm, did you have an occasion to review the voluminous police reports involved in this case?" asked David.

"Yes I did," replied Dr. Storm.

"Thank you, I have no further questions," David said.

David talked with Jean and she said that she had really appreciated the testimony of Dr. Camellia Storm. We were somewhat surprised at the complete lack of effective cross-examination by the prosecutor. Her testimony was so solid, and Will Brenner did not possess the knowledge of clinical psychology that might have placed him in a better position to challenge Dr. Storm's opinions. He was asking questions, just to be asking questions, as if he felt that the jury had found Dr. Storm too credible and he was merely trying to divert the jury's attention away from her answers to the direct examination.

Following the lunch break, David went directly to Judge Roode's chambers. Will Brenner and the judge were already there and the court reporter was in the process of setting up her recording equipment.

"Well, Mr. Brenner, Mr. Chartier has told me that the defense is going to rest at this time. The prosecuting attorney stated that he has a number of rebuttal witnesses. Mr. Chartier wants to place an objection on the record concerning prosecution witness's testimony regarding new ballistics retesting that Mr. Brenner plans to introduce in rebuttal. So go ahead, Mr. Chartier," stated Judge Roode.

"Thank you, Your Honor. This morning, I have furnished the court and the prosecuting attorney with a memorandum of law on the subject of rebuttal. That memorandum is offered in support of my motion objecting to the prosecution's introduction of new ballistics tests that he and the state police had performed over the past weekend, which he now intends to introduce in rebuttal," said David.

"I object on the basis that it constitutes new evidence that should have been introduced in his case in chief, and there is no good cause shown for its introduction now and reasons why the same was not introduced at the time of the prosecution's case in chief. The cases cited in the memorandum indicate that such introduction of new evidence concerning the angle and trajectory of the bullet path might be admitted within the sound discretion of the trial judge, only where good cause is shown for doing so. The prosecution had the ability and could have introduced such evidence in his case in chief, but failed to do so.

"I think that it is unduly prejudicial to the defense, coming at this stage of the proceeding. My expert witness has returned to California, and we went through considerable expense to obtain him and bring him to this courtroom to testify. New testing of the rifle and the production of new ballistics evidence requires that I have an opportunity for surrebuttal should it be admitted. I would further ask that the court adjourn the trial for a period of two weeks to provide me an opportunity to consult with my ballistics expert to confirm or perform additional testing, so that I can deal with the new tests performed by the State Police that are now being offered in rebuttable testimony.

"Therefore, first I object to it being received. It is untimely and not justified, as no just cause has been shown as to why it was not introduced in the prosecutor's case in chief, thus it is unduly prejudicial. Secondly, should the court rule against me in this matter, I ask for an adjournment giving me time to again secure further testimony from my ballistics expert regarding the results of the retesting of the ballistics by the prosecution," said David, summarizing his objection.

"Well, so the record is clear, it's my understanding that tests were made at the crime lab over the weekend," stated Judge Roode.

"That is correct, Your Honor," Mr. Brenner concluded.

"For what purpose, Mr. Brenner?" inquired the judge.

"To determine the angle from which the bullet was fired from the gun, to the body of John Davis. Your Honor, it was raised by an issue brought forth by the defense through the testimony of Professor Paul Cachette, who gave his opinion that the gun was fired at an upward angle," Will responded, with a familiar smirk in his expression.

"Your Honor, I might say that the record will show that Dr. Cachette's testimony was prepared from the prior evidence of the State Police. They had performed an angle test but did not seem fit to testify with regard to its significance. They have now gone out and performed new tests. This is clearly an area wherein the people had the ability and should have introduced their angle testing in their case in chief. To now go and perform new tests and to place in evidence proofs that they believe that will support their position is new evidence that should have been introduced in the prosecution's case in chief. There is no good cause shown as to why they have not done so," David argued, feeling quite nervous about the prospects of new ballistics testing.

"I would like to ask the question, Mr. Brenner, as to whether the prosecution was aware that angle trajectory evidence was to be presented, prior to the testimony of Professor Cachette?" inquired Judge Roode.

"No, Your Honor," exclaimed Will.

"Well, I think that it is unfortunate if the prosecution did not see that angle was an important consideration. Certainly, the angle of the trajectory and the distance at which the shot was fired is relevant and material. The prosecution just did not see fit to consider that matter and because the defense did, the defense was being prejudiced," David argued.

"I am going to allow the evidence of the test, and I do not believe that the evidence should be suppressed on the basis that it should have been introduced in the prosecution's case in chief. This has to do with a point having been raised by the defense."

"One of the cases which defendant cited in his memorandum is that of *People v. Lusev*. There is at page 342 of that opinion a footnote 3, wherein the Supreme Court recognizes that there may be occasional cases in which evidence that might have been admissible in the prosecution's case in chief could be admitted. The defense having raised the issue in her case, and it seems to me that this is fairly well within the principle of that footnote. In reference to the defendant's motion for continuance, I will not rule on that at this time, but will entertain the motion again if the defense wishes to reassert it following the conclusion of all the testimony," ruled Judge Roode.

After the court and counsel reentered the courtroom, Judge Roode stated, "Mr. Chartier, do you have anything further?"

"Thank you, Your Honor. The defense rests," David announced.

David turned to Jean and tried his best to assure her that he would do his best to cross-examine the prosecution's ballistics expert and try to show that their testing was not accurate as to distance or trajectory.

Chapter 14

Rebuttal Witnesses

"Mr. Brenner, do you have any rebuttal witnesses?" inquired the judge.

"Yes, Your Honor, I do. I would like to call back to the stand State Police Crime Laboratory Specialist Roger Benny," declared Will.

"You are still under oath," Judge Roode reminded the witness.

"Officer Benny, over this past weekend, did you have an occasion to perform further ballistics testing in this case?"

"Yes, I did."

"What were the results of your further testing?"

"Well, as a result of my further testing, I now have determined that the distance between the muzzle of the rifle and the shirt worn by the victim was greater than twelve inches, but less than eighteen inches, and as to the trajectory, we do not know whether it was up or down," stated officer Benny.

"I have no further questions, Your Honor," stated Will.

"Mr. Chartier, do you wish to cross-examine this witness?" Judge Roode directed his attention in David's direction and he had a slight grin on his face—*leaving David to read the judge's expression to convey the thought that—Mr. Chartier, you would be a fool to cross-examine this witness as he has just said what you have been trying to establish all along, regarding distance and trajectory.*

"No questions, Your Honor," David replied.

The judge smiled and said, "The proofs are closed, we will have the prosecution's closing arguments to the jury tomorrow morning,"

David asked Jean to come with him to have lunch in one of the local restaurants. The trial was almost over, but this was the time for a trial lawyer to do what he or she is meant to do best, that is, advocacy. Throughout the trial, the lawyer is like a director of a stage play, arranging and scheduling the witnesses and the exhibits to portray a real-life drama, not to create one that did not exist, but a true drama, with life, death, and liberty in the balance. David felt that both he and Will had put forth the best of our individual dramas, although David believed that his cause was nobler, in the last analysis.

The closing argument was the time that the trial lawyer pulls all the testimony and exhibits together with that "golden string" that aids the jury to see the entire picture as a collective mind from which it will deliberate its verdict. The effective defense trial lawyer will again remind the jury of the promises made by the lawyer in his opening statement when he outlined the evidence he was promising to prove, directing their attention to the fulfillment of those promises during the course of taking of the direct testimony and cross-examination of witnesses. He will also direct the jury's attention to the promises that the prosecution had promised to prove and how, in the last analysis, he failed to do so. The jury needs to remember the burden of proof beyond a reasonable doubt, the presumption of innocence, and deliberating only on evidence properly admitted in the trial.

Jean said that she was relieved that the testimonial phase of the trial was over but was still feeling anxiety because of the uncertainty of what was yet to come. David told her that he felt that the jury was attentive to the testimony of the witnesses and that he needed to know that she was confident in David's advocacy skills, before he began his final argument to the jury. Jean assured David that she did have confidence in him. They ate their soup and sandwiches and did not say much from that point until it was time to return to the courtroom.

Although David displayed an outer appearance of confidence, he knew that the jury was going to grapple with reaching a unanimous verdict. A verdict of acquittal could not be predicted at this point. How did they receive Dr. Storm's testimony of the battered woman? Did they believe Dr. Cachette regarding trajectory? Did they believe that it was John's blood at the threshold of the bedroom door? Would they believe Dr. Bergman's testimony, that at the instant the shot was fired, Jean was in dire fear for her life, beyond terror?

Chapter 15

Closing Argument for the Prosecution

"Mr. Brenner, you may commence your closing argument to the jury," stated Judge Roode.

"Thank you, Your Honor," Will responded.

"Good afternoon, ladies and gentlemen. May it please the court, Mr. Chartier, ladies and gentlemen of the jury, we have had a trying two weeks or more. We have gotten to know each other somewhat. One thing you probably and undoubtedly noticed about counsel, and probably the parties to the case, we haven't expressed too much familiarity with you as a jury, and I think you have been instructed, of course, not to address us in the same way. I do want to thank all of you very much for your patience. It has been appreciated by all of us. It has been a long ordeal, and I just want to thank you all very much. I think that when I say thank you, I express it on behalf of the court, Mr. Chartier, and the defendant as well.

"One of the purposes of closing argument, and let me point this out to you at the outset, closing argument is not evidence. It is argument by the attorneys. Mr. Chartier will have his opportunity, I am having mine now, to show you what we think is important in this case and to summarize for you what we consider important.

"Again, closing argument is argument. When both parties rested, well, Mr. Chartier rested yesterday; I rested about a week or so ago, at that point in time the evidence is through. The judge will instruct you probably later today.

"You have also heard during the course of this trial many objections. All of these objections have been decided and determined by Judge Roode, and that is one of his functions and purposes. He is the judge of the law. Counsel objected whenever they felt the evidence was improper, and then the decision, the final decision, rested with the judge. Again, objections are not evidence.

"We point out to you a couple of facts. There have been thirty witnesses, eighteen by the defense and twelve by the people. As to exhibits, I count a total of sixty-seven, thirty-nine for the people and twenty-eight for the defense.

"Again, one of the purposes of closing argument is to hopefully summarize and capsulate for you our respective positions. It is not my intent to rehash the entire case. That would take probably two or three days. I am going to touch upon what I consider the highlights of the important testimony that the people believe is relevant in this case.

"It is the claim of the people that there is evidence in this case beyond a reasonable doubt that: First, John Davis died on September 22, 1984, in Pictured Rocks County. Second, that his death was caused by an act of the defendant, Jean Davis, and that she shot John Davis with a .22-caliber rifle. That the .22-caliber rifle is in evidence marked as people's exhibit 2. Third, that the defendant Jean Davis intended to kill John Davis, that she intended to do unto him great bodily harm, or that she committed a willful and wanton act, the natural tendency of which was to cause death or great bodily injury. Fourth, that there was no justification or excuse for Jean Davis to kill her husband on September 22, 1984.

"The people submit in this case that there is clear evidence that John Davis did everything possible and within his powers to avoid confrontation in those early evening hours of September 22, 1984. First, he locked and secured the doors of the family residence. Next, he attempted to prevent entry into the dining room area. There, after being shoved back and away by Jean Davis, he gave a disgusted look at the people confronting him and he retreated into the bedroom and closed the door. Finally, the defendant, Jean Davis, pushed the door to the bedroom open and a fight started while he was in the bedroom on the bed.

"All of the evidence in this case indicates that John Davis remained on the bed until the time of the fatal shot. Did John Davis rant and rave at that time? No. Was he violent? No. Was he destructive? No. Did he run through the house looking for a victim to assault? No.

"What John Davis did do, however, was remain sitting on the bed, sitting there passively. He was not the aggressor in this case. I think that the evidence will show that Jean Davis was the aggressor."

As Will got started with his closing argument, he seemed to be gathering steam as he progressed with his argument, becoming almost believable, had there been no contradictory testimonial evidence, as to the facts. How could he argue in good faith that John remained on the bed until the shot was fired, when there was the upward trajectory of the bullet on its way to John's body, together with the evidence of blood at the threshold of the bedroom doorway?

"Let's start with the first witness—*as Will continued with his closing argument to the jury*—Brian Cassidy. He was the deskman on duty with the Pictured Rocks Sheriff Department, during the afternoon shift. He was on duty at approximately 7:06 pm. He received the first of two phone calls in connection with the shooting incident. The first one showed that there was a telephone call from the Davis residence. A boy said that they need an ambulance out there right away. He said that John had been shot in the throat. He said that Jean Davis had shot him.

At 7:10 p.m., the next call came in from the Davis residence and the person who was calling said that John Davis was bleeding bad and thought that he was going to die. Deputy Cassidy told him that the ambulance was on its way, and to put a compression bandage on him.

"The caller then turned the phone over to Jean Davis, and she told the deputy that John had hit her and that she got the gun and she shot him. Deputy Cassidy testified that he told her to stop the bleeding with a compression bandage and that she responded by saying that she was not going to do it.

"We next had State Trooper Dale Rose, the chief investigation officer, who has been sitting next to me at the prosecution table throughout this trial. He arrived at the scene at approximately 7:25 p.m. He entered into the Davis house and asked, 'Where is John?' Jean responded, 'He is in the bedroom.' In addition, she said to the trooper that she had shot him. She also told him that John had hit her and she shot him. The trooper said that Jean did not appear to be intoxicated.

"Trooper Rose assisted the ambulance crew. He observed John Davis's body in the position as is shown on some of the exhibits, lying on the side of the bed, with his head on the bed, and that he appeared lifeless. He took several photographs and these have been introduced as exhibits in this case.

"Trooper Rose departed the scene with Jean Davis in his custody and while in the patrol car gave her a Miranda warning and she agreed to talk to him.

"Trooper Rose testified that Jean Davis had told him that John had slugged her in the mouth and had tried stuffing ice down her throat. He had threatened to kill both she and her son, had gotten off the bed, and was going to kill her as he charged her.

"She said that she did not aim the gun, and only attempted to scare John. She said that she knew the gun was loaded only when she first saw blood come out of John's mouth.

"Deputy Tom Moore said in his testimony that he too was at the Davis home the night John Davis was shot. He said that the rifle was in plain sight in the kitchen, leaning up against the refrigerator. He said that he searched the floor of the bedroom and found a spent .22-caliber shell casing near the doorway, but did not see any blood on the floor near the doorway, as claimed by the defendant's private investigator. Deputy Moore also testified that there were a couple of dogs in the house, while he was there.

"Trooper Rose had made some sketches of the interior of the house, including the layout of the bedroom. They were small drawings but *I myself was also at the scene and I prepared the larger drawings that were incorporated into People's Exhibits 9 and 10.*"

Will had never disclosed to David that he had personally been at the scene and had made drawings of the scene that were incorporated, as exhibits in this trial.

Such conduct on the prosecution's part was highly improper and was in violation of the Code of Professional Conduct, which states that a lawyer cannot be involved in a trial, as the trial lawyer, where he may also appear as a witness. Had David known that Will had made those drawings, he certainly would have called him as an adverse witness, using leading questions to find the underlying facts of that issue.

David was hearing this for the first time during Will's closing argument. David debated in his mind whether to draw Judge Roode's attention to this matter and perhaps get Will sanctioned and/or a mistrial. Or, was it better to let the case proceed as it was unfolding, for fear that if Will was kicked off this case, a more astute prosecutor would be appointed by the court administrator's office, and the case might be more difficult to defend. David feared that Jean would not be able to endure another trial, and he felt that he had already successfully defended the open murder charge and that the jury might find her guilty of either voluntary or involuntary manslaughter. He felt that he had about the best jury that he could possibly expect to get in Pictured Rocks County. In addition, he planned to talk with Jean as soon as Will had concluded his closing argument.

"We heard from J.P. Wiseman, MD, the pathologist who testified that the .22-caliber bullet could have been deflected when hitting the second rib and had taken a downward trajectory inside the body of John Davis, didn't say that it was deflected, only that it could have been. He concluded the autopsy, saying that death was caused by a gunshot wound to the upper chest.

"We next heard from State Police ballistics expert Roger Benny, who testified that the bullet removed from John Davis's body and the bullet casing found on the floor of the bedroom were fired from the same .22-caliber weapon found in the Davis residence soon after John Davis had been shot. He also found gunshot residue on the shirt worn by John Davis. It was his opinion that the muzzle of the gun was held at a distance greater than eighteen inches, but less than five feet at the time of discharge. However, on rebuttable he testified that it was closer to the eighteen inches than the five feet. He concluded, however, that he was unable to establish that the weapon was pointed upward or downward at the time it was discharged.

"Now we have come to the testimony of Robert Davis. He is the seventeen-year-old son of Jean Davis and the son of the deceased. Try to recall the manner in which Robert testified. He appeared defensive, guarded, and reluctant to recall some of the pertinent details of that critical half-hour period from 6:30 to 7:00 p.m. on September 22, 1984. Recall also how difficult it was to admit certain occurrences before and after the shooting.

"Robert Davis, you will recall, testified that he, his uncle, and his mother Jean Davis left the bar together at about 6:25 p.m. on September 22, 1984, and that it took them about five minutes to get home. John Davis did not accompany them to the bar. They got to the residence about 6:35 p.m. and John Davis was inside the home with the doors locked. Robert was able to open the rear door with a spare key, and he and his mother entered the house. John confronted them, and Jean, Bill, and

Robert pushed John aside and entered the dining room. John went into the bedroom and began closing the door but was followed by Jean who began fighting with John telling him to leave the house. Robert testified that he and his uncle went into the bedroom and broke up the fight and that his mother was on the floor at the foot of the bed. Robert helped his mother get up and his uncle ran upstairs and brought down a rifle and put it under his mother's arm, as she was crying and asking his father to leave. He then turned to go back to go into the kitchen, heard more screaming, and then a gunshot. He turned and went back to the bedroom door and saw his mother holding a rifle at her hip, and when looking into the bedroom, saw his dad lying partly on the bed coughing blood all over, and he appeared to have a bullet hole in his neck.

"Robert testified that the last time he saw his dad alive, he was sitting on the bed with his legs to the floor. Before hearing the shot, he could hear his mother and his dad arguing, his mother crying and screaming, and said that he heard his dad say that he was going to shoot them all and then commit suicide.

"Also, during my questioning of Robert, I asked him if he could hear noise from the bed if someone gets up quickly, and he answered yes. I asked him that when he was in the kitchen, did he hear such a noise coming from the bed, and he said yes.

"I asked him again what happened immediately after the shooting, and he said that his mother shouted to call the ambulance, and Robert placed the call.

"Dr. Bergman testified that in his opinion, Jean Davis's state of mind at the time of the shooting was one of deep fear. I asked him on what he based his opinion. He said that he based his opinion on hearing what Mrs. Davis told him in his office and from reading the police reports in this case, as well as some recorded interviews between Jean Davis and her attorney, Mr. David Chartier. Any person of common sense can listen to one's story, read a report, listen to some tapes, and come up with an opinion.

"Dr. Storm did not so much testify as she lectured, and she was interesting. She lectured extensively about World War II, concentration camps, Stockholm syndrome, battered wives, battered families, motives, statistics, and averages. Her specialty obviously is battered women. She discussed the relevance of the battered spouse syndrome. Both Dr. Bergman and Dr. Storm made no mention of loss of memory, amnesia, or haziness.

"As to Jean Davis's testimony, which lasted almost two days, she expressed in minute detail every facet of her life from at least eleven years of age on up to September 22, 1984.

"I am going to submit to you a couple of thoughts in connection with this case that Jean Davis put herself in the position to shoot and kill her husband, John Davis. She was the aggressor. John Davis did not put her in that bedroom; John did not have the gun. John retreated from the confrontation. She followed; she was the aggressor. She had the gun, and she shot him. Another thought, she did not have to kill him. She could have left the room with the gun. She could have even used the gun as a club against her husband, if in fact, as she testified, he got off the bed and she was that fearful. She did not have to kill him. If her intent was to hurt him, she certainly could have hurt him.

"We will never know John Davis's feelings, his beliefs, or what the facts are, because he is not here to testify in his own defense. We have heard Jean Davis's story, but I am sure that John Davis would also have an interesting story to tell, and I think that he should have had the chance to tell his story. There are two sides to every story, like two sides of a pancake; you have only heard what Jean Davis wants you to hear.

"I would ask you, ladies and gentlemen, to think of this case very carefully when you go into the jury room to deliberate. I would ask you to render a fair and impartial verdict based on the facts in this case, and no sympathy, no compassion, just the facts.

"You were carefully selected and chosen. It took a lot of time. I listened carefully to the questions and the responses, and I was satisfied, as I am sure my fellow counsel is satisfied, that you are a fair and impartial and honest jury. All we ask is your fairness, impartiality, and common sense in arriving at a verdict in this case. Thank you."

"We will have a recess at this time," declared Judge Roode.

David could see that Jean was very upset at Will's final argument to the jury. She just could not believe that she was viewed with such great contempt. She was just about to start crying when David asked her to come outside with him and have a cigarette. He wanted to get her out of the courtroom for a few moments to talk to her about Mr. Brenner's conduct in actually preparing one or two of the exhibits that he introduced into evidence.

Rule 3.7 of the Rules of Professional Conduct states that a lawyer shall not act as an advocate at a trial in which the lawyer is likely to be a necessary witness, except where:

(1) The testimony relates to an uncontested issue;
(2) The testimony relates to the nature and value of legal services rendered in the case; or
(3) disqualification of the lawyer would work substantial hardship on the client.

Combining the roles of advocate and witness can prejudice the opposing party and can involve a conflict of interest between the lawyer and client. The opposing party may properly object where the combination of roles may prejudice that party's rights in the litigation. A witness is required to testify based on personal knowledge, while an advocate is expected to explain and comment on evidence given by others. It may not be clear whether a statement by an advocate-witness should be taken as proof, or as an analysis of the proof.

David told Jean that he had no knowledge of this conduct on the prosecutor's part, until Will mentioned it in his closing argument. David told Jean that in his opinion, the prosecutor's conduct could be sufficient grounds for a mistrial. He told her that he would not like to see her have to undergo a second trial; he believed that she probably would be acquitted of the murder charges, but that in any subsequent trial, the lesser-included offenses of voluntary or involuntary manslaughter would still be a probable verdict. He told her that if a mistrial was granted, that they might get a much more astute prosecutor assigned, putting on a better case for the people, but that the decision was hers. David would abide with her decision. David had some doubts that Jean's heart would survive a second trial.

Jean thought about the situation, as she smoked a second Virginia Slim cigarette, and finally said to David that she did not want a mistrial or a second trial and that they should proceed with David's closing argument to the jury.

Chapter 16

Closing Argument for the Defense

"Mr. Chartier, you may commence your closing argument to the jury," Judge Roode stated.

"Thank you, Your Honor," David responded.

"May it please the court, Your Honor, Mr. Brenner, ladies and gentlemen of the jury, it is now time for the defense to speak. And, as Mr. Brenner had expressed gratitude for your services and attentiveness throughout this trial, I, also, thank you for your attention, and for your dedication to your responsibilities as citizens of the State of Michigan and of the United States of America. Jury duty is a very important and solemn duty of every citizen.

"If you were to be involved in a matter wherein a complaint was filed against you or a member of your family, you would want to be tried by a jury of your peers. Our way of life, our government, and the Constitution of our country, preserves the right to trial by jury. It is a valuable right that you should never give up. We do appreciate that it takes people like yourselves who, even though it would be nicer to be out Christmas shopping, perhaps, or tending to your job, recognize that they have a special responsibility to their fellow man or woman and to our government to sit in judgment at times. It is not only a duty, but also a privilege that is not enjoyed in many other parts of the world.

"Most governments do not have the jury system, so I think we have to be grateful that we do live in America. We do have the ability to have these matters determined by people who have lived, who have experienced, who have values of a diverse nature, and to look to the composite thinking of the jury and ultimately decide what the thoughts of a defendant man or woman were, at the time of an occurrence.

"The reasonable man that you sometimes hear of is a real mystery. Do you know what he looks like? Well, in jury cases, in law cases, the reasonable man or woman is the composite thinking of the jury. It is important that we have your composite thinking, that we have your composite values, that we have your composite judgment, and that there be unanimity in your vote.

"Closing argument is a little different, quite a bit different from an opening statement. When I first addressed you, I told you that the purpose of an opening statement was to give you a bird's eye view. Mr. Brenner described it as a puzzle, a picture on the outside of a box that shows you what it should look like when it is assembled. It is an opportunity to tell you what we intend to prove.

"Closing argument, on the other hand, is advocacy. It is the moment in time when we try to refresh your recollection as to the evidence that has been received from this witness chair, evidence sworn under oath, subject to cross-examination. It is also an opportunity for the trial attorney to be an advocate, to try to convince you to see the evidence in the light most favorable to our respective positions.

"We have to be able to hear and view the evidence and understand it with our own values, with our own feelings, our own upbringing, our experiences in life, and to apply the law, as told to you by the court. An advocate is someone who must portray a drama, not create one that did not exist, but to portray one that in fact occurred. He must make you a part of that drama, to let you feel what people feel, to let you think what people think, trying to place you into the position of being there, having an awareness of what is happening around you, as you witness this drama.

"When I spoke to each of you on voir dire, I asked each one of you if you looked at Jean Davis as an innocent person, if you saw her with a shroud of innocence around her. Each one of you promised that you did and that you would throughout this trial, until charged by the court to deliberate. Only then should you find that the prosecution has proven, beyond a reasonable doubt, every element of the charges that have been brought against her or the lesser included offenses that could be returned in this case, only then would you see the shroud of innocence removed. If the prosecution has not satisfied you that it has proven every element of the charges, then the shroud of innocence will never be removed from her, and you will return a verdict of not guilty.

"It is important that we think about this. As I listened to the prosecution's closing argument, it seemed to me that all of a sudden, the tables were turned. It seemed to me that he was suggesting that I should prove beyond a reasonable doubt that Mrs. Davis is innocent. Somehow, I lost something. They did not teach us that in law school. I do not think that this judge is going to tell you that that is the standard.

"Somehow, I should have proven that it was human blood, somehow I should have proven that it was not a dog's blood, somehow I should have proven all these things. Well, even though I did not have the burden of proof, I took a crack at it, and I think that I have more than raised a reasonable doubt in a number of areas. How can there be a conviction when there is a reasonable doubt? How can there be . . . There cannot be a conviction where there is a reasonable doubt.

"The prosecution has completely lost sight of the fact that his is the burden to prove beyond a reasonable doubt every element of this offense, so that you have no doubt, no reasonable doubt that she is guilty as charged. I do not believe that this burden was any more than merely approached; it certainly was not satisfied.

"Not only does the prosecution have the burden of proof as to each and every element of the crime charged, but where I have raised the defense of self-defense, the prosecution must prove beyond a reasonable doubt that at the instant in time, Mrs. Davis was not in fear for her life, was not acting in self-defense. That is his burden, not mine.

"Somehow, in listening to his closing argument, I thought that he was saying that it was my burden. The defense in this case claims that the prosecution will not meet its burden of proof. When you think of a verdict of not guilty later in the day, when you are deliberating, think of it in terms of the people not proving. There are some jurisdictions where they have used the words *not proven*, instead of not guilty. We use the words 'not guilty,' but I submit to you that it is synonymous, not guilty is not proven, not proven beyond a reasonable doubt by the prosecution.

"What is the quantum, what is the degree? It is beyond a reasonable doubt. Mrs. Davis has claimed that she did not intend to kill her husband, but only in her terror, intended to stop him in his threatening and assaultive behavior, and that if she had not been able to defend herself she would not be in this courtroom today. He would have killed her and Robert, then probably would have set the house afire and shot himself. What did she do right after she realized that she had shot him? She told her son to call the ambulance. If she had intended to kill him, would she have told her son to call the ambulance?

"People's exhibit number two is a semiautomatic rifle. It was loaded with a clip containing six or seven cartridges in it. You need not rack anything to fire additional shots. All you need to do is keep pulling the trigger and as many times you pull the trigger, it will fire another time, and another time and another time. If she had intended to kill him, would she have shot only one time? She would have filled him with lead if she had intended to kill him.

"Mrs. Davis claims that she was terrified that John would instantly carry out his threat to kill her, her brother, and her son, he having threatened to do so numerous times since morning. After her brother had put the rifle under her arm, turning around, and leaving her holding the gun, it enraged John more; John looked at her with a strange look in his eyes. She, feeling she had no escape when he got up and charged at her, threatening to take the gun from her and shoot her, her brother, and her son Robert, she was beyond terror, alone and helpless.

"We all have moments of greatness throughout our lives, a split second within which to make a quick decision. It might be a decision, after some deliberation, to go into the ministry or not, a decision as to avoid hitting a deer. It might be a decision to act to save your own life or the life of someone you love.

"How long does that moment last? The moment of greatness that can later prove to be great or disastrous lasts only a millisecond in time. He is coming off the bed, threatening to kill her; she is alone, terrified. She knows that she cannot allow him to get the gun. It is a moment of greatness.

"Jean Davis has been under a long-term exposure to threats and malicious destructive behavior by her husband. She knew him to be an alcoholic with a split personality. When drinking, he was capable of extreme destructiveness and hurtful conduct. She claims, although she did not intend to kill him, she was nonetheless justified or excused in shooting, because of her actual fear, at that moment, and that her conduct was in self-defense of her, her brother, and her son's life, and the protection of their home.

"She was afraid. She was afraid that John would take the gun from her and kill them all. She was in profound terror, profound terror at the moment the shot was fired, and she believed that she was going to die.

"Now we must remember, and the court will tell you that we do not calmly look back in reflection and ask ourselves, well . . . was Jean Davis justified in thinking about what she thought? Let us take a look at it and see if she was justified and make our determination; that is not the test. The test is what was Jean's state of mind at that moment in time. At that moment in time, that moment of greatness; what was her state of mind then? Not what my state of mind might have been or someone else's state of mind, but what was Jean's at that moment in time. That is the test.

"So crucial is that issue to the case that I hesitate to leave the subject and go on to something else because I have to feel that you really understand that. You really must understand that.

"Jean Davis is charged with murder. There was no premeditation or deliberation. I advocate now that there was no intent to kill; there was only an attempt to stop him, and there was justification. She was, at that moment in time in profound terror, and the law will tell you that a person may take the life of another in self-defense. I believe that the judge will rule, as a matter of law, that she is not guilty of first-degree murder, and you are not to consider first-degree murder.

"Second-degree murder requires intent to kill or intent to do great bodily harm or willful and wanton disregard. In this case, there was no intent to kill. There was no intent to do great bodily harm, and there was no willful and wanton conduct.

"The judge, I believe, will tell you that willful and wanton conduct is a defined term. I believe he will define willfulness as meaning the defendant knowingly and consciously created the danger, intending to inflict injury. Someone who is, at that moment, merely defending herself cannot be deemed to have willfully, knowingly, and consciously created the danger intending to inflict injury. Wantonness, I believe, will be described to you as meaning that the defendant knowingly and consciously created the danger with knowledge of its probable consequences. Again, we are talking about someone defending a threat, meeting force with force.

"Although he had no gun, he had the look in his eye. She had experienced death threats many times; she knew that this time he was going to do it. John was built like a bull, weighing two hundred thirty-five pounds; he had beaten her so many times before.

"You will be told that as part of the elements of second-degree murder, that you must find, beyond a reasonable doubt, that her actions were not justified. Is self-defense justification? The court will tell you yes, self-defense is justification. You must look to her state of mind at the time to determine whether it was self-defense. In addition, the people must prove beyond a reasonable doubt that it was not self-defense or you must find her not guilty. If you find justification, if she acted in self-defense in saving her life, the life of her brother and the life of her son, you must acquit her of everything because even with the lesser-included offense of manslaughter, justification will acquit her.

"The court will talk to you about voluntary manslaughter; the court will talk to you about involuntary manslaughter, and the court will talk to you about gross negligence. In addition, I believe that the court will tell you about involuntary manslaughter, death from a firearm intentionally aimed, without malice, as well as careless, reckless, or negligent use of a firearm with injury or death resulting.

"Notwithstanding every one of these lesser-included offenses, before you can return a verdict, you would have to determine that the prosecution has met its burden beyond a reasonable doubt in proving that she was not in fear for her life and that she did not act in response to that fear. And if you find that that fear is there, or there is a reasonable doubt in her favor, that she was indeed in fear for her life and acted as a result thereof, you must find her not guilty."

David was feeling quite emotional at this stage of the closing argument. Telling the jury about the possible verdicts, he found himself becoming extremely nervous about the lesser—included offenses, feeling that the jury will be looking for something to convict her on, in spite of the possibility of their not finding her guilty of second-degree murder.

"The court will talk to you about your verdict form, a sheet of paper that will be taken with you into the jury room. You will see that it says that you may return one verdict only in this case; check only one line on this sheet. It begins with *not guilty*. The next verdict is *guilty of murder in the second-degree*. The next is *voluntary manslaughter*, then *involuntary manslaughter*, and the last is *careless use of a firearm with death resulting*.

However, I advocate to you that her defense of self-defense to murder is a defense to all. She is not guilty.

"I was talking about the prosecution's burden of proof. Look at the questions in this case. The body was partially on the bed. Testimony of Robert Davis places Mrs. Davis at the threshold to the bedroom door. There is absolutely no evidence whatsoever to establish that she was ever closer inside that room, at the instant the shot was fired, than right there at the threshold of the bedroom door. Did the people show her to be anywhere other than right at the bedroom doorway? Did the people ever offer anything to say that after she left the room, following the fight, that she had reentered that room? There is absolutely no evidence whatsoever to establish that she was ever closer inside that room, at that moment in time, than right at the threshold of the doorway.

"Look at the measurements between the door threshold and the bed, five feet ten inches. What does the ballistics show? Sure, Lieutenant Roger Benny said eighteen inches to five feet. However, when I had him on the stand and I asked him of all the tests that he performed, which is the most similar to the pattern found on the shirt, he said eighteen inches. On rebuttal, he admits that the distance was not greater than eighteen inches. How then is the bullet going to reach John, leaving that pattern on the shirt, if he is on the bed? It is a distance of five feet ten inches to the bed. The ballistics shows eighteen inches. The shirt was eighteen inches from the gun. Could he then be on the bed? He is not on the bed. Whose evidence was it? It was the State Police evidence. It was Lieutenant Roger Benny's evidence. What did Dr. Cachette find? He found the distance to be eighteen inches to two feet. We can forget about that five-foot distance because Lieutenant Benny is now tied to a specific answer and that was eighteen inches. As a rebuttal witness, his testimony supported that of Dr. Cachette. He would like to have had that greater range to support the prosecution's theory of the case, but he is now tied to his answer, and if the man is going to sit here and tell the truth, he has to answer the question honestly and fully.

"So what else goes together? Dr. Cachette testified that the gun was at a slight upward angle. You saw the pattern when he had me hold the shirt up to my chest. It was an elliptical pattern showing an angular shot.

"On cross-examination, it came out of the mouth of State Police Lieutenant Roger Benny. He did not want to admit to it, but yesterday when I pressed, pressed, and pressed him for the answer, asking if the pattern that he took was elliptical, he finally said, 'Yes.' We have looked at the gun residue pattern on the shirt, and yes, it is an elliptical pattern and Lieutenant Benny now cannot dispute the testimony of Dr. Cachette.

"The blood at the door of the bedroom, as you recall from the testimony of this defendant, came to John's mouth the instant the shot was fired. If you will look at the photographs taken by my investigator Mr. Don White, you can see the blood on the carpet near the door. One of the blood spots is right near the center of the doorway.

"I contend that it would have been easy for the officers to miss a blood spot on the carpeting at night, using a flashlight to search for evidence. The evidence was there all the time. I am not trying to blame the officers, but it was there. I did not put it there, and I think that Mr. Brenner's speculation about a dog being in heat and dropping blood is completely unsupported by the evidence and has been suggested as a 'red herring' to divert your attention from the reality that the presence of John's blood at that location is consistent with the testimony of Jean Davis.

"The distance is right, the angle is right, and the blood is there. Mrs. Davis testified that as soon as she shot, blood came out of his mouth. You know from the testimony of Dr. Wiseman that John Davis was shot through the heart, through the aorta, and through the lung. He would immediately cough up blood with that kind of injury. She testified that after the shot, he stepped back a couple of steps and fell onto the bed. It is indeed only two steps to the bed.

"The evidence has shown that John was again very drunk and very violent, having threatened the family on September 22, 1984, as well as threatening suicide. He struck Jean, jammed ice down her throat, and was becoming more and more difficult for Jean's brother Bill and her son to intervene in defense of Jean. The assaults were becoming more and more violent.

"Jean left during the day, hoping that things would be better when she returned. Dr. Bergman said that it is typical of Jean, when she experiences stress; she is going to try to leave. Even when she tried to complete the psychological testing, the sentence test, she did not complete it, and when he went into the room and she was gone. Dr. Bergman testified that Jean's response to the stress of the sentence test was more valuable to his diagnosis than if she had finished the test because it demonstrated to him how she reacts to stress, she leaves. She leaves if she can.

"She could not take the beatings anymore; Dr. LaGale said she would die. He said that she would suffer another heart attack, probably a fatal attack. Jean knew that John's psychiatrist had told her that he was capable of fulfilling his threats to kill her and the family and that she should not try to leave him under those circumstances.

"Again, we are talking about her state of mind with regard to her husband, at the time of firing the gun, as he charged her. His suicide threats made more credible his threats to kill the family. He had nothing to lose, he had absolutely . . . nothing to lose. His attacks, more desperate, more violent, convinced her that he was very likely to kill her that very evening.

"On the day in question, Jean was surprised to see the gun, she immediately felt terror because she knew that John would try to get the gun.

"She was shocked to understand that there was still a gun in the house, the police were supposed to have removed all of the guns. Where did this one come from? She questioned in her mind. It was too late; John had already seen the gun and now he was intent on getting a hold of it.

"Jean was now alone, having been abandoned by her brother after John had said to him, 'You haven't got the guts to pull the trigger; you won't use that.' Jean's brother then moved behind Jean, stuffed the gun under her right arm and he quickly departed, leaving Jean to face this drunken, crazy, raging bull alone.

"Unexpectedly, without Jean's knowledge, her brother Bill had introduced an instrumentality into that scene, that moments prior was not there, exacerbating a previously bad situation, now making it much worse than before. Abandoned, she knew that John would get the gun and would not hesitate to kill her and the family. John came off the bed saying, 'I'm going to kill you.' She was looking at the strange look in his eyes, when she fired the gun.

"The testimony of Dr. Wiseman, regarding the trajectory, do you remember it? Do you remember that he said to me, 'Mr. Chartier, you are absolutely correct,' when I said that the trajectory of the of a .22-caliber bullet inside the body could not determine the trajectory of the bullet on its way to the body. He said, 'Mr. Chartier, you're absolutely correct.' Do you remember that? I had reminded him of the shooting of President Reagan and the picture that was in *Time* magazine showing the .22-caliber bullet changing its trajectory after it had struck a rib. Dr. Wiseman testified that he had not read about it but that he had heard about it.

"The people have shown no trajectory, they did not show it through Dr. Wiseman, nor did they show it through the testimony of their ballistics expert. It was my witness, Dr. Cachette, that testified about a slight upward trajectory of the bullet on its way to the body of John Davis, and there could not have been a downward trajectory if he was on his feet but would have to be a downward trajectory if John was sitting on the bed.

"With the distance right, the presence of blood at the doorway, with the trajectory right, we know that John was not on the bed when he was shot, but was lunging at Jean, almost reaching the gun when it was fired.

"Dr. Bergman said that Jean was in profound fear, beyond terror when she fired. He said that she thought that she was facing eminent death. She did not intend to kill him, but only to stop him, when she fired the shot. She never felt the trigger pulled.

"Is it surprising that she does not remember saying some of the things she did? What did she say? 'I shot John, he beat me and I shot him, he is not going to beat me anymore.' She does not remember saying those things, but assuming that she did, everything that she is purported to have said is consistent with our theory of the case. She was a long-time continuing spousal abuse victim, who had to defend her life against a drunken, crazy husband, bent on killing her and the family, burning the family home, and committing suicide.

"Dr. Storm explained the dynamics of family violence to you. I agree that Dr. Storm did not spend time studying Jean Davis, but she did that for a reason; it was all in the plan. She wanted to come to you and talk in terms of the subject of family violence. After all, I had already had a clinical psychiatrist interview and evaluate Mrs. Davis, and that was Dr. Bergman.

"The purpose of her testimony was to enlarge your minds and your awareness of the problem of domestic violence, so that you had a feeling and an understanding regarding battered wives. I was talking with Dr. Storm, and she told me of a recent case in Michigan where an ex-husband came back and killed the whole family. The wife's divorce case was to become final the next day. Although Dr. Storm came here to testify about the subject of family violence, she nonetheless has related her testimony to both Jean Davis and to her late husband John. She wanted you to have awareness and an appreciation for the psychological dynamics that occur in the parties to that marital relationship and how it progressively changes as the violence increases in frequency and severity. It was and is my desire to advocate that you remember the things that she said, concerning the psychology of the relationship, the dynamics of that relationship, and to evaluate it in conjunction with the facts that you have learned from this witness chair, as it applies to this case.

"You heard Dr. Bergman; he said that she had no intent to kill, that she was in fear of dying, a profound fear, beyond terror.

"I had asked Robert Davis whether his father ever told him about his (John Davis's) childhood and whether he had ever been beaten. He said that he had been beaten by both his parents.

"Dr. Storm testified that the batterer is a product of a violent home. He is dependent upon his wife, and she is the only close relationship, although that dependency may not be obvious until she leaves. He lacks insight into his own behavior; he minimizes his own violence. He has an intense fear of being left by his wife, is jealous, controlling, and expecting her to meet all his needs. He is suspicious, has periods of depression, views himself as a victim, and the assaults serve to reduce his feelings of anxiety, depression, and periods of depersonalization. He is very sensitive of feelings of rejection, has very low self-esteem, is self-punitive in the extreme, and may be suicidal. He feels powerless, but violence makes him feel powerful.

"Dr. Storm testified that until the battering occurs, there is no psychological profile of the woman. It can be any woman. However, after she has been subjected to the violence, a psychological profile develops. The woman becomes low in self-esteem, feels guilt and shame about the beatings, feels that she deserves being beaten, becomes depressed, and may even become suicidal herself. She is dependent, has emotional outbursts, chronic anxiety, fear of being alone, and underestimates the threat.

"She has the irrational hope that he will change. Dr. Storm testified that an outsider might question why she does not just leave. In reality, the husband would become more violent if she left and would probably fulfill his threats to kill the entire family. It is not a simple solution, she is going to be beaten if she stays; she is going to be killed if she leaves. Her day-to-day goal is to try to remain safe for that day, if she can.

"The legal system did not help her, and I might say, although this trial might appear to some to be an indictment against our prosecutor, I did not intend it to be such. He is not alone. Dr. Storm told you that they are involved in a program to educate police and prosecutors about how to deal with this matter of family violence. She testified that our past thinking is not productive, and it is only through these cases, that they are becoming aware of the fact that they had numerous opportunities to intervene effectively before a homicide occurs. I wanted to make a point, and that is, showing the ineffectiveness of our legal system in dealing with the problem of domestic violence.

"When I showed Dr. Storm the letter that Jean had received from our prosecutor, I asked her what psychological effect that would have on a person who received that letter. She said that it would make her feel abandoned, more alone, more helpless, isolated. I asked her what would be the psychological effect of knowing of her heart condition, her short life expectancy, the continuing danger of being subjected to further assaults, and that she may have a fatal heart attack in the process. Dr. Storm said that it would greatly enhance her sense of life threat. Further, knowing that her husband had threatened suicide would greatly enhance her knowledge and fear that he would follow through with his threats to kill her.

"I wanted to portray a drama and have you experience that drama from the eyes and emotions of Jean Davis. To do this, it was necessary, I felt, as her advocate, to take each of you back in time. You saw her in your mind's eye as a little girl, one in a family of eight children, with a loving mother, who seemed always to take good care of her children. You grew up with her and experienced her frustrations in school and of her dreams of having a family of her own someday. You were there when she was first married and bore her two children by her first husband. You then saw the tragedy of her discovering that he was missing and of learning that her marriage was a sham, a cruel trick and that it was void from the beginning. You experienced her courtship with John Davis, shared in her excitement of a new life in Milwaukee, a new life of stability, security, love, and compassion.

"You witnessed her concern over the thought of her husband giving up his job in Wisconsin, and with it, her security, to return to Michigan. You heard her say that she felt she owed him a chance to prove that their life in Michigan could be just as good and just as secure as what he had provided her in Wisconsin. However, we all saw the disappointment that she felt when comparing what she had left in Milwaukee with what she had moved to in Michigan. You felt her inner strength as you watched her clean up that pigsty that they moved into and saw her make a home.

Her disappointment and concern over John's inability to keep a job, she described to us all. It only confirmed her fears that she had entertained before leaving Milwaukee.

"The car accident and the injuries to John were the turning points in their lives. He became violent and resentful to her and to the children, burdened with frustration and the painful feelings that he was less than a man. He was the product of a violent home and child abuse, and he himself resorted to the very violence that he had suppressed since his youth.

"He then could find his masculinity, his power, only in beating his family, in asserting complete dominance and terror over them. You witnessed the many violent assaults and beatings that Jean and the children endured. I asked you to look at the photograph of her body after she was beaten with a two-by-four when she tried to put out a fire that he had set on the living room floor in an attempt to destroy the family home.

"You saw her life and her nature change; she began to fight back when possible, and the children and her brother intervened on her behalf. Leaving for short periods was her answer, leaving until the anger and frustration passed. You saw him beat her in the home, throw her from a speeding car onto the highway, and leave her unconscious near the guardrail. You witnessed the violent destruction of the furniture with his crutches, and heard the children tell of his crazy look in his eyes, saw the distortion of his face in your mind, as he became a raging bull terrorizing Jean and the children, heard of his growls and then of the destruction.

"You witnessed the arson of the residence and the house next door, heard the terror in her voice as she thought that her house was being destroyed. You, through her testimony, have witnessed the death of her eight-year-old son, and felt the anguish that crushed her heart. You feared for her life in surgery and received with her the crushing reality of her short life expectancy.

"You heard the gunshots fired at the children standing on the stairway and the glass blown from the windows. Your life passed before you in an instant as you looked down the barrel of his .308-caliber rifle with rage in his eyes. You know that she cannot leave; surely, she would die if she tried.

"It is a vicious cycle indeed, frustrated by her efforts to get help from our legal system she lived with the constant fear and thoughts of how to survive. You witnessed her irrational hope that someday, someone, somewhere would help John and that they would again live a life as happy and secure as they once knew.

"You saw the terror of September 22, 1984, and felt her concern when she realized that her brother Bill had placed a gun under her arm. She knew that once John saw the gun, he would want to get it from her and then kill her and the family. She knew that she could not allow him to get the gun; she was willing to die trying to prevent it. You saw John lunge at her, saying that he was going to take the gun and kill her and the family. You witnessed her insecurity when her brother left her alone, there at the threshold of the bedroom doorway, abandoned, in profound fear, beyond terror. John was so close, blood came to his mouth; it was over, no more beatings.

"As Jean Davis's defense advocate, I speak to you but once. Mr. Brenner has spoken to you, and now he has a second opportunity to address you, at the conclusion of my closing argument. However, I shall never speak to you again during this trial. I want you to listen carefully to Mr. Brenner's presentation that follows, knowing that I shall never be afforded a second opportunity to speak to you again; I want you to wonder what I would say to counter Mr. Brenner's further comments, if I could speak again.

"You are the sole judges of the guilt or innocence of Jean Davis. Never again, in the entire world, will her fate in this case be determined. She was crushed by the events of her life; she was demoralized by the loss of her son, her heart failure, the abuse she endured, her inability to find justice from our legal system, help for her husband, and her terror. Each of you, as members of the jury, has sworn to be faithful to your oath, to justice, and faithful to yourselves. I beg of you, not to abandon her, not to shame her, not to punish her further. She is a good person; I plead with you to find her not guilty and finally set her free. Thank you," said David, concluding his closing remarks to the jury.

"We will recess at this time," said Judge Roode.

It is over, thought David; did he say enough, did he offend the jury, was he too technical, too emotional, or too hard on the prosecution? The instant he finished his closing argument and plea to the jury, doubts set in, did he do a good job of defending Jean? He wished that he had said a dozen other things and perhaps omitted saying some other things. Has he lost the case for her; will the jury disregard all that he has said? It was typical for David to do an instant analysis of his closing, beating himself up emotionally for what he imagined was a poor performance as a criminal trial attorney. Now comes the toughest part, listening to the prosecutor's rebuttal argument, not being able to address the jury again, perhaps failing to object to things Will might say in rebuttal, not being confident that Judge Roode would sustain or overrule the objections, leaving the jury with a possible poor impression of David, appearing desperate. David hated this part of defending criminal defendants in trial. However, such was the criminal trial procedure. The prosecution has the burden of proving guilt beyond a reasonable doubt and has the opportunity of having the last word to the jury.

David reluctantly accepted that he does not have control of the results of a trial, never has had that kind of control. The control is always with the judge or the jury. David was able to be the best advocate he could be and that is all that he could be. The control was not with him. If everyone was faithful to his or her oaths, the judge, the lawyers, and the jury, the correct result was supposed to occur. However, sometimes it does not occur, but the American System of Justice, although in continual need of improvement, is yet the best system in the world.[3]

David spent a few minutes at the rear of the courthouse with Jean. David now frequently smoked cigarettes during breaks in the trial along with her. He was upset with himself taking up smoking again after so many years. It was almost time to go back into the courtroom to listen to Will's rebuttal closing argument to the jury.

Chapter 17

Prosecution Rebuttal

"Mr. Brenner, do you wish to exercise your right to rebuttal argument?" asked Judge Roode.

"Thank you, Your Honor. Members of the jury, as Mr. Chartier indicated to you, the people do have the final word, the last word. One reason that we do have the last word is because we have the burden of proof, and we do have a high standard. There is a high standard and high degree of proof required in every criminal prosecution, whether it is a murder case, an assault, breaking and entering, or a speeding case. That burden requires proof beyond a reasonable doubt. Mr. Chartier said that Mrs. Davis did not intend to kill John Davis, but only that she intended to stop him. Well, I submit to you that she had other means of stopping him. The victim cannot speak; he is dead. Stopping him with a bullet is murder. There were no other witnesses supporting her claim of wanting only to stop him. Mr. Chartier brings up another interesting point that the shooting of John Davis was to protect herself and her family, a moment of greatness, and the question in this case was Jean Davis's state of mind at the time the shot fired. You cannot go into her mind, you cannot use a computer card, and you cannot use a punch card. However, you can do it by looking at her actions and listening to her words, as she said to John that 'if Bill does not make you leave, I would.' Why did she want him to leave? It was his home too. What was he doing at that moment in time that demanded that he leave the house? However, I submit to you that her actions and her words, at that period, between 6:30 p.m. and 7:00 p.m., were such that she intended to kill her husband. No one forced her to accept the gun from her brother Bill. She held on to it and she used it to kill her husband. Mr.

Chartier said that blood came to her husband's mouth as soon as the shot fired. If he was shot, where she claims, and blood came to his mouth and then goes back four or five feet to the bed, there certainly would be a trail of blood all the way to the bed; there was no trail.

"Mrs. Davis testified that John's psychiatrist in Newberry and his psychiatrist from Tomah, Wisconsin, told her that John had a split personality when he drank. All of you are listening to the testimony of Jean Davis telling you what she wants you to hear. We do not know about these psychiatrists; they were not here to testify. John was probably an alcoholic.

"The defense would put several people on trial in this case. The police were certainly on trial, the prosecuting attorney's office was on trial, and John Davis was on trial. Mrs. Davis resented her husband for relocating to Michigan from Milwaukee, for putting her in that position, having to clean up a pigsty in an attempt to make a home for the family. These seeds caused her to build up the intent, over the years. She wanted him out of the house on September 22, 1984; it was her house, her furniture, her children; she wanted him out; he would not leave; she killed him.

"Mr. Chartier talked of the right of self-defense, but there is a higher command, thou shall not kill is embedded in our law in the state of Michigan, you shall not commit murder, you shall not commit manslaughter. Mr. Chartier argued that the prosecution did not prove all of the elements of the crime of murder or manslaughter. I will touch on these elements:

- first, John Davis died in Pictured Rocks County on September 22, 1984;
- second, that his death was caused by an act of the defendant, Jean Davis;
- third, that defendant intended to kill John Davis, do him great bodily harm, or committed a willful and wanton act, the natural tendency of which was to cause death or great bodily injury; and
- fourth, there was no justification or excuse for Jean Davis to kill her husband, John Davis, on September 22, 1984.

"There was no self-defense; she could have retreated. I ask that you find the defendant guilty of second-degree murder and I want to thank you for your attention," Will said, finalizing his closing rebuttal argument to the jury.

David thought about his defense of Jean and wanted to remain focused on the trial and the upcoming instructions to the jury that will come from Judge Roode.

At this point in the trial, the judge tells the jury what the law is. He describes the burden of proof, the presumption of innocence, rules of evidence, the jury's obligation to follow the law, the jury's right and obligation to deliberate concerning the facts of the case, coming to a unanimous agreement regarding the facts, and then applying the law as given by the judge.

David told Jean that he would not be going to lunch with her and that he wanted only to think about the case as he remained in the courtroom through the lunch hour. He knew that Jean was very apprehensive, as the trial was nearly completed. David wondered what he had accomplished. If he could get Jean acquitted of all charges, it would be great, thought David, but the likelihood was that the jury would find her guilty of one of the lesser-included offenses—*voluntary or involuntary manslaughter*—as a compromise verdict. David felt, however, that if self-defense was good enough for an acquittal of the first-degree murder, then it should also be good enough to acquit her for second-degree murder and the lesser-included offenses as well.

In spite of it all, David felt that his defense of Jean Davis served another purpose, irrespective of the jury's verdict. The testimony, elicited from the witnesses during this trial, brought to light a serious social problem in the state of Michigan and throughout the country concerning the issue of spousal abuse in the home, an issue that is seldom, if ever, discussed among families and the community. We read about it in books, in the papers, watch movies about it, and continue to be shocked on learning that one has killed the other and possibly the entire family. We do not know how to feel about it. Until now, we did not know the psychological dynamics occurring with people subjected to ongoing spousal abuse. We did not understand the isolation, the physical injuries, the fear, the terror that spousal abuse victims live through on a daily basis. The *Iron Town Mining Journal* reporter was in the courtroom throughout the trial, and the daily newspaper continually ran updates on the course of the trial and the issues exposed through the trial process. David felt pleased to think that this very trial might help to bring to the forefront the dire circumstances of abused victims, the topic of spousal abuse. People might actually talk about it with their families.

Chapter 18

Judge Roode's Instructions to the Jury

At about 1:15 p.m., the court reconvened.

Judge Roode began his instructions to the jury, "Members of the jury, the evidence and the arguments in this case have been completed, and I will now instruct you as to the law. Following the instructions I am about to give to you, two of your number will be deleted by lot, and the remaining twelve will go to the jury room to deliberate and decide on your verdict. Remember, you are sworn to deliberate and decide this case justly. Sympathy or prejudice must not influence your decision.

"It is my duty as judge to instruct you on the law you are to apply to this case, and it is your duty to follow the law as it is given to you. From time to time, I have given you some instructions. You should consider all of my instructions as a connected series, which together form the law you are to follow. You should not pick out one of some instructions and disregard others.

"It is your duty as jurors to determine the facts. You are the sole and exclusive judges of the facts. You alone determine the weight, the effect, and the value of the evidence as well as the believability of the witnesses. You must consider and weigh the testimony of all witnesses in evidence. You alone are to determine whether to believe any witness or evidence and the extent to which any witness or evidence should be believed. Your decision as to any fact in this case is final.

"Basic in our system of criminal justice is the principle that a person accused of a crime is presumed to be innocent. This presumption of innocence started at the very beginning of this case and continued throughout the trial, and should continue during your deliberations. Each one of you must be satisfied beyond a reasonable doubt after deliberating that the defendant is guilty before you can return a verdict of guilty. You must begin you deliberations with the presumption of innocence foremost in your minds.

"The fact that the defendant was arrested and is on trial is no evidence against her. There must be evidence introduced in this trial that convinces you of the defendant's guilt beyond a reasonable doubt. The law does not require a defendant to prove her innocence or produce any evidence whatsoever. The burden of proving guilt is upon the prosecution throughout the entire course of the trial, and at no time does the burden of proof shift to the defendant.

"This burden of proof means that every element of the crime charged must be proven by evidence beyond a reasonable doubt. A reasonable doubt is a fair doubt growing out of the testimony, the lack of testimony, or the unsatisfactory nature of the testimony in the case. It is not a mere imaginary or possible doubt, but a fair doubt based on reason and common sense. It is such a doubt as to leave your minds after a careful examination of all the evidence in the case in the condition that you cannot say that you have an abiding conviction to a moral certainty of the truth of the charge here made against the defendant.

"The information, that is, the charge in this case, charges that on September 22, 1984, in this county, the defendant, Jean Davis, did murder John Davis. You are instructed that I have determined that the evidence, as a matter of law, will not sustain a verdict of first-degree murder. You should therefore consider that the information charges the defendant with the crime of murder of the second degree.

"Murder is the killing of a person by another with a certain mental element. For murder, the defendant must have intended to kill or have intended to do great bodily harm or have willfully and wantonly disregarded the strong and plain likelihood that death would result, and she must have done so under circumstances that did not justify, excuse, or lessen the crime.

"The defendant has pleaded not guilty to this charge. To establish this charge, the prosecution must prove each of the following elements beyond a reasonable doubt:

- first, that the deceased died on September 22, 1984, within Pictured Rocks County;
- second, that his death was caused by the act of the defendant, that is, that John Davis died as a result of a gunshot fired by the defendant;
- third, if you find that the death was caused by the defendant, then you must determine whether the defendant is guilty of any crime, and
- fourth, for murder you must find that the defendant intended to kill or that she intended to do great bodily harm, or that she committed a wanton and willful act, the natural tendency of which is to cause death or great bodily harm. There must be a strong and plain likelihood that death or serious bodily harm will result, and the defendant must have willfully and wantonly disregarded the knowledge of the possible consequences of death or a serious injury.

"The killing of one human being by another may be entirely innocent. It is not the act of killing in itself which makes it a crime, but the state of mind with which it is done. A killing is not murder if it is justified or excused. Neither is it murder if it occurs under circumstances that make the killing the lesser crime of manslaughter or some other lesser-included offense.

"Where certain intent is a necessary element in a crime, the crime cannot have been committed, when the intent did not exist. Intent is a decision of the mind to knowingly do an act with a conscious objective of accomplishing a certain result. There can be no crime of murder under our law when there is no intent to kill, to do great bodily harm, or to do an act, the natural tendency of which is to do great bodily harm. In addition, the burden rests upon the prosecution to show beyond a reasonable doubt that the defendant at the time of doing the alleged act had that wrongful intent.

"The intent with which a person does an act is known by the way she expresses it to others or indicates it by her conduct. The intent with which a person does an act can sometimes be determined from the manner in which it is done, the method used, and all other facts and circumstances, but only if that intent is established by the evidence.

"In determining the question of intent, you should consider any evidence reflecting the mental condition of the defendant at the time of the act. You may consider her appearance, conduct, and manner in determining whether the defendant's judgment or common sense was disturbed, consider whether the defendant appeared intoxicated, and what effect, if any, such condition had on her mental faculties. Evidence of intoxication may be used in defense of this charge, and all such evidence should be weighed in determining whether or not the defendant had the necessary intent to commit this crime.

"If you find that the defendant, for any reason whatsoever, did not consciously and knowingly act with the intent to kill, to do great bodily harm, or to do an act, the natural tendency of which is to do great bodily harm, the crime cannot have been committed, and you must find the defendant not guilty of the crime of murder.

"If from all the evidence you have a reasonable doubt as to whether or not the defendant knowingly and consciously acted with that intent, then you must find the defendant not guilty of the crime of murder.

"A gun, of course, is a dangerous weapon. You may infer an intention to kill from the use of a dangerous weapon when it is used in such a manner that the death of a person would be very likely. You may infer that a person intends the usual results that follow from the use of a dangerous weapon.

"You must consider all of the facts and circumstances in determining what the state of mind of the defendant at the time of the act was. This may be inferred from the kind of weapon used, the nature of the wounds inflicted, the circumstances surrounding the killing, the acts, conduct, and language of the accused, or any other circumstances in evidence. In determining whether a person who has killed another is guilty of murder, the nature and extent of the injury or wrong, which was actually intended, must be usually of controlling importance. There cannot be a conviction of murder unless the injury intended was one of a very serious character, which might naturally and commonly involve loss of life or grievous mischief. If all the evidence does not convince you beyond a reasonable doubt that the defendant either intended to kill or consciously created a very high risk of death with knowledge of the probable consequences, then you must find the defendant not guilty of the crime of murder.

"Now I shall instruct you what are termed lesser-included offenses to the charge of murder of the second degree. If all the elements of the crime of murder of the second degree have not been proven beyond a reasonable doubt, but all the elements of a lesser-included offense have been proven beyond a reasonable doubt, it would be your duty to find the defendant guilty of such lesser-included offense. The lesser-included offenses which I shall discuss with you are three in number, voluntary manslaughter, involuntary manslaughter, and careless use of a firearm with death resulting.

"Now, first I will discuss voluntary manslaughter. The crime of murder may be reduced to voluntary manslaughter if the killing were committed under the influence of passion or in the heat of blood produced by an adequate provocation and before a reasonable time has elapsed for the blood to cool.

"Manslaughter is distinguished from murder in that with voluntary manslaughter, first the mind or reason of the defendant is at the time of the act disturbed or clouded by mental or emotional excitement to the extent which might make an ordinary person likely to act rashly or without due deliberation or reflection and from passion rather than judgment.

"Second, the cause of such disturbance must be something which would cause ordinary persons to act rashly. The law does not state what things are sufficient to produce such a reaction. Anything that would naturally tend to produce such a state of mind in ordinary persons is sufficient.

"Third, the killing must result from such provocation or passion. That is, the killing must have occurred before a reasonable time has elapsed for the blood to cool and for reason to resume its control. No precise time can be laid down. The test is whether a reasonable time has elapsed under these particular circumstances.

"To repeat, the crime of murder may be reduced to voluntary manslaughter if the killing be committed under the influence of passion or in heat of blood produced by an adequate provocation and before a reasonable time has elapsed for the blood to cool.

"Now, as to involuntary manslaughter, if the evidence does not convince you beyond a reasonable doubt that the defendant intended to kill, you must consider whether she acted with an unreasonable disregard for human life. It is sufficient for murder in the second degree if the defendant consciously created a very high degree of risk of death if she had knowledge of those consequences.

"However, if you find that the defendant's acts did not amount to such criminal purpose aimed against life, you must find the defendant not guilty of murder or voluntary manslaughter, which involves also the same intent to kill, and consider whether she is guilty of involuntary manslaughter.

"In order to establish the crime of involuntary manslaughter, the prosecution must prove each of the following elements beyond a reasonable doubt. First, that John Davis died on or about September 22, 1984; second, that his death was caused by an act of the defendant; third, that the defendant caused the death without lawful justification or excuse; fourth, that when she did the act which caused death, the defendant must have been acting in a grossly negligent manner.

"Gross negligence means more than carelessness. It means willful, wanton, and reckless disregard of the consequences, which might follow from a failure to act and an indifference to the rights of others.

"In order to find that the defendant was guilty of gross negligence, you must find beyond a reasonable doubt: first, that she knew of the danger to another, that is, that this was a situation requiring ordinary care and diligence to avoid injuring another; second, that she had the ability to avoid harm to another by exercise of such ordinary care; and third, that she failed to use such care and diligence to prevent the threat and danger when to the ordinary mind it must have been apparent that the result was likely to cause serious harm to another.

"Involuntary manslaughter may also be defined in another way, that is, there is a second form of involuntary manslaughter. A person who kills an individual commits the crime of involuntary manslaughter if the death results from the discharge of a firearm pointed intentionally but without malice.

"To establish this charge, this kind of involuntary manslaughter, the prosecution must prove each of the following elements beyond a reasonable doubt:

- first, that John Davis died on or about September 22, 1984;
- second, that his death was caused by the act of the defendant;
- third, that the defendant caused the death without lawful justification or excuse;
- fourth, that the death resulted from the discharge of a firearm;

- fifth, at the time of such discharge, the defendant was pointing or aiming the firearm at John Davis;
- sixth, at the time of the discharge, defendant intended to point or aim the firearm at the deceased.

"Now, as I have already explained to you, when certain intent is a necessary element in a crime, the crime cannot have been committed when the intent did not exist. Intent is a decision of the mind to knowingly do an act with a conscious objective of accomplishing a certain result. There can be no crime of involuntary manslaughter from an intentionally aimed firearm under our law where there is no intent to point or aim the firearm at the deceased, and the burden rests upon the prosecution to show beyond a reasonable doubt that the defendant at the time of doing the alleged act had that wrongful intent.

"Now, you know that involuntary manslaughter involves a non-intentional killing, either resulting from gross negligence, as in the first form explained to you, or from intentionally pointing a firearm under the second form of involuntary manslaughter given.

"Besides voluntary and involuntary manslaughter, there is involved or included in the charge against the defendant the lesser-included offense of careless, reckless, or negligent use of a firearm with death resulting. Any person who carelessly, recklessly, or negligently, but not willfully or wanton, allows a firearm under his or her immediate control to be discharged is guilty of this crime if another person is killed.

"To establish this charge, the prosecution must prove each of the following elements beyond a reasonable doubt:

- first, that John Davis was killed;
- second, that his death resulted from the discharge of a firearm;
- third, at the time of the discharge, the firearm was within the immediate control of the defendant, and the defendant caused or allowed the firearm to be discharged;
- fourth, the discharge was the result of carelessness, recklessness, or negligence on the part of the defendant and,
- fifth, that the discharge was not the result of willfulness, or wantonness, on the part of the defendant.

"If it were discharged because of willful and wanton misconduct or negligence on the part of defendant, it would be manslaughter. However, the lesser-included charge of careless, reckless, or negligent use of a firearm involves a careless, reckless, or negligent act that was not willful or wanton.

"The evidence must convince you beyond a reasonable doubt that the defendant was guilty of some carelessness, recklessness, or negligence in the discharge of this firearm. The evidence must establish beyond a reasonable doubt that the defendant was guilty of at least ordinary negligence.

"In order to understand this term, you should bear in mind that there are different kinds of negligence under the law. You must distinguish between slight negligence and ordinary negligence. Slight negligence is characterized by acts, which are not naturally and inherently dangerous to life, which only an extremely careful person would have foreseen is likely to produce injury to another.

"The fact that an accident occurred is not in itself any evidence of negligence. Whatever is unavoidable, by the exercise of due and reasonable care, is not a crime. Slight negligence is not a crime and is that degree or kind of negligence, which is below, or less than ordinary negligence. In this case, if you find that the defendant was negligent, but that her negligence was only slight negligence, then you must return a verdict of not guilty.

"Ordinary negligence is defined as want of reasonable care, that is, failing to do what an ordinary, reasonable person would have done under the conditions and circumstances then existing or doing what an ordinary sensible person would not have done under the conditions and circumstances then existing in view of the probable injury.

"Ordinary negligence occurs in the doing of acts, which are naturally and inherently dangerous to life, which a reasonable person ought to foresee are likely to produce injury to another. Ordinary negligence is greater than or above slight negligence and is characterized by thoughtlessness, heedlessness, or inattention.

"Now, I mentioned that under this included offense of careless, reckless, or negligence use of firearms with death resulting, to be guilty of that crime, it must be established that the discharge was not the result of willfulness or wantonness, because if it was, then the crime would be manslaughter rather than careless use of a firearm.

"Willfulness means that the defendant knowingly and consciously created the danger intending to inflict injury. Wantonly means that the defendant knowingly and consciously created the danger with knowledge of its probable consequences.

"Now, I want to instruct you concerning self-defense. One of the defenses raised in this case is that the defendant acted in lawful self-defense. The law recognizes the right of a person to use force or even to take a life in defense of her own person under certain circumstances.

When a person acts in lawful self-defense, such actions are excused, and the defendant is not guilty of any crime.

"In considering whether or not the defendant acted in lawful self-defense, you should carefully consider all of the evidence in light of the following rules. First, at the time of the act, the defendant must honestly believe that she is in danger of being killed or of receiving serious bodily injury. If she so believes, she may immediately act and defend herself even to the extent of taking human life if necessary. Although it may now turn out that the appearances were false and that she was mistaken as to the extent of the real danger, she is to be judged by the circumstances as they appeared to her at the time of the act.

"Second, the degree of danger, which must be feared, is serious bodily harm or death. A person is not justified in killing or inflicting great bodily injury upon another in order to protect herself from what appears to be a slight or insignificant injury. In deciding whether, at the time the defendant feared for her life or safety, you should consider all the surrounding circumstances, the condition of the parties, including their relative strength, whether the other party is armed with a dangerous weapon, or had other means to injure the defendant, the nature of the threat or attack of the other party, previous acts of brutality or threats of the other party of which the defendant was aware.

"Third, the act or acts taken by the defendant must have appeared to her at the time to be immediately necessary. A person is justified in using only such an amount of force as may appear necessary at the time at the time to defend herself from danger. In considering whether the degree of force appeared to be necessary, you should consider the excitement at the moment and what alternatives the defendant knew existed.

"A defendant in a state of excitement is not held to fine distinctions of judgment about how much force is necessary for her to use to protect herself. A person who is assaulted while in her own home or dwelling is under no obligation to try to escape from her dwelling but may stand her ground and repel the attack with as much force as appears necessary for the defense of her person.

"The defendant is not required to prove that she acted in self-defense. The prosecution has the burden of proof of guilt beyond a reasonable doubt and this includes the responsibility of proving that the defendant was not acting in self-defense.

David got the feeling from Judge Rood's demeanor in giving the instructions that he somewhat sympathized with Jean's plight before the law. He continued with his instructions and told the jury about self-defense and how it can be the basis for acquittal. He explained to the jury the theories of both the prosecution and of the defense.

David glanced at Jean as she listened intently at the judge's instructions, trembling as if she was hearing a verdict being rendered against her.

Will appeared confident of receiving a verdict as to the 2nd degree murder or at a minimum voluntary manslaughter. David could tell that he wanted such a conviction on which to end his long career as a prosecutor and David feared the worst even though he had given Jean the best defense that any seasoned criminal trial lawyer could have given her. Still, David had doubts that just would not go away. David and Jean were both suffering with the reality that they still had no control of the results.

Judge Rood further instructed the jury, saying, "During the course of the trial, there has been some evidence tending to show that one of the witnesses, Robert Davis, made earlier statements, which were inconsistent with the testimony made during the course of the trial. As you were previously instructed, such out-of-court statements are not evidence, which you consider to satisfy or prove any of the elements of the crime charged, since such statements were not made under oath, during the course of this trial. You should consider whether the witness made those out-of-court statements and whether they conflict with or contradict some or all of the sworn testimony of that witness. You may consider prior earlier statements in determining whether, or not, you believe the testimony of the witness, Robert Davis, that he made during the course of the trial.

"When you go to the jury room, your deliberations should be conducted in a businesslike manner. You should first select a foreperson. He or she should see to it that the discussion goes forward in a sensible and orderly fashion and that each juror has the opportunity to discuss the issues fully and fairly.

"A verdict in a criminal case must be unanimous. In order to return a verdict, it is necessary that each of the twelve of you agree upon that verdict. In the jury room, you will discuss the case among yourselves, but ultimately each of you will have to make up your own mind. Any verdict must represent the individual considered judgment of each juror.

"It is your duty to consult with your fellow jurors and to deliberate with a view to reaching agreement. Before deciding the case, consider the views of your fellow jurors. This means that you should give respectful consideration to one another's views and talk over differences of opinion in a spirit of fairness and frankness.

"It is natural that differences of opinion will arise. When they do, each of you should not only express your opinion, but also the facts and reasons upon which you base it. By reasoning the matter out, it is often possible for all the jurors to agree.

"In the course of your deliberations, do not hesitate to reexamine your own views and change your opinion, if you are convinced it is wrong. However, none of you should consider surrendering your honest conviction as to the weight and effect of the evidence or lack of evidence, solely because of the opinion of your fellow jurors or the mere purpose of returning a verdict.

"Do not concern yourselves during your deliberations with what the penalty might be if you find the defendant guilty. The question of guilt and the question of penalty are decided separately. It is the duty of the judge to fix the penalty whenever a defendant is found guilty. Possible penalties should not influence your decision.

"If you wish to communicate with the court while you are deliberating, please have your foreperson write a note and deliver it to the bailiff. It is not proper to talk directly with the judge, attorneys, court officers, or other persons involved in the case, even if the discussion has nothing to do with the case.

"During your deliberations, you should not disclose the state of your deliberations to others outside of the jury room. Therefore, unless you reach a verdict, do not disclose this information even in the courtroom.

"Now, counsel have agreed that all of the exhibits in the case will be delivered to the jury room so that you may examine them there, if you wish, during your deliberations.

"Now, as to the form of the verdict, several copies of the verdict form will be handed to you. This form states that you may return only one verdict on this charge. Check the line saying not guilty, or the line for guilty of murder in the second degree, or one of the three following lines for voluntary manslaughter, for involuntary manslaughter, or for careless use of a firearm with death resulting.

"Again, I inform you that there should be only one verdict; only one line on this sheet should be checked. The written form has no significance; your foreperson may use it as a guide on announcing your decision, but it need not be signed by any or all of you."

"May I ask counsel to approach the bench?" asked Judge Roode, wherein a discussion was held off the record, after which the judge continued.

"The instructions have been completed, and I will ask now that the clerks, with the assistance of the bailiff, give a good shake to the box that bears the names of the fourteen jurors, and two of the names should be withdrawn and these people will be excused," said Judge Roode.

"Juror no. 29, Robin Bloggers," announced the clerk.

"Mr. Bloggers, you will be excused. We thank you very much for your services," said Judge Roode.

"Juror no. 52, Trish Henson," announced the clerk.

"Mrs. Henson, we also thank you very much for your services; and after you get your wraps from the jury room, you may leave the courtroom, if you desire, or you may stay in the courtroom, if you please," stated Judge Roode.

—*whereupon the two jurors retrieved their belongings from the jury room*—

"Clerk, you may now administer the oath to the bailiff," said Judge Roode. Whereupon the clerk swore the bailiff, under penalty of law, and administered the oath, charging the bailiff not to allow any communication to pass in or out of the jury room, aside from a note to the judge, posing a special request of the jury, to keep the jury room secure from all other persons and to not disclose the state of the jury's deliberations should he come into possession of that knowledge, after which the clerk gave the forms of verdicts to the bailiff to be given to the jury upon their entering the jury room to start their deliberations.

—*At 2:09 pm, on December 24, 1984, the jury began their deliberations.*—

"Court will be in recess," announced Judge Roode.

Chapter 19

The Verdict

"All rise!" announced the bailiff, after returning to the courtroom, having secured the jury in the jury room. He then stated, "The court shall be in recess, until further order of the court."

David turned to Jean and could not conceal his concern, saying, "Jean, I feel good that the jury cannot consider a first-degree murder charge, but I'm still worried about the second-degree murder charge, as well as the lesser-included charges. I had hoped that we could have proceeded on just the second-degree murder charge, but I think the jury will see the self-defense issue as raising substantial doubt; the prosecution clearly did not prove beyond a reasonable doubt, the absence of self-defense."

It was at Will Brenner's insistence that the lesser-included offenses instruction be given to the jury. David did not like it, but had no legal basis to oppose it. He saw the lesser-included offenses as a problem, in that juries sometimes are eager to hold the defendant responsible for causing the death and will return a verdict on one of the lesser offenses to appease the prosecution while giving the defendant relief from the greater charge of murder. However, in David's mind, if the self-defense issue makes the killing of John a justified act, it should also apply to the lesser-included negligent-based offenses as well.

Jean looked very worried at this point of the trial. All that was able to be said was said and the matter was now with the jury to determine Jean's fate. There was just nothing more that David could have said or done to allay her fears.

—At about 3:05 pm, in the courtroom, in the presence both counsel, Judge Roode announced, "We have received a note from the jury that reads as follows: Could we please have the printed forms of distinction among the lesser offenses, especially for voluntary and involuntary manslaughter," reading the note received from the jury.

"Could counsel please approach the bench?" requested Judge Roode, and a whispered discussion was taking place between counsel and the judge.

Judge Roode spoke for the record, saying, "I discussed this with counsel and have agreed that we will photocopy the copies I used of the following standard jury instructions, 16:4:02, 16:4:04, 16:4:05, 16:4:06, 11:3:01, 11:3:02, 11:3:03, and 11:3:04. Is that correct, gentlemen?"

"That is correct," Will stated.

"The defense has no objections. I think that it is fine," David announced.

—At about 9:20 pm, on December 24, 1984, the jury informed the bailiff that they had arrived at a verdict.—

David was very nervous having the teacher on the jury. He was known to all of the other members of the jury, and his discussions in the jury room, should he favor conviction, would be highly regarded by the other members of the jury. As the jury began entering the courtroom, David was especially concerned when the teacher avoided eye contact with him and looked only in the judge's direction. David felt that it was a telltale sign that the jury was not going to acquit.

"Mr. Clerk, you may inquire as to a verdict," stated Judge Roode.

"Ladies and gentlemen of the jury, have you agreed upon a verdict, and if so, who will speak for you?" inquired the clerk.

"I am the foreman," stated Mr. Graham.

"What is your verdict?" inquired the clerk.

"Our verdict is involuntary manslaughter," responded Foreman Graham.

"Ladies and gentlemen of the jury, do you say that you find the defendant guilty of the offense of involuntary manslaughter?" inquired the bailiff.

"Yes," was the oral response of some, and others merely nodded their heads in agreement.

"All right, very well. I will ask all of the members of the jury to please rise and listen to your verdict as recited by your foreman. You say on your oaths that you find the defendant guilty of the offense of involuntary manslaughter. So say you, Mr. Foreman?" inquired Judge Roode,

"I do," stated Foreman Graham.

"And so say you, members of the jury?" asked Judge Roode.

—The clerk poled each juror by name and all jurors responded "Yes."—

"You may be seated. Clerk, you may record the verdict. This matter will be continued then for sentencing to January 25, 1985, which is the second motion day in January. And I assume, Mr. Brenner, there will be no objections if the bond is continued, until that time," stated Judge Roode.

"No objections," responded Will.

"All right, I want to say to you, members of the jury, something that I say to all jurors, that I am continually proud of people like you, my fellow citizens, who accept this duty that is thrust upon you and that you do not ask for, and yet discharge so conscientiously and responsibly. And, on behalf of your fellow citizens, I thank you for your services," stated Judge Roode.

"Now I ask that everyone else remain in the courtroom until the jury has had the opportunity to get their wraps and depart from the building, and you are dismissed," stated Judge Roode.

—At about 9:31 p.m., court recessed.—

Jean was openly smiling upon hearing the jury's verdict. She was just relieved to understand that she was acquitted of the murder charge, but did not yet know how to feel about a conviction for involuntary manslaughter and the possible sentence she might receive from the court.

David packed up his files, and both he and Jean departed the courthouse with mixed feelings of joy and of disappointment. After all, he had won a great victory for Jean, but was left with a definite feeling that he failed in not convincing the jury that the self-defense issue applied to the lesser offenses as well.

Jean, getting into her car, said to David that she would call him after a few days, but that she just did not feel like discussing the case any further today.

There were times, during the closing arguments to the jury, that David felt such extreme emotion come over him, thinking that he was not going to be able to finish addressing the jury, without breaking down and crying. He had felt so much anxiety and fear for his client that his voice would be noticeably weak and stressed at various stages, while delivering his summation to the jury. At no other time in the life of a trial does the trial attorney come to realize the limit of his control of the outcome of a case. During all those years of trying cases, David had felt that his presence as a trial advocate for his client resulted in favorable verdicts that he had performed so well as a criminal defense attorney that the result as voiced by the jury was preordained, once David had filed his appearance in a case. David had suffered in all those years from a self-centered delusion that his advocacy controlled the outcome of the trial. It was really quite painful, yet liberating, for David to find that he, in reality, had no control of the results of a trial that the control was always going to be with the judge or the jury, that David could be the best advocate he could be and that was all he could be.

After years of trying cases for criminal defendants, David was aware of the limits of the power of the advocate in the American system of justice. That realization precisely reflected the best thinking and intentions of the framers of the U.S. Constitution, that the ultimate control should be reflected in the verdict of a jury of the defendant's peers, not in the verdict of the judge, the prosecutor, nor in the verdict of the counsel for the defense. However, there is no guarantee of justice in the jury's verdict, but if everyone performs their individual roles—*the prosecutor, the defense, the judge, and the members of the jury*—to the best of their ability, justice is supposed to be the result. There are times, however, when errors occur in the course of trial, and a defendant is wrongfully convicted through the jury's verdict. In recognition of this, post-trial proceedings may and sometimes should provide relief from the jury's verdict.

David wasted no time in filing a Motion for a Directed Verdict of Acquittal, Notwithstanding the Verdict of the Jury[4] or, alternatively, a Motion for a New Trial, claiming that the jury's verdict of guilty of involuntary manslaughter was against the great weight of the evidence. David worked tirelessly in drafting the motions, researching the law, and writing additional supporting briefs. However, both motions were thereafter denied at a special hearing on March 24, 1985, and sentencing was set for the following day March 25, 1985, at 9:00 a.m. in the Pictured Rocks Circuit Court room.

Chapter 20

Sentencing

"Hear yea! Hear yea!" commanded the bailiff. "Court is now in session, the Honorable Judge William F. Roode, presiding."

Jean was again trembling as she sat next to David, this time worrying about the fate awaiting her under the gavel of Judge William F. Roode. She and Robert had been living at their home in Township AuTrain, but their relationship was not the same as before the shooting. Robert was becoming more resentful with time. She turned and looked around the courtroom to see her son staring back at her with a look of loss, condemnation, and increasing resentment for shooting his father. There did not seem to be anything she could do or say to console him.

"Mr. Chartier, would you bring the defendant up before the bench?" He then asked her if she had anything to say to the court prior to his passing sentence.

Jean thought about how she might address the judge and what she might say to him. David had told her that the judge would be giving her a chance to address the court, just prior to the judge pronouncing the sentence. Jean began, "Your Honor, I'm awful scared to go to prison and I don't know if my heart will let me live through the experience, but I hope that I can make it . . . at least I won't be beaten every day. I am sorry that John is dead, but I wish we could have gotten some help for him; then all of this would not have been necessary."

"Very well," responded Judge Roode. While picking up his notes, he said, "We are here today for the sentencing of Ms. Jean Davis on the jury's verdict of involuntary manslaughter. The court has met with counsel in chambers to discuss the presentence report of the Department of Corrections, has reviewed the sentencing guidelines with both counsel, has heard the arguments of the attorney for the people, the attorney for the defendant, and has listened to the words of the defendant in her address to the court.

"I must first state that I do not see this defendant as a threat to anyone. I do not believe that she intended to kill her husband, but meant only to stop him in his assaultive behavior. I find that she has a very serious heart condition, and I believe that a lengthy prison sentence might end up being a death sentence. But her husband died as a result of her criminal conduct, as found by the jury, and I now, departing downward from the guidelines, pronounce a sentence of a minimum of six months under the jurisdiction of the Michigan Department of Corrections and a maximum of fifteen years, with early community placement," decreed Judge Roode.

"Your Honor," David called out to the judge, "will the court grant a Stay of Execution of Sentence, pending an appeal to the Michigan Court of Appeals?"

"The court will take your motion under advisement until tomorrow, but in the meantime will remand the defendant to the custody of the Pictured Rocks County sheriff," declared Judge Roode. "I want counsel in my chambers at 1:00 p.m. tomorrow and, Sheriff, I want the defendant in the courtroom at that time, as well."

"Court is adjourned until tomorrow at 1:15 p.m.," declared the judge.

Jean was again upset that she was to be held in jail overnight. David tried to console her, telling her that he would try to encourage the judge to continue her bond, under a stay of execution of sentence, while her appeal was pending. David felt emotional exhaustion, worried for Jean, yet grateful that Judge Roode imposed the minimum sentence. He could have been much sterner in imposing sentence, but must have been quite moved by the life that she lived, in constant fear of being beaten, suffering so many injuries and heart attacks, and finding that the legal system had repeatedly failed her.

The following day, David was again in the courtroom and had been summoned into Judge Roode's chambers to meet with Will and the judge to discuss the question of a stay of execution of sentence and the continuation of bond, pending a contemplated appeal to the Michigan Court of Appeals. Will argued against a stay of execution of the sentence and to continuing Jean's bond, pending an appeal. The judge, however, was persuaded to follow David's argument that Jean was not a threat to anyone and felt that the real estate continuing to be pledged to the court would be sufficient to insure Jean's appearance in court for further proceedings, as might be determined by the court. They returned to the courtroom and Judge Roode ordered Jean's release from the custody of the Pictured Rocks County Sheriff, pending the results of her appeal and possible further incarceration, should the appellate court sustain the jury's verdict. The more that David thought about Jean's prospects of getting the Michigan Court of Appeals to overturn the jury's verdict, the more remote the prospect appeared to him, notwithstanding that a good faith argument was to be raised in support of the appeal.

Jean seemed quite relieved to be at liberty again and told David that she wanted to go back to her home and be with Robert as much as she could because he seemed to be more upset about the absence of his father as time went on.

For eight months, Jean tried to live as much of a normal life as possible, keeping her doctor appointments, meeting and playing cards with a few of her lady friends, shopping, cooking, and keeping the house clean and neat. Her relationship with Robert continued to be strained, and he seemed to prefer spending his nights away from the home and away from Jean. This was heartbreaking for her, as she dearly wished to have a close relationship with him. She now was beginning to understand the deep impact that the long-term abusive home environment had on Robert and the post-traumatic effect of the violent death of his father, after being shot by his mother. Robert obviously had not understood nor appreciated the terror that his mother endured when his dad was threatening death to her, his uncle Bill, and himself. He acknowledged that she was scared, but irrationally thought that his dad would not have hurt them, had she not killed him. Jean told David that she knew that Robert resented her and she did not know what to do about it.

Chapter 21

The Appeal and Court of Appeals Decision

The State Appellate Defender Office in Detroit was responsible to bring the appeal on Jean's behalf before the Michigan Court of Appeals. Before the appeal could commence, however, the trial transcript of over two thousand pages had to be typed by the Pictured Rocks County Court stenographer. It was completed and sent to the State Appellate Defender Office on April 6, 1985.

Arguments for reversal of the conviction raised by the attorneys handling Jean's appeal included:

A) that the verdict of the jury was contrary to the law,
B) that the verdict of the jury was contrary to the great weight of the evidence,
C) the court erred in admitting, over defense objections, statements of the defendant after she had requested counsel,
D) the court erred in admitting rebuttal testimony of new ballistic testing done after the close of the prosecution's case in chief,
E) the court erred in denying defendant's motion for a continuance of the trial,
F) the court erred in denying defendant surrebuttal testimony, and

G) the court denied the defendant procedural due process by permitting the sheriff—*who had also been a witness in the trial*—to serve a guardian of the jury, during jury deliberations.

On November 26, 1985, the Michigan Court of Appeals issued a unanimous decision, affirming the verdict of the jury, and David was ordered by the court to have Jean report to the Pictured Rocks County Jail, to be transferred to the Michigan Department of Corrections to begin her prison incarceration. Jean had packed a few toilet articles and a change of clothes to take with her to the Michigan Women's Prison in Saginaw, and David drove Jean to the jail to begin her trip downstate to the women's prison.

Before Jean was placed in the prison van for the drive downstate, she was again handcuffed, shackled at the ankles, and wore belly chains through which her handcuffs were attached. She expressed to David her continuing concern regarding Robert. She was hopeful that his resentment toward her would diminish while she was away and that they could once again share the close mother-son relationship that they had always had prior to her shooting his father. Jean had encouraged Robert to talk with a counselor or a priest, but he would not do that, telling her that she should not worry about him.

Life in prison was very difficult for Jean. She did not associate with the other inmates, although she had no problem talking with a number of women, some of whom had killed husbands or boyfriends following prolonged abuse in the home. However, Jean constantly longed to be in her own home. She had no communication with Robert, although she repeatedly wrote to him and tried calling him whenever she could use a telephone. She had chest pains nearly every day and feared that she might not live to see her home again.

David had asked Judge Roode to consider releasing Jean from prison due to her failing health and presented Judge Roode with a letter from Jean's cardiologist Dr. LaGale, encouraging her early release. The doctor had talked with Jean a number of times by telephone, and he wrote to the judge that Jean continues to experience frequent angina even at rest. He wrote that with her strong emotions, coronary artery bypass surgery, with patency of only one of the two bypass grafts, Jean was at great risk of dying. He went on to tell the judge that he feared that she was not getting the medical attention that she deserves while in prison. He stated in his letter, that in his opinion Jean would not come out of prison alive, if she was not released soon.

Chapter 22

Jean's Release from Prison and Homecoming

On January 5, 1986, the fortieth day of Jean's imprisonment, she was called into the warden's office and informed that Judge Roode had ordered her immediate release from prison and further ordered that she be transported back to her home in AuTrain Township. Jean felt elated at the prospect of returning home, and she called David to tell him of the news. David asked Jean to call him again after she arrived home and promised to come out to her home to talk with her and to Robert about hopeful things. Transportation was not arranged until the following morning, and after four hours on the road, Jean was very happy to be crossing the Mackinac Bridge into the Upper Peninsula. She had been thinking of plans for the balance of the winter. She had not celebrated Christmas, but now the New Year had filled her with hope. She had finally talked on the telephone with Robert prior to leaving the prison and had told him that she was coming home and was excited to see him.

It was about 3:00 p.m. of the afternoon of January 6, 1986, when the prison van dropped Jean off at the driveway to her home. She looked at the house and noted the smoke coming from the chimney, and although the drive was not plowed, she did not mind trudging through eight inches of snow to reach the house. The wind was brisk and the temperature was in the 20s, but she felt a warm feeling as she entered the rear door into the kitchen and called out, "Robert, honey, I'm home." There was no immediate response and she wondered if he was in the house; she was just about to call his name again when he came down the stairs and appeared in the living room with a .308-caliber rifle in his hands, saying, "Welcome home, Ma—*sobbing*—I've been waiting for you," whereupon he raised the rifle and said, "You shouldn't have shot Dad," and he fired the rifle, striking her directly in the chest, blowing a hole in her chest the size of a grapefruit, killing her instantly. A moment prior, she had stood in her kitchen, filled with happiness, hopes for the New Year, and had wanted to enjoy life being a good mother to Robert. Her body was spread across the kitchen floor in a pool of blood. Robert looked at his mother's lifeless body—*still sobbing*—and then bolted from the rear door of the house, carrying the rifle and running in his stocking feet across the snow-covered forty at the rear of the house, reaching the brush pile where his father had once hid from the police. Robert then sat on the ground next to the brush pile, and while feeling the blowing snow strike his face . . . *crying aloud . . .* he raised the barrel of the rifle to his mouth, and with the aid of a stick, pushed the trigger, causing the rifle to fire, blowing his head from his neck and spraying blood and brains upon the surrounding snow and the snow-covered brush pile where his body lay. As his lifeless body lay there, a lone chickadee landed in an adjacent bush, and sang its lonely song . . . *chic-a-dee-dee-dee* . . .. The north wind continued to blow, and heavier snow filled the air. Aside from the wind and the occasional chirping of a single chickadee, there were no other sounds.

End Notes

[1] *Res gestae* is defined in part in Black's Law Dictionary, Fourth Edition, West Publishing Company as: [Things done.] . . . Res gestae is considered as an exception to the hearsay rule. In its operation, it renders acts and declarations which constitute a part of the things done and said admissible in evidence, even though they would otherwise come within the rule excluding hearsay evidence or self-serving declarations. The rule is intended to include, not only declarations by the parties to the suit, but includes statements made by bystanders and strangers, under certain circumstances . . .

[2] Michigan Criminal Laws and Rules © 2003 a Thomson business/ Michigan Rules of Evidence 804 (b)(2)—Statement Under Belief of Impending Death. In a prosecution for homicide or in a civil action or proceeding, a statement made by a declarant while believing that the declarant's death was imminent, concerning the cause or circumstances of what the declarant believed to be impending death.

[3] Years later, David would attend a criminal trial in the USSR in 1987, while on a professional legal exchange with the Soviet Constitutional Lawyers. The Soviet defendant had been held incommunicado for up to one year, the judge and two lay assessors—both of whom are appointed by the judge—investigated the case. The defendant was brought into the courtroom to listen to the judge read a long indictment, saw the back of his defense attorney's head at the table before him—never having yet met him—and was asked how he intended to plea. There was no jury; the judge was not unbiased. In the Soviet Union, there

was no burden of proof on the prosecution, no jury, no presumption of innocence, no rules of evidence, and the role of the defense was not to defend, but to accept responsibility, show remorse, and plead for clemency. The same was true in China, as David would observe in that future 1987 year during a professional legal exchange with the eight hundred Chinese lawyers who had survived the cultural revolution

[4] **MCR 6.419 Motion for Directed Verdict of Acquittal**

- **After Jury Verdict.** After a jury verdict, the defendant may file an original or renewed motion for directed verdict of acquittal in the same manner as provided by MCR 6.431(A) for filing a motion for a new trial.
- **Inclusion of Motion for Judgment of Acquittal.** The court must consider a motion for a new trial challenging the weight or sufficiency of the evidence as including a motion for a directed verdict of acquittal.

About the Author

A trial lawyer helps one woman regain her freedom in Revord's New Book

Wetmore, MI—She would be severely beaten and likely killed if she stayed, but certainly killed if she tried to leave. Was it self-defense, or was it murder? To defend his client, one lawyer from Michigan's Upper Peninsula must fmd the truth in forensic evidence and through a sensational trial, portray to the jury a drama of the life of Jean and John Davis. Ralph Revord's Beyond Terror tells readers this gripping story of a battered wife who suddenly is left no choice but to end years of domestic violence by killing her abusive husband.

Attorney David Chartier was spending quality time with his family in their cabin near the Upper Twin Lake when a phone call from a highly distressed woman broke the peace and serenity of that evening. It was Jean Davis, David's longtime client, calling from the Michigan State Police Post where she is being held for her husband's murder. After years of physical and emotional abuse, Jean abruptly realized that her only chance of staying alive was to kill her husband.

So begins David's investigation, examination, gathering and analysis of forensic evidence that will provide a defense for his client. Beyond Terror follows the proceedings of the trial, beginning with David's investigation at the scene until the final verdict from the jury and appellate decision of the Court of Appeals. A shocking and unexpected end to the novel awaits readers.

A trial lawyer for more than fifty years himself. Revord delivers this fictional story—based largely on real events—with much precision, capturing the technicalities and the drama involved in criminal proceedings. For more information on "Beyond Terror", log on to www.raoulrevordbeyondterror.com.

Printed in July 2023
by Rotomail Italia S.p.A., Vignate (MI) - Italy